Better Homes and Gardens®

EATING HEALTHY COOK BOOK

Edwin Kiester, Jr. and Sally Valente Kiester
and the Editors of Better Homes and Gardens® Books

© Copyright 1986 by Meredith Corporation, Des Moines, Iowa
All Rights Reserved. Printed in the United States of America
First Edition. First Printing
Library of Congress Catalog Card Number:85-73118
ISBN:0-696-00675-8

BETTER HOMES AND GARDENS® BOOKS
Editor: Gerald M. Knox
Art Director: Ernest Shelton
Managing Editor: David A. Kirchner
Copy and Production Editors: James D. Blume, Marsha Jahns,
    Rosanne Weber Mattson, Mary Helen Schiltz, Carl Voss

Food and Nutrition Editor: Nancy Byal
Department Head, Cook Books: Sharyl Heiken
Associate Department Heads: Sandra Granseth,
    Rosemary C. Hutchinson, Elizabeth Woolever
Senior Food Editors: Julia Malloy, Marcia Stanley, Joyce Trollope
Associate Food Editors: Barbara Atkins, Linda Henry, Lynn Hoppe, Jill Johnson,
    Mary Jo Plutt, Maureen Powers, Martha Schiel, Linda F. Woodrum
Recipe Development Editor: Marion Viall
Test Kitchen Director: Sharon Stilwell
Test Kitchen Photo Studio Director: Janet Pittman
Test Kitchen Home Economists: Jean Brekke, Kay Cargill, Marilyn Cornelius, Jennifer Darling,
    Maryellyn Krantz, Lynelle Munn, Dianna Nolin, Marge Steenson, Cynthia Volcko

Associate Art Directors: Linda Ford Vermie, Neoma Alt West, Randall Yontz
Assistant Art Directors: Lynda Haupert, Harijs Priekulis, Tom Wegner
Senior Graphic Designers: Jack Murphy, Stan Sams, Darla Whipple-Frain
Graphic Designers: Mike Burns, Sally Cooper, Deb Miner, Brian Wignall,
    Kimberly Zarley

Vice President, Editorial Director: Doris Eby
Executive Director, Editorial Services: Duane L. Gregg

President, Book Group: Fred Stines
Director of Publishing: Robert B. Nelson
Vice President, Retail Marketing: Jamie Martin
Vice President, Direct Marketing: Arthur Heydendael

EATING HEALTHY COOK BOOK
Editors: Jill Johnson, Marcia Stanley, Linda F. Woodrum
Copy and Production Editors: Rosanne Weber Mattson, Carl Voss
Graphic Designers: Deb Miner, Stan Sams
Electronic Text Processor: Donna Russell
Contributing Photographers: Mike Dieter, Jim Hedrich, Wm. Hopkins, William K. Sladcik, Inc.
Food Stylists: Kathleen E. German, Dianna Nolin, Janet Pittman, Bonnie Rabert
Scientific and Nutritional Consultant: Keith B. Taylor, M.D.,
    George DeForest Barnett Professor of Medicine, Stanford University.
    Former Director General of the Health Education Council of Great Britain.
    Co-author of *Clinical Nutrition*, a standard medical reference text.

Our seal assures you that every recipe in
the *Eating Healthy Cook Book* has been tested in the
Better Homes and Gardens® Test Kitchen.
This means that each recipe is practical and reliable,
and meets our high standards of taste appeal.

On the front cover:
Brandied Beef (p.68), Broccoli-Pasta Toss (p.146), Thick Banana Milk Shake (p.207), Rosy Berry Punch (p. 206).

CONTENTS

Feeling good and looking good have a lot to do with how you treat your body every day. What you eat and how much you exercise affect your physical and mental well-being. It's important to know how these factors work together with your individual body makeup, so you can improve your chances, and your family's chances, of living a long, healthy life.

That's what the *Better Homes and Gardens® Eating Healthy Cook Book* is all about—putting all the ingredients together for a healthy lifestyle. This book sorts out the nutrition information you've been hearing on topics such as cholesterol, sodium, caffeine, and diet specialists. It gives you both sides of controversial nutrition issues, so you can make up your own mind about what's right for your family.

But this book goes beyond just talking about nutrition. You'll find more than 175 pages of recipes for delicious, healthy foods that you and your family will enjoy. Every recipe exemplifies sound nutrition for a healthy lifestyle—each is low in fat, cholesterol, sodium, and calories. And just as important, all the food tastes great!

Using a food diary for three days will help you chart every spoonful of food that passes your lips.

EVALUATING YOUR EATING HABITS

CHAPTER 1

Most of us eat three—or more—meals a day and can't remember at lunch what we ate for breakfast. A good starting point for a program of healthy eating is to assess your diet, and your nutritional status, today. From that foundation, you can construct a life-style that will give you good health for years to come.

CONTENTS

The Greeks had a word—

or ten—for the relationship

between diet and health:

"Let food be your medicine,

and medicine be your food."

Hippocrates said that a

healthy body would cure

itself, and made diet, not

drugs, the cornerstone of

good health.

o one can absolutely guarantee that any food or group of foods can make you run faster, breathe easier, live longer, look better, feel stronger, act smarter, or think straighter. The fact is, though, that how we feel and function is intimately connected to what we eat. As a matter of basic chemistry, human beings are collections of molecules, and so is food. The body takes from food the molecules it needs to build and rebuild tissues and to fuel its activities. The process of chemical transformation and utilization is called metabolism. The sum of all the metabolic processes is called nutrition. The aim of sound nutrition is to provide the body with the proper amounts of the proper molecules at the proper time in the proper manner.

To establish a healthy nutrition program for yourself, you need to know two things: what foods you're eating now, and what happens after you've eaten them. On page 18, you'll find a model food diary to help you with the first step. As for how this morning's granola fuels this afternoon's tennis game, let's take a brief look at the principles of nutrition, its history, and how the philosophy and information about it have changed during the past few years.

The study of diet goes back beyond ancient Greece and Hippocrates, the father of medicine. However, much of our knowledge is very recent. It was not until 1912, for instance, that a Polish biochemist, Casimir Funk, made perhaps the landmark discovery. Funk was researching an epidemic of a disease called beriberi, which had become widespread in parts of the world where rice was the mainstay of the diet.

Because the disease had spread so suddenly and widely, many doctors thought it was caused by an unknown germ. Funk showed that beriberi was limited to persons who primarily ate polished rice, which had recently been introduced. Persons who still ate unpolished rice were protected. Funk eventually isolated the protective substance from the rice bran and called it a "vitamin," because he thought it was a form of chemical called an amine and it was vital to life. We now know this first identified vitamin as thiamine, or vitamin B_1. Since then, 12 additional vitamins have been identified, as well as other substances essential to human health. New discoveries are still being made.

For years, doctors thought about nutrition in medical terms, almost like a prescription. Vitamins were considered weapons against disease—thiamine to combat beriberi, vitamin C to fight scurvy, and so on. But gradually, as these "dietary-deficiency diseases" have come under control, nutrition scientists have identified a far more ominous dietary health problem. Eating *too much* of the wrong foods posed an increasing threat to human health.

The chronic illnesses of the United States and other industrialized countries—heart disease, high blood pressure, cancer, diabetes—have now been closely linked to the high-protein, high-fat diet and slothful life-style of modern society. Thanks mainly to rich food, one-fifth of the U.S. population is seriously obese, a condition that increases the risks of chronic disease. As office jobs have replaced physical labor as a means of livelihood for the majority, overconsumption of food has been complicated by underuse of energy.

Thus the new goal of nutrition is protection against the creeping diseases of excess rather than the dramatic treatment of acute illness. And its aim goes a step beyond. Sound nutrition is now seen in positive terms—the cornerstone of a healthful life-style that will last and extend through the years. Not only what you eat but how you live is emphasized in today's nutrition.

The human diet, nutrition chemists now know, contains literally thousands of organic compounds. Most of them do virtually nothing for us except add a little flavor to the food or provide an additional bit of energy. Forty-five of these nutrients, however, are substances we absolutely cannot do without.

These essentials to human life are usually lumped into six categories: protein, fats, carbohydrates, vitamins, minerals, and water. Sometimes protein, fats, and carbohydrates are classified as macronutrients because we need them in quantity; vitamins and minerals, which are needed in far smaller amounts, are termed micronutrients. Water, which makes up some 70 percent of the body, is the most crucial nutrient of all: we can survive for weeks without the other nutrients, but we cannot last without water beyond a few days.

EVERY NUTRIENT HAS A ROLE

Each nutrient plays a specific but critical role in human metabolism. We need only a pin-prick of copper daily, for instance, but if we do not get it on a regular basis, our red blood cells do not form properly. We must have carbohydrates for instant energy, and fats for reserve energy; protein, the body's construction material, is necessary not only for building muscle and tissue but for synthesizing enzymes, hormones, and other body chemicals. Vitamins, the chemical catalysts, help certain body processes to take place. The mineral calcium helps to build strong bones and teeth. Sodium and potassium regulate the body's water balance inside and outside the cells.

We tend to classify foods as "protein," or "carbohydrate," but in fact, virtually nothing we eat consists purely of one nutrient or another. A typical hot dog weighing 56 grams, for instance, contains seven grams of protein. But it also contains 15.9 grams of fat, about a gram of carbohydrates, water, and trace amounts of minerals and vitamins.

"In nutrition, many mysteries remain to be solved. If the nation's top nutrition scientists created their best synthetic diet which reflected all our nutrition knowledge, such a diet would not sustain life."

—Dr. Howard Jacobson, Institute of Nutrition University of North Carolina

With the exception of the minerals and water, all the nutrients consist principally of the three elements carbon, hydrogen, and oxygen, often arranged in highly complex ways. (Protein also contains nitrogen, as we shall see in Chapter 7.) These three elements also comprise most of the basic biological substances of the body, as indeed they do of all living things. The elements are held together by links called chemical bonds. For the body to use these elements to construct other molecules for its own purposes, it must first sever the bonds and break the substances down into simpler, more usable compounds. These processes include digestion and absorption in the intestinal tract, and additional changes in the liver and other organs.

We are all familiar with the early stages. We put a forkful of food into the mouth, and the teeth grind and pulverize it, and mix it with saliva so that it passes easily down the throat. Powerful enzymes attack it to begin the breakdown process. In the stomach, these enzymes are mixed with the food by the churning and squeezing of the stomach muscles and chemical transformation begins. The resulting compounds move into the small intestine, where further breakdown takes place before the products of breakdown pass through the intestinal walls to be transported by the blood or lymph to the body's trillions of cells.

The precise details of the process differ among the nutrients. Carbohydrates, for instance, are utilized immediately, so their breakdown process is swifter. All carbohydrates are made up of sugars—simple sugars or monosaccharides (fructose, glucose) found in fruit or honey; double sugars or disaccharides (sucrose, lactose); and polysaccharides, long and complex chains of sugars that make up starches, cellulose, and pectin.

Specialized enzymes break down the double sugars into simple sugars, so they can be absorbed. Another enzyme first breaks the giant starch molecule into smaller fractions, and others transform those, too, into simple sugars. The resulting glucose, the body's basic fuel, is then carried to the cells to power their individual functions. If more is produced than the body can use at one time, the excess is converted to a polysaccharide called glycogen and stored in the liver.

CONCENTRATED ENERGY

Fat is concentrated energy: Each gram of fat contains more than twice the energy of a gram of carbohydrate. The breakdown process is designed to prepare it both for immediate use and also for storage. Unlike the other nutrients, fat is not soluble in water; bile, secreted by the liver and stored in the gallbladder, and enzymes from the pancreas render it water-soluble so it can pass through the intestinal walls. A new form of fat is produced within the walls and passes first into the lymphatic system and then into the bloodstream for processing by the liver and the muscles of the body and finally is stored in adipose tissue—what we commonly call fat.

Proteins are composed of amino acids, linked together in incredibly long chains called polypeptides. Amino acids are the basic building blocks of the tissues and many body chemicals. Enzymes from the pancreas break the proteins down into smaller and simpler groupings of amino acids so they can pass through the intestinal wall and be properly utilized to build tissues and body chemicals.

Most of the utilization of the nutrients goes on within the individual cells. The cells must be supplied with these life-sustaining substances on a continuing basis, for they are quickly used up: Even as we sleep, the ongoing processes of our bodies are consuming energy at the rate of 90 calories an hour. Even when we receive a continuing supply of carbohydrate, some fats are called upon to provide energy, and when carbohydrate is not available, fats must provide almost all the energy requirement. When both are exhausted, protein is broken down to furnish body fuel. Conversely, when we eat more fat than we can efficiently store, we see the effects in the waistline. When we eat extra protein, much may be converted to—and stored as—fat.

You often hear one or another nutrient touted as a "super food" more important to the diet than the others. But in fact we must have each of the 45 essential nutrients in proper quantity to achieve good health. The role of modern nutrition is to establish a diet that provides the nutrients in proper and healthy balance.

Indeed, the Food and Nutrition Board of the National Research Council stated in issuing the most recent RDAs:

"We are aware of no convincing evidence of unique health benefits accruing from consumption of a large excess of any individual nutrient."

Americans are buying less red meat, the U.S. Department of Agriculture reports, but the decline is gradual, not sharp. In 1977, retail meat sales amounted to 153 pounds per person. In 1982, sales were down to 139.3 pounds. All types of meat were affected, but pork had dropped most.

Does the dinner in the photo *above* look familiar? If it does, it's because that combination of meat, potatoes, rich gravy, and mountainous dessert is still what all too many Americans eat as a main meal—night after night after weight-producing night.

How about the dinner *at right?* The spiced beef and vegetable dinner is the kind of meal Americans should be eating—and the kind you will find in this book.

The American diet *is* changing, no doubt about that. According to the U.S. Department of Agriculture food consumption surveys, which have recorded the food intakes of families of every income level since 1910, Americans now consume less pork, fewer eggs, less milk, less butter, and less ice cream than they did in the 1960s; they eat more chicken, fish, fruits and vegetables, and cereals and grain products. They use more vegetable oil rather than animal fat in cooking. They drink almost twice as much orange juice.

But we still have a long way to go. The same surveys show that affluent, meat-eating Americans still obtain 40 percent of their daily calories from fat, less than 50 percent from carbohydrate. (In 1910, the U.S. diet was more than 60 percent carbohydrate.) The 12 percent of calories derived from protein has remained the same for more than half a century. But today 70 percent comes from meat rather than protein-rich vegetables.

We eat nearly 15 grams of salt a day via processed foods and salt we add in cooking or at the table; and we average nearly 125 pounds of refined sugar per year, almost as much as the candy-loving British, plus increasing amounts of corn syrup. Another survey shows that the typical sedentary male office worker consumes nearly 4,000 calories a day, the average female nearly 3,000.

Alarmed by these figures, a U.S. Senate committee in 1977 suggested that Americans should drastically alter their diets and issued dietary guidelines for Americans to follow. The committee estimated that if these goals were realized, there would be an 80 percent

drop in obesity, a 25 percent decline in heart-disease deaths, a 50 percent decrease in deaths from diabetes, and a 1 percent increase in longevity. The guidelines have been modified by the Departments of Agriculture and Health and Human Services in pamphlet No. 232, *Nutrition and Your Health: Dietary Guidelines for Americans.* These guidelines are the basis for this book. They are:

    1) Eat a variety of foods.

    2) Maintain desirable weight.

    3) Avoid too much fat, saturated fat, and cholesterol.

    4) Eat foods with adequate starch and fiber.

    5) Avoid too much sugar.

    6) Avoid too much sodium.

    7) If you drink alcoholic beverages, do so in moderation.

No specific recommendations were made for individual nutrients, but the Senate committee and others have suggested that total fat be reduced at least to 30 percent of calories (other authorities have even recommended lowering it to 20 percent), that cholesterol be limited to 300 milligrams a day, and that sodium be kept below five grams daily.

The spiced beef and vegetable dinner meets these standards, as do other recipes in the *Eating Healthy Cook Book.* Low in fat, calories, and sodium and high in fiber, this main dish is simultaneously nutritious and delicious.

The main dish features lean beef seasoned with honey, orange juice, curry powder, ginger, and low-sodium soy sauce. High carbohydrate content comes from the pilaf of brown rice and bulgur wheat, fiber from the whole-wheat Italian bread fortified with wheat germ. The mousse with fresh fruit (using unflavored gelatin, honey and yogurt) is high in both fiber and vitamin C.

The meal provides a little more than 500 calories per serving, one-third of a suggested 1,500-calorie-a-day diet. It furnishes about seven grams of fat, 45 milligrams of cholesterol, and about one-third of the daily protein needs. In addition, it contains only 397 milligrams of sodium. Accompanied by a glass of skim milk, it is a menu for healthy eating.

Latest wrinkle in planning a nutritious diet: the personal computer. Software is available which weighs in the RDAs and other recommendations for all essential nutrients, calculates them with your age, sex, body frame, and activity level, and prints out daily menus suited to your needs.

Putting together a nutritious daily diet is a bit like conducting a symphony orchestra. You need the proper blend of shrills on the piccolo and bleats on the bassoon to end up with a harmonious product. Similarly, you must skillfully orchestrate the nutrients in your diet if you are to achieve healthy eating.

The table of Recommended Dietary Allowances (RDAs), shown on pages 16–17, is your musical "score." Prepared by an elite scientific panel for the Food and Nutrition Board of the National Research Council, the RDAs suggest specific amounts of 17 essential nutrients you should attempt to consume each day. The list includes protein; the fat-soluble vitamins A, D, and E; seven water-soluble vitamins; and six minerals.

SAFE AND ADEQUATE RANGES

The RDAs also recommend proper energy intake (fats and carbohydrates) and list "safe and adequate" ranges for 12 other nutrients about which not enough is known to make more precise recommendations. The "safe and adequates" are three vitamins, six trace minerals, and the electrolytes: sodium, potassium, and chlorine.

The RDAs are revised periodically to incorporate new data about the effects of various nutrients on the body. The current version was compiled in 1980. The tables make specific recommendations by sex and age group, classifying the needs of infants, children 10 and under, males and females in five age categories over 11 years, and pregnant women and nursing mothers.

The RDAs can be a helpful guide in planning healthy menus, but they have limitations. The Food and Nutrition Board emphasizes that they are guidelines, not commandments etched in stone. For one thing, they are calculated on the basis of whole population groups; your own needs could differ considerably from those of others in your age group. The amount of exercise you get and the climate you live in both can drastically alter your needs for certain nutrients. A 45-year-old male laborer who does construction work in a sweltering climate has different needs from an executive of the same age who pushes paper in an air-conditioned office.

Although the RDAs are categorized by age group, there can be differences within the groups. All persons over 50 are lumped together, but the board agrees that a 70-year-old requires less protein (but probably more calcium) than a 50-year-old.

Moreover, the figures deliberately overstate the needed amounts of a given nutrient. The levels are set high to compensate for individual differences, so that everyone is sure to get an adequate amount. The safety cushion isn't so thick that meeting the standard would harm anyone. Thus, falling a bit short of the RDAs isn't cause for worry. *Exceeding* the RDA consistently (as many of us do, for example, for protein) means that we are taking in far too much of the given nutrient.

Finally, the RDAs are meant to suggest an *average* daily intake, not a daily must. Hitting each RDA right on the button every day would require real feats of culinary ingenuity. You're more likely to exceed the allowance for one nutrient, undershoot on another, and be right on target with a third. The committee suggests that you try to strike a balance over five days to a week.

Within these limitations, how can the RDAs help you plan a healthy diet? Because the recommendations have been drawn up by a scientific panel, they call for a bit of arithmetic. The allowances are expressed in metric measures of grams, milligrams, and micrograms, rather than the common measures we are familiar with—ounce, pound, cup, teaspoon, tablespoon.

OTHER PROBLEMS

Another problem occurs because most foods do not list the amount of nutrients per serving, and most people simply have no idea of the nutrient composition of, say, a chicken drumstick. The nutrition analysis tables accompanying the recipes in this book provide that information (see pages 22–23). Agriculture Department Home and Garden Bulletin No. HG-72, *Nutritive Value of Foods,* available through government printing offices, also lists the kind and amount of nutrients in typical servings of many common foods and can be used as a reference.

Another way to calculate your nutrient intake is by using the United States Recommended Daily Allowances (USRDAs), which, despite their slightly—and confusingly—different name, are based on the RDAs. These are the nutrition-analysis figures you find on some package labels, listing the percentage of the daily nutrient requirement met by a typical serving of the product.

The USRDAs have been established by the U.S. Food and Drug Administration as a uniform labeling system for certain processed foods. They are *not* required on all foods, only those to which vitamins and minerals have been added or for which nutrition claims are made. The listing is voluntary for other foods, although in practice the nutrient breakdown per serving is included on many nationally marketed products.

The USRDAs are simpler than the RDAs, but they also are less precise. To make them easier to understand, the USRDAs are based on only a single figure for each nutrient, instead of providing different information for varying situations and age groups. That figure is the highest recommended allowance for each RDA. That means that the USRDA for vitamin A, for example, is set at 1,000 retinol equivalents, another nutrition measure. A single serving of oatmeal, with one-half cup of vitamin-D-fortified whole milk, meets 20 percent of that daily requirement. The USRDA for a 10-year-old is 700 retinol equivalents, so that the oatmeal and milk meets nearly 30 percent of the daily recommendation for a child of that age.

In the case of iron, the USRDA is set at 18 milligrams, because this is the RDA for menstruating adult women, who have the highest need for the mineral. The USRDA for riboflavin is established at 1.7 milligrams, because that's the requirement for adult men, who need the most of this vitamin.

To further complicate matters, the USRDAs for calcium, phosphorus, biotin, pantothenic acid, copper, and zinc are made exceptions under the law. The USRDAs for calcium and phosphorus are actually lower than the highest RDA value. They are somewhat arbitrarily set at 1 gram each because of the wide variability in age-based requirements for these important minerals.

Juggling all these figures can be a bit confusing, but remember that it's not like balancing your checkbook. You needn't calculate your daily food intake down to the last microgram. Using the food diary, the nutrition analysis tables in this book, and the package labels on your foodstuffs, you can closely approximate the RDA for your age-sex group, and shape your diet accordingly.

This table of Recommended Dietary Allowances is intended as a guideline for sound diet, not a statistical must. To use it, find your age and height; "weight" represents the ideal for the category. The figure for each nutrient is the amount you should average, not necessarily meet each day. The recommendation meets the needs of 90 percent of healthy persons, but consistently exceeding or falling short of the figure could have harmful effects on your health.

	AGE Years	WEIGHT Pounds	HEIGHT Inches	PROTEIN Grams	VITAMINS VITAMIN A Micrograms RE	VITAMIN D Micrograms	VITAMIN E Milligrams α-TE	
Infants	0.0–0.5	13	24	lbsx1.0	420	10	3	
	0.5–1.0	20	28	lbsx.0.9	400	10	4	
Children	1–3	29	35	23	400	10	5	
	4–6	44	44	30	500	10	6	
	7–10	62	52	34	700	10	7	
Males	11–14	99	62	45	1000	10	8	
	15–18	145	69	56	1000	10	10	
	19–22	154	70	56	1000	7.5	10	
	23–50	154	70	56	1000	5	10	
	51 +	154	70	56	1000	5	10	
Females	11–14	101	62	46	800	10	8	
	15–18	120	64	46	800	10	8	
	19–22	120	64	44	800	7.5	8	
	23–50	120	64	44	800	5	8	
	51 +	120	64	44	800	5	8	
Pregnant				+30	+200	+5	+2	
Lactating				+20	+400	+5	+3	

| | | | | | | | MINERALS | | | | | |
VITAMIN C Milligrams	THIAMINE Milligrams	RIBOFLAVIN Milligrams	NIACIN Milligrams	VITAMIN B_6 Milligrams	FOLACIN Micrograms	VITAMIN B_{12} Micrograms	CALCIUM Milligrams	PHOSPHORUS Milligrams	MAGNESIUM Milligrams	IRON Milligrams	ZINC Milligrams	IODINE Micrograms
35	0.3	0.4	6	0.3	30	0.5	360	240	50	10	3	40
35	0.5	0.6	8	0.6	45	1.5	540	360	70	15	5	50
45	0.7	0.8	9	0.9	100	2.0	800	800	150	15	10	70
45	0.9	1.0	11	1.3	200	2.5	800	800	200	10	10	90
45	1.2	1.4	16	1.6	300	3.0	800	800	250	10	10	120
50	1.4	1.6	18	1.8	400	3.0	1200	1200	350	18	15	150
60	1.4	1.7	18	2.0	400	3.0	1200	1200	400	18	15	150
60	1.5	1.7	19	2.2	400	3.0	800	800	350	10	15	150
60	1.4	1.6	18	2.2	400	3.0	800	800	350	10	15	150
60	1.2	1.4	16	2.2	400	3.0	800	800	350	10	15	150
50	1.1	1.3	15	1.8	400	3.0	1200	1200	300	18	15	150
60	1.1	1.3	14	2.0	400	3.0	1200	1200	300	18	15	150
60	1.1	1.3	14	2.0	400	3.0	800	800	300	18	15	150
60	1.0	1.2	13	2.0	400	3.0	800	800	300	18	15	150
60	1.0	1.2	13	2.0	400	3.0	800	800	300	10	15	150
+20	+0.4	+0.3	+2	+0.6	+400	+1.0	+400	+400	+150	*	+5	+25
+40	+0.5	+0.5	+5	+0.5	+100	+1.0	+400	+400	+150	*	+10	+50

RE represents retinol equivalents, a method of calculating vitamin A activity in the body.

α-TE or α-tocopherol equivalents are a standard for measuring vitamin E activity.

+ indicates additional nutrient units a pregnant or lactating woman must add to her normal daily intake.

* indicates that a pregnant or lactating woman usually cannot receive sufficient iron from dietary sources alone during pregnancy and that supplements are necessary.

TIME	PLACE	ACTIVITY	FOOD	AMOUNT
	kitchen	reading paper	coffee	1 cup
			cream	1 tsp.
			sugar	1 tsp.
			poached egg	1 medium
			white toast	1 slice
			margarine	1 pat
10 AM	office	computer terminal	coffee	1 cup
			cream	1 tsp.
			sugar	1 tsp.
			Danish pastry	1
NOON	McDonald's	talk with co-worker	Big Mac	1
			French fries	1 reg. svg.
			7-Up	1 cup
5 PM	car	driving home	Snickers chocolate bar	1
7 PM	dining room	talk with family	chicken, baked	2 drumsticks
			potato, baked	1 medium
			margarine	2 pats
			carrots, fresh, cooked	½ cup
			salad, lettuce	3 lea
			tomato	½
			French dressing	1 tbsp.
			red wine	1 4 oz. glass
8:30 PM	kitchen	filling out food diary		

You start a household budget by taking stock of what you're spending now. In the same way, a diet program begins with an honest appraisal of your present eating habits. That means keeping a diary in which you record every meal, snack, nibble, and gulp.

The table in the photograph *at left* shows how you can set up your own food diary. List all food and drink that passes through your lips for at least three days. Five days are preferable. The longer the record, the more complete picture you'll get of your eating habits. Include at least one Saturday or Sunday, since most of us eat differently on weekends than from Monday through Friday. Don't skip "bad days" or "unusual" days. Remember that a diary is not a test. Information from bad days may help you to identify trouble spots in your diet.

Write down each food as soon as you have eaten, which makes it easier to remember, and estimate the amounts consumed. Don't forget the candy bar or soft drink at your desk in the afternoon, or the potato chips you munched while watching reruns of *Love Boat*.

Write in a full description of each food, including things you added. A surprising percentage of calories and fats in the American diet come from that splash of cream in the coffee, the dollop of butter on the baked potato, and the jelly on the breakfast toast. List added salt and sugar, too.

As nearly as possible, describe how the food was prepared. Fried? Deep fried? Roasted? Baked? Was it a casserole? What fat was used in frying? What ingredients went into it? For restaurant meals in particular, such a complete record can be difficult, but try to approximate it. For processed or packaged foods, consult the list of nutrients found on most labels.

Also list where you ate, whom you were with, and what you were doing. People eat at many places besides the dinner table, and some of us snack almost automatically and unthinkingly in certain situations, like gobbling popcorn during a movie. A record helps you to avoid the situation in the future and can be important in a weight-loss diet.

When you see it in stark black and white, you'll probably find your food intake surprising—and dismaying. Many of us who consider ourselves light or picky eaters are startled to discover how much we really consume. And, even though no one else need see your diary, there's a tendency to fudge a bit by underestimating portions or, more commonly, actually cutting back on what you eat while keeping the diary, only to later revert to your old habits. Again, remember that your goal is an honest look at your normal eating habits. There are no right and wrong answers.

After three to five days of entries like those above, you can begin your self-assessment. Use a pocket calorie chart of the type you can purchase in a supermarket and the nutrition analysis breakdown on pages 278–279 to calculate calories and nutrients for each food eaten. Then total these figures for each day. Estimate from the tables the proportion of calories from fat, carbohydrate, and protein. The table also should enable you to estimate the daily percentage of saturated fat and of cholesterol.

Make similar totals for the other days in the diary, then add the daily figures for calories and each nutrient. Compute your average daily intake by dividing this total by the number of days you have kept a record.

The result will be an accurate profile of your customary diet. It will help you to identify trouble spots and reveal how you measure up to the dietary guidelines.

In the example on page 18, the total number of calories for the day is approximately 2,000, about average for a 120-pound nonpregnant American woman in her 30s, slightly higher than the dietary guidelines recommend. Intake of macronutrients for the day is 86 grams of protein, 82 grams of fat, and 130 grams of carbohydrate. About one-fourth of the fat is saturated.

But note where the diary-keeper obtains some of her calories. Nearly 400 are "empty"—derived from wine, soft drinks, and refined sugar in the coffee. Another 300 calories come from butter and cream; 150 more from salad dressing and margarine. A candy bar contributes 147. Eliminating or reducing some of these items could bring the diary-keeper's consumption under 1,500 calories, an adequate daily amount if properly balanced.

The day's protein from chicken, Big Mac, and egg exceeds by nearly 50 percent the government recommendation of 40–60 grams of protein daily. However, the dinner could come within the proposed ceiling by substituting a salad for the Big Mac, or forgoing a second piece of chicken. A late-night neighborhood walk instead of television might break the snacking habit.

More important than specific changes, however, the diary will help you to establish rules to follow in your quest for healthy eating.

RISKS OF POOR NUTRITION

It's interesting to note that nutritional problems today are more likely to come from what we eat than from what we don't eat. That wasn't the case in our parents' and grandparents' days, when pellegra, rickets, scurvy, and other diseases of poor diet were a threat to health and longevity. These diseases have virtually disappeared from the U.S. They occur so rarely that the federal government's Center for Disease Control doesn't even tabulate the cases. Better diet and enriched and fortified foods have almost wiped them out. However, alcoholics, elderly persons on a "tea and toast" diet, food faddists, the inner-city impovershed, and the rural poor may suffer from long-term lack of essential nutrients. Dietary-deficiency diseases remain a major health problem in the Third World.

Among the dieases of poor nutrition that doctors continue to see are anemia (a blood disorder with many causes) and goiter. The nutritional form of anemia results from lack of dietary iron. Iron now is added to many foods. Goiter, the enlargment of the thyroid gland in the neck, results from lack of dietary iodine. This condition can be prevented by use of iodized salt.

Less-common diseases include scurvy, which is lack of vitamin C, rare these days because of widespread availabilty of fresh citrus fruit, and rickets, which leads to bone deformity in growing children. Rickets, usually due to vitamin D deficiency, has largely been overcome by use of vitamin D in milk. Beriberi, caused by lack of thiamine, was once common among Asians who ate polished rice. Symptoms include nerve damage and heart failure. Pellegra is a consequence of lack of niacin, resulting in skin disorders, mental confusion,diarrhea, and ultimately, death. It occurs primarily among persons eating a very low-protein diet, usually with corn as the staple.

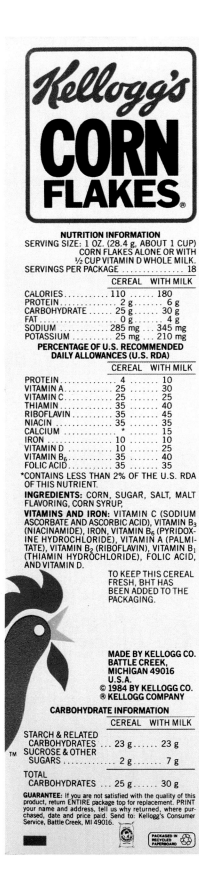

NUTRITION INFORMATION
SERVING SIZE: 1 OZ. (28.4 g, ABOUT 1 CUP)
CORN FLAKES ALONE OR WITH
½ CUP VITAMIN D WHOLE MILK.
SERVINGS PER PACKAGE 18

	CEREAL	WITH MILK
CALORIES	110	180
PROTEIN	2 g	6 g
CARBOHYDRATE	25 g	30 g
FAT	0 g	4 g
SODIUM	285 mg	345 mg
POTASSIUM	25 mg	210 mg

**PERCENTAGE OF U.S. RECOMMENDED
DAILY ALLOWANCES (U.S. RDA)**

	CEREAL	WITH MILK
PROTEIN	4	10
VITAMIN A	25	30
VITAMIN C	25	25
THIAMIN	35	40
RIBOFLAVIN	35	45
NIACIN	35	35
CALCIUM	*	15
IRON	10	10
VITAMIN D	10	25
VITAMIN B₆	35	40
FOLIC ACID	35	35

*CONTAINS LESS THAN 2% OF THE U.S. RDA
OF THIS NUTRIENT.
INGREDIENTS: CORN, SUGAR, SALT, MALT
FLAVORING, CORN SYRUP,
VITAMINS AND IRON: VITAMIN C (SODIUM
ASCORBATE AND ASCORBIC ACID), VITAMIN B₃
(NIACINAMIDE), IRON, VITAMIN B₆ (PYRIDOX-
INE HYDROCHLORIDE), VITAMIN A (PALMI-
TATE), VITAMIN B₂ (RIBOFLAVIN), VITAMIN B₁
(THIAMIN HYDROCHLORIDE), FOLIC ACID,
AND VITAMIN D.

TO KEEP THIS CEREAL
FRESH, BHT HAS
BEEN ADDED TO THE
PACKAGING.

MADE BY KELLOGG CO.
BATTLE CREEK,
MICHIGAN 49016
U.S.A.
© 1984 BY KELLOGG CO.
® KELLOGG COMPANY

CARBOHYDRATE INFORMATION

	CEREAL	WITH MILK
STARCH & RELATED CARBOHYDRATES	23 g	23 g
SUCROSE & OTHER SUGARS	2 g	7 g
TOTAL CARBOHYDRATES	25 g	30 g

GUARANTEE: If you are not satisfied with the quality of this
product, return ENTIRE package top for replacement. PRINT
your name and address, tell us why returned, where purchased, date and price paid. Send to: Kellogg's Consumer
Service, Battle Creek, MI 49016.

PACKAGED IN
RECYCLED
PAPERBOARD

WHAT YOU CAN LEARN FROM A FOOD LABEL

By government regulation, ingredients must be listed on the label of certain foods, but listing is optional for others. You'll usually find ingredients listed for most nationally marketed products, including processed meats and poultry, most canned and packaged goods, and cereals.

The nutrition information must be presented in a standard format. As shown on the cereal box at left, the serving size and the number of servings per box are listed, along with the amount of protein, fat, and carbohydrate per serving. The percentage of the U.S. Recommended Daily Allowance met by each serving must be shown for protein and seven specified vitamins and minerals (thiamine, riboflavin, niacin, calcium, iron, and vitamins A and C). The quantities of other vitamins and minerals, sodium, potassium, cholesterol, and saturated and polyunsaturated fats also may be included, although their listing is optional.

Government regulations also stipulate that ingredients must be listed in descending order by weight. Thus, in the cornflakes package at left, the largest single ingredient is milled corn, followed by sugar, salt, and malt flavoring. Chemical additives used to preserve freshness or to improve flavor or color also are usually listed at the end of the ingredients section, although the listing is not required by the government.

A s a health-conscious individual, you are undoubtedly familiar with nutrition labeling on packaged foods. These labels spell out the the number of calories and nutrient amounts you consume when you eat that product. We've made this same type of information available to you in the form of nutition analyses for all the recipes in the *Eating Healthy Cook Book.*

Nutrition analysis eliminates guesswork when you plan your daily menus. With a quick check, you'll know whether the foods you want to prepare meet your eating goals. You'll find this nutrition information at the front of each chapter in the form of a chart, like the one on the opposite page. The recipe titles are listed, along with each of the nutrient values for one serving of that recipe.

From the charts, you'll quickly know the exact amount of calories, protein, carbohydrate, fat, cholesterol, sodium, and potassium you'll get from one serving of a recipe. In addition, you can know the percentage each serving provides of the United States Recommended Daily Allowances (U.S. RDA) for protein, vitamin A, vitamin C, thiamine, riboflavin, niacin, and iron.

With these facts at your fingertips, you can use the charts to compare the nutrient values of the recipes so you can choose the foods that best fit your needs. For instance, if you're concerned about cholesterol, you can choose low-cholesterol recipes. If you need more protein in your diet on a particular day, you can easily find the recipes that contain significant amounts of protein.

Here are some tips on using the nutrition analysis charts.

●When a recipe ingredient has a variable weight (such as a 2½- to 3-pound broiler-fryer chicken), the nutrition analysis was calculated using the lesser weight.

●The nutrition analyses of recipes calling for fresh ingredients were calculated using measurements for raw fruits and vegetables.

●Recipes calling for meats used the cooked weight in their nutrition analyses.

●When two ingredient options appear in a recipe (such as reduced-calorie mayonnaise or salad dressing), the nutrition analysis was calculated using the ingredient given first.

●Suggested garnishes and ingredients that are listed as "optional" or "if desired" were not counted in the analyses.

●If a food is marinated or basted, the nutrition analysis reflects the entire amount of marinade or basting sauce, even if only part of it is used.

●If a recipe has a subrecipe within it, the analysis for the subrecipe was included in the nutrition analysis for the recipe. For example, for Waffles with Blueberry Sauce on page 143, the analysis for the waffles includes the analysis for Blueberry Sauce.

●The title of each recipe and the page number of each recipe is listed down the left side of the chart. The titles are grouped in alphabetical order for each chapter.

●The first column after the recipe titles lists calories. There you'll find the number of calories per serving for each recipe.

●Also listed across the top of each chart are nutrients. The next six columns, after calories, show you the number of grams or milligrams per serving of each nutrient for the recipes. And the last eight columns on each chart show you the percent of the U.S. RDA obtained for each nutrient in a serving of the recipe. (For more information about the U.S. RDAs, see pages 14 and 15.)

SAMPLE NUTRITION ANALYSIS CHART	PER SERVING							PERCENT U.S. RDA PER SERVING							
	CALORIES	PROTEIN (g)	CARBOHYDRATES (g)	FAT (g)	CHOLESTEROL (mg)	SODIUM (mg)	POTASSIUM (mg)	PROTEIN	VITAMIN A	VITAMIN C	THIAMINE	RIBOFLAVIN	NIACIN	CALCIUM	IRON
Apricot-Sauced Chops (p. 92)	277	26	8	15	83	98	397	40	14	4	56	14	26	1	7
Barbecue-Sauced Pork Roast (p. 89)	288	30	11	13	93	84	648	46	12	15	64	18	31	5	14
Bean-Sauced Pasta (p. 124)	438	20	71	9	20	573	920	31	43	61	24	18	19	23	35
Beef and Apples (p. 70)	280	23	30	8	61	63	485	35	31	11	7	11	23	3	18
Beef and Barley Bake (p. 80)	240	22	30	4	49	274	841	34	104	64	48	46	60	22	105
Beef and Pasta Salad (p. 81)	175	16	18	4	24	277	396	25	46	43	9	15	11	19	11
Brandied Beef (p. 68)	228	23	11	7	61	101	495	35	86	13	8	14	23	5	19
Broccoli-Tofu Strata (p. 121)	182	13	16	8	83	237	288	20	19	51	9	17	4	29	11
Broiled Flank (p. 77)	131	19	2	5	60	150	175	30	0	0	2	9	15	1	14
Bulgur-Stuffed Salmon Steaks (p. 114)	496	31	29	28	85	201	708	47	20	16	16	22	8	24	18
Chicken and Fruit Salad (p. 106)	368	17	63	5	39	325	404	26	5	51	18	8	28	5	16
Chicken Burrito Stack-Ups (p. 104)	250	19	20	11	48	102	519	30	14	38	9	12	29	15	12
Chicken Salad for Two (p. 106)	194	23	12	6	65	114	495	36	9	33	5	13	35	10	8
Curried Beef and Cabbage (p. 76)	294	26	26	10	80	123	767	40	12	94	12	17	30	8	25
Curried Beef and Fruit (p. 79)	451	26	53	16	55	94	494	40	8	17	19	12	36	5	25
Curried Pork Stew (p. 82)	289	17	37	10	33	195	1021	25	104	71	27	13	30	5	15
Curry Chicken Kabobs (p. 103)	223	29	14	6	112	142	730	44	83	45	13	26	51	5	14
Deep-Dish Tuna Pie (p. 117)	325	24	23	15	45	229	360	36	59	8	14	15	46	17	13
Egg and Rice Skillet (p. 125)	282	15	38	9	280	273	520	23	74	223	17	18	13	17	16
Fish 'n' Shrimp Mornay (p. 108)	312	28	33	5	95	205	579	44	6	30	18	20	17	24	13
Fruit Scallop Plate (p. 109)	187	13	23	5	26	265	622	19	23	68	11	5	7	5	10
Garden Tenderloin Rolls (p. 87)	226	24	12	9	65	245	709	37	90	36	38	28	33	4	13
Gingersnap Pot Roast (p. 74)	266	31	14	9	90	124	364	47	45	18	7	15	24	3	23
Grilled Pork Burgers (p. 84)	230	23	13	9	65	263	391	36	2	19	33	17	23	4	7
Harvest Pot Pie (p. 122)	276	17	27	12	22	301	505	26	41	99	17	21	15	32	16
Healthful Joes (p. 76)	273	21	32	8	50	353	566	32	35	16	17	13	26	7	27
Healthy Cheese Soufflé (p. 125)	297	17	7	22	222	389	197	26	19	1	4	22	1	37	5
Herbed Lamb Kabobs (p. 96)	232	17	21	9	59	460	409	26	9	96	10	15	20	2	9
Honey-Ginger Chicken (p. 98)	192	27	14	3	72	169	242	41	0	4	4	6	58	2	6
Honey-Orange Beef (p. 68)	304	22	40	7	49	183	541	34	32	96	15	14	26	6	20
Hot Tuna Toss (p. 116)	290	29	32	4	58	220	461	45	26	58	15	8	69	4	17
Italian Eggplant Casserole (p. 119)	353	23	42	10	31	425	1105	35	68	116	22	26	18	51	23
Lean Irish Stew (p. 96)	233	14	30	7	39	236	837	22	159	42	13	11	22	5	12
Lean Taco Salad (p. 81)	357	32	25	15	95	353	1422	49	145	196	20	25	39	20	51
Low-Fat Moussaka (p. 97)	185	14	15	7	57	225	543	21	18	23	11	16	14	14	13
Macaroni and Cheese with Vegetables (p. 122)	306	16	32	12	37	590	429	25	34	65	14	22	8	36	8
Marinated and Grilled Leg of Lamb (p. 95)	252	32	2	12	110	78	390	49	1	10	12	20	34	2	14
Marinated Fish Fillets (p. 111)	111	15	2	5	41	90	346	23	0	10	5	3	10	1	2
Meatballs in Mushroom-Yogurt Sauce (p.75)	331	26	33	9	67	148	556	40	25	6	18	27	32	11	21
Mexicali Stew (p. 72)	283	21	33	9	44	495	768	32	91	101	11	15	21	18	30
Mexican Chops and Vegetables (p. 93)	321	26	33	11	69	373	621	40	71	105	53	20	31	6	17
Minestrone (p. 119)	333	20	59	4	7	489	1438	30	110	60	36	26	26	31	36

Since nutrition has become a "hot" topic, giving advice about the subject also has become popular—and lucrative. Self-styled "nutrition counselors" and "diet clinics" have set up shop around the country, promising to solve diet problems for a fee. A few states have begun to establish standards, but in most places anyone can claim to be a nutritionist. Therefore, you must examine qualifications carefully, and be on guard against unqualified persons and quacks.

Be wary of those who promise to treat an "illness" with diet, especially a self-diagnosed "illness" that would be difficult to confirm by medical tests, such as a "glandular insufficiency" or "hypoglycemia." Another warning signal is a "nutritionist" who pushes a specific "super food," rather than emphasizing the overall quality of the diet. And since dietary needs of most persons can be met at the dinner table, ethical nutritionists seldom prescribe expensive vitamins, minerals, or food supplements.

The most reliable source of information on nutrition and diet is a registered dietitian. The 50,000 men and women who carry the initials R.D. after their names have met a rigorous set of criteria established by the American Dietetic Association. They must have completed a four-year course of academic study at an accredited college or university, plus a dietetic internship in a hospital or institution, or a three-year work experience program. They must also pass a registration examination and take continuing education courses to keep up to date. Many R.D.s hold a master's or doctoral degree.

At one time most dietitians worked for institutions, planning menus for large food-service programs such as a university cafeteria, or assisting hospitals with patient meals. Or they were on hospital staffs to help doctors draw up specialized diets for convalescing patients or those with chronic illnesses.

More recently, many R.D.s have gone into private practice or set up small clinics to help individuals with their diets. They may provide general nutrition advice, or, with a doctor's referral, set up an individually tailored diet set up for particular needs and life-style.

Your family doctor also knows more about nutrition than in the past. Once nutrition was crowded out of the medical-school curriculum, but today most medical schools teach at least one nutrition course, according to the American Association of Medical Colleges. Continuing education and convention programs also offer doctors a better understanding of the relationship between nutrition and good physical health.

Local health departments, college and university nutrition departments, and the Society for Nutrition Education also are reliable sources of information, as are local chapters of the American Dietetic Association, American Diabetes Association, American Red Cross, and American Heart Association, which also offer nutrition courses in schools or community centers free or for a nominal charge.

The next time you're cooking for one, make Cider-Turkey Soup and Dilled Potato Salad (see recipes, page 50). They're just the right amount for one.

Menus

CHAPTER 2

Good eating habits are easy to practice when you start with delicious recipes. To help you get into the habit of a healthy diet, we've put together some excellent examples. The following daily menus show you how to combine a variety of foods wisely to meet your body's needs. Whether you're feeding a busy family or just yourself, going all out for company or keeping it casual, cutting back on meat or cutting back on last-minute cooking, you'll find a menu to fit the situation.

CONTENTS

MAKE-AHEAD
MENU

Your body tells you it's time to eat, but there's no time to cook the nourishing meal you're hungry for. It's easy to understand how you could fall into the fast food frenzy of grabbing something quick to pacify your appetite. But don't!

By cooking in spare moments before the urge to eat strikes, you can sit down to an already-ready meal that's both satisfying and nutritious.

MAKE AHEAD

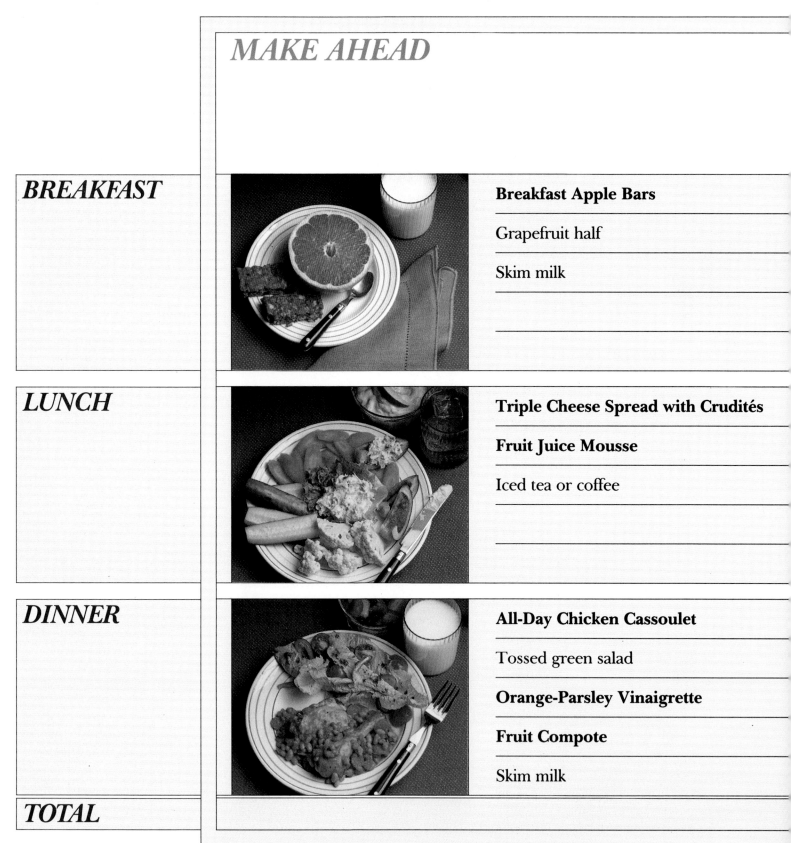

BREAKFAST

Breakfast Apple Bars

Grapefruit half

Skim milk

LUNCH

Triple Cheese Spread with Crudités

Fruit Juice Mousse

Iced tea or coffee

DINNER

All-Day Chicken Cassoulet

Tossed green salad

Orange-Parsley Vinaigrette

Fruit Compote

Skim milk

TOTAL

	PER SERVING						PERCENT U.S. RDA PER SERVING							
CALORIES	PROTEIN (g)	CARBOHYDRATE (g)	FAT (g)	CHOLESTEROL (mg)	SODIUM (mg)	POTASSIUM (mg)	PROTEIN	VITAMIN A	VITAMIN C	THIAMINE	RIBOFLAVIN	NIACIN	CALCIUM	IRON
182	3	23	10	0	75	169	4	8	4	6	2	3	1	5
38	1	10	0	0	1	167	1	3	69	3	1	2	1	1
85	8	12	0	4	126	404	13	10	4	6	20	1	30	1
253	20	10	16	23	405	411	30	51	45	27	15	7	31	11
105	1	17	4	0	6	134	1	0	6	0	1	0	1	1
0	0	0	0	0	0	0	0	0	0	0	0	0	0	0
249	28	20	6	67	190	712	43	44	16	15	12	40	7	19
60	3	13	1	0	27	638	5	33	360	13	11	8	4	10
97	0	2	10	0	1	39	0	4	14	1	0	0	1	1
59	1	14	0	0	2	238	1	4	82	4	3	2	1	1
85	8	12	0	4	126	404	13	10	4	6	20	1	30	1
1213	**73**	**133**	**47**	**98**	**959**	**3316**	**111**	**167**	**604**	**81**	**85**	**64**	**107**	**51**

Fit the food-fixing for today's menu into YOUR schedule. Breakfast Apple Bars and Fruit Compote can be made weeks ahead and frozen. Mix up the Triple Cheese Spread and the Orange-Parsley Vinaigrette in advance. Allow 3 to 24 hours for the Fruit Juice Mousse to chill. And while your day speeds by, let dinner's main dish, All-Day Chicken Cassoulet, cook unattended in the crockery cooker.

Making foods ahead is a successful device to help manage your time. Wise use of leftovers is another time-saving hint you can try with the foods on this menu. Save the remaining Breakfast Apple Bars *for another night's dessert or pack them in a sack lunch. Use any surplus* Triple Cheese Spread *as a cracker spread for a snack and reserve any unserved fresh vegetables for tossed salad or soup ingredients. If there is any* Fruit Compote *left, serve it as a breakfast fruit cup or as a topping for angel cake, ice milk, or sherbet.*

BREAKFAST APPLE BARS

Honey sweetens these moist, fruity bars.

    Nonstick spray coating
½ **cup whole wheat flour**
½ **cup quick-cooking rolled oats**
½ **teaspoon baking soda**
¼ **teaspoon ground cinnamon**
¼ **cup cooking oil**
¼ **cup applesauce**
3 **tablespoons honey**
½ **teaspoon vanilla**
½ **of a 6-ounce package (¾ cup) mixed dried fruit bits**
¼ **cup chopped walnuts**

Spray a 10x6x2-inch baking dish with non-stick coating. In a medium mixing bowl stir together flour, oats, baking soda, and cinnamon. Combine oil, applesauce, honey, and vanilla. Stir applesauce mixture into flour mixture till combined. Stir in dried fruit and nuts. Transfer to the prepared baking dish and spread evenly.

Bake in a 350° oven for 15 to 20 minutes or till a wooden toothpick inserted near center comes out clean. Cool in the dish on a wire rack. Cut into bars. Store in a tightly covered container at room temperature or in the freezer. Makes 16 bars (8 servings).

TRIPLE CHEESE SPREAD *with* CRUDITÉS

A trio of cottage, Swiss, and Parmesan cheeses in the spread provides complete protein for a meatless lunch.

1 **cup low-fat cottage cheese**
½ **cup shredded Swiss cheese (2 ounces)**
¼ **cup grated Parmesan cheese**
2 **tablespoons skim milk**
⅛ **teaspoon dried dillweed**
⅛ **teaspoon pepper**
¼ **cup unsalted sunflower nuts**
¼ **cup finely shredded carrot**
1½ **cups assorted fresh vegetables (cauliflower flowerets, cucumber spears, bias-sliced carrots, *or* green pepper wedges)**

In a blender container or food processor bowl combine cottage cheese, Swiss cheese, Parmesan cheese, milk, dillweed, and pepper. Cover and process till smooth. Transfer to a container. Stir in sunflower nuts and carrot. Cover and chill. Serve with fresh vegetables. Makes 1⅓ cups (4 servings).

FRUIT JUICE MOUSSE

Light and refreshing.

1 **teaspoon unflavored gelatin**
⅔ **cup cold water**
½ **of a 6-ounce can (⅓ cup) frozen apple juice concentrate**
¼ **teaspoon finely shredded lemon peel**
2 **teaspoons lemon juice**
¼ **teaspoon ground cinnamon**
1 **small apple, cored, peeled, and shredded**
½ **of a 4-ounce container frozen whipped dessert topping, thawed Apple slices**

In a medium saucepan soften gelatin in water for 5 minutes. Heat and stir the gelatin mixture till gelatin is dissolved. Remove from heat. Stir in apple juice concentrate, lemon peel, lemon juice, and cinnamon. Chill till partially set (consistency of unbeaten egg whites). Fold in apple and dessert topping. Transfer to a 2-cup bowl or soufflé dish, or to 4 individual dessert glasses. Refrigerate for 3 to 24 hours before serving. Garnish with apple slices. Makes 4 servings.

ALL-DAY CHICKEN CASSOULET

Cook the navy beans the night before. Then in the morning, put all the ingredients in the crockery cooker to simmer till dinnertime.

- ½ cup dry navy beans
- 1½ to 2 pounds chicken pieces, skin removed
- ¾ cup sodium-reduced tomato juice
- ½ cup chopped celery
- ½ cup sliced carrot
- ½ cup chopped onion
- 1 clove garlic, minced
- 1 bay leaf
- 1 teaspoon instant beef bouillon granules
- ½ teaspoon dried basil, crushed
- ½ teaspoon dried oregano, crushed
- ½ teaspoon dried sage, crushed
- ¼ teaspoon paprika

Rinse beans. In a medium saucepan combine beans and 2 cups *water*. Bring to boiling. Boil, uncovered, for 10 minutes. Drain. Add 2 cups more *water*. Return to boiling; reduce heat. Cover and simmer about 1½ hours or till beans are tender. Drain; cover and chill.

In an electric slow crockery cooker combine beans, chicken pieces, sodium-reduced tomato juice, celery, carrot, onion, garlic, bay leaf, bouillon granules, basil, oregano, sage, and paprika. Cover and cook on low-heat setting for 8 to 10 hours. Remove and discard bay leaf. Makes 4 servings.

ORANGE-PARSLEY VINAIGRETTE

This citrus dressing gives even the simplest tossed salad extraordinary flavor.

- 3 tablespoons olive oil *or* salad oil
- 1 teaspoon finely shredded orange peel
- 3 tablespoons orange juice
- 2 tablespoons finely snipped parsley
- 1 tablespoon white wine vinegar *or* vinegar
- ¼ teaspoon dried marjoram, crushed Dash pepper

In a small screw-top jar combine the oil, orange peel, orange juice, parsley, vinegar, marjoram, and pepper. Cover and shake well to mix. Chill. Shake again just before using. Makes about ½ cup (4 servings).

FRUIT COMPOTE

No sugar added!

- 1 cup sliced fresh *or* frozen strawberries
- ½ cup fresh *or* frozen blueberries
- ½ cup fresh *or* frozen peach slices, halved
- ¼ teaspoon finely shredded orange peel
- 1 cup orange-pineapple juice *or* orange juice Coconut, toasted (optional)

In a mixing bowl combine strawberries, blueberries, and peaches. Stir in orange peel. Pour juice over fruit. Divide fruit-juice mixture evenly among four 1-cup freezer containers. Seal, label, and freeze.

Before serving, let stand at room temperature about 3 hours or till thawed. Or, thaw in refrigerator for 6 to 8 hours. Sprinkle with toasted coconut, if desired. Makes 4 servings.

ON-the-GO
MENU

A busy life-style allows little time for cooking. It also may mean eating out regularly. Because the fast pace you keep may put stress on your body, sound nutrition is vital to keep your body and mind in top-notch working order.

Relax! With quick, wholesome recipes to fix at home, as well as a working knowledge of what you should eat in restaurants, you can overcome the time crunch and eat right. In addition to the recipes in this menu, search out the many other recipes in the book labeled "Quick Recipe."

ON-the-GO

BREAKFAST	**Pineapple-Rice Compote**
	Toast with margarine
	Skim milk
LUNCH	Salad-bar salad
	Crisp rye cracker
	Sodium-reduced vegetable juice
	cocktail
DINNER	**Pronto Mini Pizzas**
	Lettuce wedge with reduced-calorie
	salad dressing
	Banana Shakers
SNACK	Unsalted peanuts
	Tomato Beer
TOTAL	

| | PER SERVING | | | | | | PERCENT U.S. RDA PER SERVING | | | | | | | |
CALORIES	PROTEIN (g)	CARBOHYDRATE (g)	FAT (g)	CHOLESTEROL (mg)	SODIUM (mg)	POTASSIUM (mg)	PROTEIN	VITAMIN A	VITAMIN C	THIAMINE	RIBOFLAVIN	NIACIN	CALCIUM	IRON
236	3	56	0	0	4	302	5	2	70	20	2	8	3	8
114	3	15	5	1	188	37	4	3	0	6	4	5	3	5
85	8	12	0	4	126	404	13	10	4	6	20	1	30	1
543	49	39	23	59	1373	1364	75	118	598	23	58	16	55	28
23	1	5	0	0	50	32	1	0	0	2	1	0	0	2
51	0	10	0	0	56	588	0	88	87	3	4	9	4	8
430	40	48	6	81	172	699	62	15	20	22	30	51	16	32
43	1	7	1	0	204	184	2	7	11	3	3	2	2	3
124	3	20	4	16	61	249	5	5	12	4	11	1	13	1
838	38	30	70	0	7	1009	58	0	0	31	11	123	10	18
62	1	6	0	0	15	194	1	13	15	2	1	3	0	3
2549	147	248	109	161	2256	5062	226	261	817	122	145	219	136	109

Take advantage of time-saving cooking techniques to prepare this menu. Cook the Pineapple-Rice Compote *in just minutes. Use the broiler to cook the* Pronto Mini Pizzas, *again, in just minutes. And let an electric blender make* Banana Shakers *for you with the push of a button. Of course, the technique that saves you the most time in the kitchen is going out to eat for the salad-bar lunch!*

·QUICK RECIPE·

PINEAPPLE-RICE COMPOTE

This fruity breakfast cereal is a super-simple way to start any day.

> 1 15¼-ounce can crushed pineapple (juice pack)
> 1⅓ cups orange juice
> 4 teaspoons brown sugar
>   Dash ground allspice
> 1⅓ cups quick-cooking rice

In a medium saucepan stir together the *undrained* pineapple, orange juice, brown sugar, and ground allspice. Bring to boiling. Remove from heat; stir in rice. Cover and let stand 5 minutes. Transfer to serving bowls. Sprinkle with additional allspice, if desired. Makes 4 servings.

SALAD BAR LUNCH: No matter how fast you're moving, take a minute to think of healthier alternatives to the norm. For instance, at the salad bar for lunch today, pile on the greens and vegetables that carry few calories and go easy on the heavier mixtures such as potato and macaroni salads. Be sure to reach for high-protein items such as cottage cheese, chopped egg, legumes, sunflower nuts, and lean meats, if available. Choose a reduced-calorie salad dressing, if it's provided. And be sure to avoid drenching the greens—most salad dressings are high in sodium.

·QUICK RECIPE·

PRONTO MINI PIZZAS

Toasted pita bread rounds make crispy crusts for these individual pizzas.

> 1 pound fresh *or* frozen ground raw turkey
> 4 large whole wheat pita bread rounds
> 1 cup sliced fresh mushrooms
> ½ cup chopped onion
> 2 cloves garlic, minced
> 1 cup sodium-reduced tomato sauce
> ½ teaspoon fennel seed, crushed
> ¼ teaspoon dried oregano, crushed
> ½ cup shredded mozzarella cheese (2 ounces)

Thaw ground turkey, if frozen. Place pita bread rounds on a baking sheet. Broil about 3 inches from heat about 1 minute per side or till toasted. Set aside.

In a medium skillet cook turkey, mushrooms, onion, and garlic over medium heat till turkey is lightly browned and vegetables are tender. Stir in tomato sauce, fennel seed, and oregano. Cook and stir 1 minute more.

Divide meat mixture evenly between the toasted pita rounds. Sprinkle with mozzarella cheese. Return to the broiler; broil about 3 inches from heat for 1 to 2 minutes or till cheese is melted. Makes 4 servings.

·QUICK RECIPE·
BANANA SHAKERS

Freezing the sliced banana makes the drink colder and more refreshing to sip.

- **1 cup unsweetened pineapple juice**
- **1 cup skim milk**
- **1 cup vanilla ice milk**
- **2 ripe large bananas, peeled, sliced, and frozen**
- **2 teaspoons vanilla**

In a blender container combine pineapple juice, skim milk, ice milk, frozen sliced banana, and vanilla. Cover and blend mixture till smooth. Makes 4 servings.

·QUICK RECIPE·
TOMATO BEER

While the adults sip on Tomato Beer or its non-alcoholic version, let the kids enjoy a glass of vegetable juice cocktail or fruit juice.

- **2 12-ounce cans light beer, sparkling mineral water, *or* carbonated water, chilled**
- **2 6-ounce cans sodium-reduced vegetable juice cocktail, chilled**
  Several dashes bottled hot pepper sauce
- **4 lemon slices *or* celery sticks (optional)**

In a small pitcher combine cold beer, mineral water, or carbonated water; sodium-reduced vegetable juice cocktail; and hot pepper sauce; stir till well combined. Pour over ice in 4 tall glasses. Garnish each with a lemon slice or celery stick, if desired. Makes 4 servings.

THE KNACK OF SNACKING: You need not sacrifice snacking to eat a well-balanced diet. If you're wise about what you munch, you can supplement the main meals of the day with a wholesome, between-meal pickup.

Instead of downing a snack that provides calories and nothing more (commonly known as "empty" calories), take advantage of the opportunity to boost your nutrient intake. A light meat sandwich, a nut mix, or yogurt provides protein that meals eaten on the run might lack. Fresh fruits and vegetables make low-calorie, high-vitamin nibbles. And for sensible alternatives to soft drinks, switch to fruit-, vegetable-, or milk-based beverages.

MEATLESS

MENU

Meatless meals make sense! Besides sometimes being easier on the budget, they bring new and different textures and flavors to your eating routine.

Eating meatless meals involves more than leaving meat out of your sandwich. With a little planning, you can combine foods, as described in the tip on page 44, to equal the protein level of the meat you've omitted.

MEATLESS

BREAKFAST

Hot Spiced Oatmeal

English muffin half with margarine

Orange juice

LUNCH

Vegewiches

Garden Gazpacho

Apple

Skim milk

DINNER

Vegetarian-Style Chili

Salad with reduced-calorie dressing

Low-sodium crackers

Cherry-Yogurt Freeze

Skim milk

TOTAL

	PER SERVING							PERCENT U.S. RDA PER SERVING							
CALORIES	PROTEIN (g)	CARBOHYDRATE (g)	FAT (g)	CHOLESTEROL (mg)	SODIUM (mg)	POTASSIUM (mg)	PROTEIN	VITAMIN A	VITAMIN C	THIAMINE	RIBOFLAVIN	NIACIN	CALCIUM	IRON
226	7	48	2	1	300	472	10	26	3	15	8	5	7	13
109	4	16	4	0	44	2	5	3	0	7	4	5	5	4
84	1	20	0	0	2	355	2	3	121	10	2	2	2	1
495	22	63	20	0	1471	984	34	87	94	12	14	35	18	45
118	3	13	7	0	192	651	4	38	121	8	6	8	5	9
89	0	23	1	0	0	173	0	2	14	2	1	1	1	2
85	8	12	0	4	126	404	13	10	4	6	20	1	30	1
404	20	53	15	15	181	1222	30	76	54	48	41	62	36	104
79	6	12	2	1	37	824	10	61	224	13	36	21	13	12
144	3	24	4	0	3	63	5	0	0	15	8	9	0	7
130	4	28	1	2	41	200	7	2	1	2	8	1	8	1
85	8	12	0	4	126	404	13	10	4	6	20	1	30	1
2048	**86**	**1324**	**56**	**27**	**2523**	**5754**	**133**	**318**	**640**	**144**	**168**	**151**	**155**	**200**

We're willing to bet you won't miss the meat in today's menu. That's because we've replaced it with a variety of satisfying substitutes. Whole grains (oats, wheat, barley, and rye), milk products (yogurt, cheddar cheese, and skim milk), legumes (garbanzo beans, kidney beans, and peanuts), ground sesame seed, and fresh fruits and vegetables deliver protein without letting the thought of meat cross your mind.

·QUICK RECIPE·

HOT SPICED OATMEAL

1½	**cups water**
¾	**cup quick-cooking rolled oats**
½	**cup mixed dried fruit bits**
1½	**teaspoons honey**
½	**teaspoon ground cinnamon**
¼	**teaspoon salt**
⅛	**teaspoon ground nutmeg**
¼	**cup skim milk**

In a small saucepan bring water to boiling. Gradually stir in oats, dried fruit bits, honey, cinnamon, salt, and nutmeg. Cook, stirring occasionally, for 1 minute. Cover and remove from heat. Let stand for 3 minutes. Divide mixture between 2 bowls. Pour *half* of the skim milk over each. Makes 2 servings.

VEGEWICHES

Look for tahini in the supermarket or a health food store. Similar to thick peanut butter in consistency, it adds sesame flavor to spreads and salad dressings.

1	**15-ounce can garbanzo beans, drained**
¼	**cup tahini (sesame seed paste)**
3	**tablespoons lemon juice**
2	**cloves garlic, minced**
¼	**teaspoon salt**
¼	**teaspoon paprika**
½	**cup snipped parsley**
½	**medium zucchini *or* yellow crookneck squash, sliced**
1	**small carrot, sliced**
½	**small onion, sliced and separated into rings**
2	**slices rye bread, toasted**

In a blender container or food processor bowl combine the garbanzo beans, tahini, lemon juice, garlic, salt, and paprika. Cover and blend or process till mixture is smooth,

stopping and scraping the sides as necessary. Stir in parsley. Cover and chill.

Place zucchini or squash, carrot, and onion in a steamer basket. In a medium saucepan place basket over boiling water. Cover and steam for 3 to 5 minutes or till vegetables are crisp-tender. Remove vegetables; cover and chill.

Spread *2 tablespoons* of the bean mixture on *each* slice of toasted bread. (Cover and chill the remaining spread. Save for another use.) Top each with half of the vegetables. Serve sandwiches open-face. Makes 2 servings.

GARDEN GAZPACHO

For this cool soup, either use hot-style vegetable juice cocktail or use regular vegetable juice cocktail and spike it with several dashes of hot pepper sauce.

2	**medium tomatoes**
1	**small cucumber, seeded and chopped (1 cup)**
1	**6-ounce can (¾ cup) hot-style vegetable juice cocktail**
¼	**cup finely chopped green pepper**
2	**tablespoons snipped parsley**
1	**tablespoon lemon juice**
1	**tablespoon olive oil *or* cooking oil**
1	**small clove garlic, minced**
¼	**teaspoon dried tarragon, crushed**
¼	**teaspoon dried basil, crushed**
	Dash pepper

To loosen the tomato skin for easier peeling, spear a tomato with a fork and plunge it into boiling water for 10 seconds. Immediately immerse it in cold water. Peel tomato and discard skin. Repeat with other tomato. Core and coarsely chop tomatoes.

In a medium mixing bowl combine tomatoes, cucumber, vegetable juice cocktail, green pepper, parsley, lemon juice, oil, garlic, tarragon, basil, and pepper. Cover and chill. Transfer to soup bowls. Makes 2 servings.

VEGETARIAN-STYLE CHILI

Here's proof you don't need meat to make a hearty chili. Use kidney beans, barley, cheddar cheese, and peanuts to meet your protein needs.

- 1 **8-ounce can red kidney beans**
- 1 **cup sodium-reduced tomato juice**
- 1 **7½-ounce can sodium-reduced tomatoes, cut up**
- ½ **cup water**
- ½ **cup chopped onion**
- ¼ **cup sliced carrot**
- ¼ **cup sliced celery**
- 1 **clove garlic, minced**
- 1 **bay leaf**
- 1 **teaspoon chili powder**
- ¼ **teaspoon dried basil, crushed**
- ⅛ **teaspoon pepper**
    Few dashes bottled hot pepper sauce
- 3 **tablespoons pearl barley**
- ¼ **cup shredded cheddar cheese (1 ounce)**
- ¼ **cup unsalted peanuts, coarsely chopped (optional)**

In a medium saucepan combine *undrained* beans, tomato juice, *undrained* tomatoes, water, onion, carrot, celery, garlic, bay leaf, chili powder, basil, pepper, and hot pepper sauce. Bring to boiling; reduce heat. Stir in barley. Cover and simmer about 1 hour or till barley is tender. Remove bay leaf. Transfer to soup bowls. Sprinkle each serving with half of the cheese. Sprinkle each serving with half of the peanuts, if desired. Makes 2 servings.

CHERRY-YOGURT FREEZE

You'd feel guilty eating this frosty dessert if you didn't know it had only half the calories of cherry ice cream!

- 1 **16-ounce package frozen unsweetened pitted dark sweet cherries, thawed**
- 2 **teaspoons unflavored gelatin**
- 2 **8-ounce cartons vanilla low-fat yogurt**
- ¼ **cup sugar**
- 2 **egg whites**
- ⅓ **cup sugar**

Drain cherries, reserving juice. Cut up cherries and set aside. In a small saucepan soften gelatin in reserved juice for 5 minutes. Heat and stir the gelatin mixture till the gelatin is dissolved. Remove from heat and cool.

Stir together cherries, gelatin mixture, yogurt, and ¼ cup sugar. Transfer mixture to a 12x7½x2-inch baking dish. Cover and freeze about 1 hour or till edges are partially frozen. Transfer to a chilled large mixer bowl. Beat with an electric mixer till fluffy.

Wash beaters. Beat egg whites till soft peaks form (tips curl). Gradually add ⅓ cup sugar, beating till stiff peaks form (tips stand straight). Fold egg whites into yogurt mixture. Cover and freeze about 6 hours or till firm. Scoop to serve. Makes 10 servings.

COOKING-for-ONE

MENU

Nutritious eating on your own is a challenge, but it's getting easier! Supermarkets are stocking more small-quantity and individually wrapped items, many of which are sodium- or calorie-reduced. Many health-conscious recipes today are designed to serve fewer people. What's more, eating for your body's sake has become a delicious trend.

The simpler and quicker your nutritious meals-for-one, the better your chances of sticking to your standards. The menu that follows sets a good example.

COOKING-*for*-ONE

BREAKFAST

Bagel with peanut butter

Peach Smoothie

LUNCH

Cider-Turkey Soup

Dilled Potato Salad

Melba toast

Skim milk

DINNER

Barbecued Beef on Lettuce

Steamed broccoli spears

Melon Salad Dessert

Coffee or tea

TOTAL

	PER SERVING							PERCENT U.S. RDA PER SERVING							
CALORIES	PROTEIN (g)	CARBOHYDRATE (g)	FAT (g)	CHOLESTEROL (mg)	SODIUM (mg)	POTASSIUM (mg)	PROTEIN	VITAMIN A	VITAMIN C	THIAMINE	RIBOFLAVIN	NIACIN	CALCIUM	IRON
254	10	34	9	0	293	145	15	0	0	15	10	22	3	10
200	11	41	0	5	152	752	16	31	17	7	29	8	33	4
275	29	28	5	72	354	719	44	64	149	7	14	29	7	16
106	4	22	1	2	162	602	7	3	77	7	6	8	8	7
15	1	3	0	3	3	9	1	0	0	0	0	0	0	0
85	8	12	0	4	126	404	13	10	4	0	20	1	30	1
224	25	8	10	80	205	562	38	20	23	10	14	29	4	23
20	2	3	0	0	8	207	4	39	116	5	9	3	7	3
137	4	18	7	1	36	617	5	108	117	5	4	5	6	4
0	0	0	0	0	0	0	0	0	0	0	0	0	0	0
1316	94	169	32	167	1339	4017	143	275	503	56	106	105	98	68

The three-point theme to this menu is fast, fresh, and light. For example, whirl together the ingredients for the Peach Smoothie *in 5 minutes. Both* Cider-Turkey Soup *and* Dilled Potato Salad *boast lots of fresh vegetables and, as a result, fresh taste. And for dinner, serve* Barbecued Beef on Lettuce *instead of on a bun.*

·QUICK RECIPE·

PEACH SMOOTHIE

To chill the peaches in a hurry, stick the can in the freezer about 20 minutes before opening it.

>   1   **8½-ounce can peach slices (juice pack), chilled**
> ¼   **cup nonfat dry milk powder**
>   1   **teaspoon vanilla**
>   **Dash ground nutmeg**
>   2   **ice cubes**

In a blender container combine *undrained* peach slices, nonfat dry milk powder, vanilla, and nutmeg. Cover and blend till smooth. Add ice cubes. Cover and blend till combined. Makes 1 serving.

·QUICK RECIPE·

CIDER-TURKEY SOUP

It's pleasantly seasoned with gingerroot, basil, and orange peel.

> ¾   **cup apple cider *or* apple juice**
> ¼   **cup water**
>   3   **tablespoons sliced green onion**
> ½   **teaspoon grated gingerroot *or* ⅛ teaspoon ground ginger**
> ⅛   **teaspoon salt**
> ⅛   **teaspoon dried basil, crushed**
>   **Dash pepper**
> ⅔   **cup cubed cooked turkey**
> ¼   **cup shredded zucchini**
> ¼   **cup shredded carrot**
> ⅛   **teaspoon finely shredded orange peel**

In a small saucepan combine cider or juice, water, green onion, gingerroot or ginger, salt, basil, and pepper. Bring to boiling; reduce heat. Cover and simmer for 5 minutes.

Add turkey, zucchini, carrot, and orange peel. Return to boiling; reduce heat. Cover and simmer for 3 to 5 minutes more or till heated through. Makes 1 serving.

DILLED POTATO SALAD

Instead of using a mayonnaise mixture, dress this potato salad with a low-fat herbed yogurt dressing.

>   1   **small potato, unpeeled and cubed (½ cup) *or* 2 whole tiny new potatoes**
> ¼   **cup chopped cucumber**
>   2   **radishes, sliced**
>   2   **tablespoons chopped green pepper *or* sweet red pepper**
>   2   **tablespoons plain low-fat yogurt**
>   1   **teaspoon tarragon vinegar *or* vinegar**
> ⅛   **teaspoon dried dillweed**
>   **Dash salt**
>   **Dash pepper**
>   **Cucumber slices (optional)**

In a small saucepan cook potatoes in boiling water for 8 to 10 minutes or till tender. Drain.

In a small mixing bowl combine potatoes, chopped cucumber, radishes, and green or sweet red pepper. Stir together yogurt, vinegar, dillweed, salt, and pepper. Add yogurt mixture to potato mixture and toss to coat. Cover and chill for at least 1 hour. Spoon mixture onto a salad plate ringed with cucumber slices, if desired. Makes 1 serving.

BARBECUED BEEF on LETTUCE

Try dolloping the top of each serving with cool and creamy plain low-fat yogurt.

4 ounces lean ground beef
2 tablespoons chopped onion
⅓ cup water
1 tablespoon tomato paste
1 teaspoon red wine vinegar *or* vinegar
¼ teaspoon sugar
¼ teaspoon chili powder
⅛ teaspoon celery seed
Dash Worcestershire sauce
1 cup shredded lettuce

In a small skillet cook ground beef and onion till meat is brown and onion is tender. Drain off fat.

Stir in water, tomato paste, vinegar, sugar, chili powder, celery seed, and Worcestershire sauce. Bring to boiling; reduce heat. Simmer, uncovered, for 8 to 10 minutes or to desired consistency.

Place shredded lettuce on a serving plate. Top with the meat mixture. Makes 1 serving.

MELON SALAD DESSERT

It's really a salad, but it tastes like dessert.

½ of a small cantaloupe
1 tablespoon plain low-fat yogurt
1 tablespoon frozen whipped dessert topping, thawed
¼ teaspoon snipped fresh mint *or* a pinch dried mint, crushed
1 tablespoon sliced celery
1 tablespoon chopped walnuts
Leaf lettuce
Mint sprig (optional)

Remove seeds from the cantaloupe. With a melon ball cutter, scoop cantaloupe into balls. With a spoon carefully scoop any remaining cantaloupe from the shell and cut into bite-size pieces. Reserve remaining cantaloupe pieces for another use. Reserve the shell.

In a small mixing bowl combine yogurt, dessert topping, and snipped mint. Stir till well combined. Add celery, walnuts, and cantaloupe balls. Toss to coat.

Line the cantaloupe shell with lettuce. Spoon the cantaloupe mixture into the shell. Garnish with a mint sprig, if desired. Makes 1 serving.

GROUND BEEF TIPS: *Begin by buying the leanest ground beef available. The lower the fat content, the fewer the calories. Next, be sure to drain off as much fat as you can after cooking. Drain crumbly ground beef in a colander, blotting with a paper towel to absorb clinging grease. Drain cooked beef patties on a double thickness of paper towels and blot the tops.*

Here's a handy single-serving storage tip. Because butchers usually package ground beef by the pound and all you need for one serving is 4 ounces, divide the pound into four parts. Wrap and freeze the parts you won't be using right away. This avoids thawing the entire pound of meat for one serving.

SUNDAY-SPECIAL
MENU

Sundays are perfect times for get-togethers with family or friends. Indeed, sharing good food makes the gathering extra special. Start out with a late-morning brunch that keeps the energy high throughout the afternoon. After a full day of fun, offer a light soup-and-sandwich supper. Later on, bring out healthful nibbles for snacking.

SUNDAY-SPECIAL

BRUNCH

Spinach-Cheese Crepes

Easy Zucchini-Orange Salad

Pumpkin Nut Bread

Hot cider

SUPPER

Sweet Potato Soup

Chicken in the Rye

Skim milk

SNACK

Popcorn

Apple

Iced tea

TOTAL

	PER SERVING						PERCENT U.S. RDA PER SERVING							
CALORIES	PROTEIN (g)	CARBOHYDRATE (g)	FAT (g)	CHOLESTEROL (mg)	SODIUM (mg)	POTASSIUM (mg)	PROTEIN	VITAMIN A	VITAMIN C	THIAMINE	RIBOFLAVIN	NIACIN	CALCIUM	IRON
253	16	20	13	63	345	397	24	110	16	11	20	6	36	11
31	1	7	0	0	2	194	2	9	61	4	4	3	4	2
160	3	24	6	15	77	149	5	17	2	7	4	4	5	6
85	0	21	0	0	5	215	0	0	3	3	2	1	1	4
121	4	25	1	2	95	397	7	118	31	7	10	3	13	4
293	32	28	6	77	373	410	49	11	16	15	14	67	7	14
85	8	12	0	4	126	404	13	10	4	6	20	1	30	1
23	1	5	0	0	0	15	1	0	0	1	0	1	0	1
89	0	23	1	0	0	173	0	2	14	2	1	1	1	2
0	0	0	0	0	0	0	0	0	0	0	0	0	0	0
1140	65	165	27	161	1023	2354	101	277	147	56	75	87	97	45

You can eat only two meals a day and still have a nutritious menu. For instance, this menu revolves around brunch, the meal that's too late for breakfast and too early for lunch. With such a satisfying brunch at midday, make the evening meal light. Later on, pop some popcorn and add fresh fruit for light snacking.

SPINACH-CHEESE CREPES

To freeze Whole Wheat Crepes, stack each between two layers of waxed paper to keep them separated. Overwrap the stack in a moisture- and vaporproof bag, then place it in a plastic container. Freeze for up to 4 months. Thaw as many crepes as you need at room temperature about one hour before using.

To shorten your time in the kitchen on Sunday, make the Whole Wheat Crepes ahead and freeze them.

- 1 **10-ounce package frozen chopped spinach**
- 1 **cup finely chopped carrot**
- 2 **tablespoons chopped onion**
- 1 **tablespoon margarine**
- 2 **tablespoons whole wheat flour *or* all-purpose flour**
- ¼ **teaspoon pepper**
- ⅔ **cup skim milk**
- 1 **cup shredded cheddar cheese (4 ounces)**
- ½ **cup low-fat cottage cheese**
- 12 **Whole Wheat Crepes (see recipe, right)**
- ½ **cup shredded cheddar cheese (2 ounces)**

Cook spinach according to package directions, *except* omit salt. Drain well. Meanwhile, in a medium saucepan cook carrot and onion in margarine till tender but not brown. Stir in flour and pepper. Add milk. Cook and stir till thickened and bubbly. Cook and stir 1 minute more. Stir in 1 cup cheddar cheese till melted. Remove from heat.

Fold spinach and cottage cheese into the thickened mixture in the saucepan. Spoon about *3 tablespoons* of the spinach mixture onto the *unbrowned* side of *each* crepe and roll up. Place crepes, seam side down, in a 12x7½x2-inch baking dish.

Bake, covered, in a 375° oven for 20 to 25 minutes or till heated through. Uncover and sprinkle with ½ cup cheddar cheese. Bake, uncovered, for 2 to 3 minutes more or till cheese is melted. Makes 6 servings.

WHOLE WHEAT CREPES

- ½ **cup all-purpose flour**
- ½ **cup whole wheat flour**
- 1½ **cups skim milk**
- 1 **egg**
  Nonstick spray coating
  Shortening

In a mixing bowl combine all-purpose flour and whole wheat flour. Add milk and egg. Beat with a rotary beater or wire whisk till combined. Spray a 6-inch skillet with nonstick coating. Heat the skillet over medium heat; remove from heat. Spoon in about *2 tablespoons* batter. Lift and tilt the skillet to spread batter. Return to heat; brown one side only.

Invert the pan over paper towels to remove crepe. Repeat to make about 18 crepes, lightly greasing skillet with shortening as necessary. *Do not* spray the *hot* skillet with nonstick coating. Makes 18 crepes (9 servings).

EASY ZUCCHINI-ORANGE SALAD

What could be a simpler, more nutritious salad dressing than fresh orange juice?

- 2 **medium oranges**
- 2 **medium zucchini, cut into julienne strips**
- ¼ **cup sliced green onion**
- 2 **tablespoons snipped parsley**

Finely shred enough orange peel to measure 1 teaspoon; set aside. Remove and discard remaining peel from oranges. Section oranges over a medium bowl, allowing sections and juice to fall into the bowl. Add peel, zucchini, green onion, and parsley to bowl; toss to coat. Cover and chill, stirring occasionally. Makes 6 servings.

PUMPKIN NUT BREAD

Make this pumpkin bread the day before, so it's ready to serve the next morning.

- 1¼ **cups all-purpose flour**
- ¾ **cup whole wheat flour**
- 2 **teaspoons baking powder**
- ½ **teaspoon ground ginger**
- ¼ **teaspoon ground cloves**
- ¾ **cup packed brown sugar**
- ⅓ **cup shortening**
- 1 **egg**
- 1 **egg white**
- 1 **cup canned pumpkin**
- ¼ **cup skim milk**
- ½ **cup chopped walnuts**
- ½ **cup raisins**
  Nonstick spray coating

In a mixing bowl stir together all-purpose flour, whole wheat flour, baking powder, ginger, and cloves; set aside. In a large mixer bowl beat together brown sugar and shortening till combined. Beat in egg and egg white. Add pumpkin and milk and mix well. Stir in flour mixture. Gently fold in chopped nuts and raisins.

Spray a 9x5x3-inch loaf pan with nonstick coating. Spoon batter into the prepared loaf pan. Bake in a 350° oven for 55 to 60 minutes or till a wooden toothpick inserted near center comes out clean. Cool in the pan for 10 minutes. Remove and cool thoroughly on a wire rack. Wrap and store overnight before slicing. Makes 1 loaf (18 servings).

CHICKEN in the RYE

- 3 **whole medium chicken breasts (about 2¼ pounds total), skinned, boned, and halved lengthwise**
- ¼ **cup dairy sour cream**
- 2 **teaspoons lemon juice**
- 1 **teaspoon Dijon-style mustard**
- ¼ **teaspoon dried tarragon, crushed**
- 12 **slices rye bread**
- 6 **lettuce leaves** *or* **1½ cups fresh alfalfa sprouts**
- 2 **medium tomatoes, thinly sliced (12 slices)**

Place chicken breasts on the rack of an unheated broiler pan. Broil 4 to 5 inches from the heat for 8 to 10 minutes total or till chicken is tender, turning once. Cool chicken. Thinly slice across the grain.

Combine sour cream, lemon juice, mustard, and tarragon. To make sandwiches, spread *half* of the bread slices with sour cream mixture. Top with lettuce or sprouts, chicken, tomato slices, and remaining bread. Cut each sandwich in half. Makes 6 servings.

SWEET POTATO SOUP

- 3 **medium sweet potatoes, peeled and sliced (about 3 cups)**
- 2 **cups water**
- 1 **medium parsnip, chopped**
- 1 **medium onion, chopped**
- ¾ **teaspoon instant chicken bouillon granules**
- ¼ **teaspoon ground nutmeg**
- 1½ **cups skim milk**
- ¼ **cup plain low-fat yogurt**

In a large saucepan combine sweet potatoes, water, parsnip, onion, bouillon granules, and nutmeg. Bring to boiling; reduce heat. Cover and simmer for 20 to 30 minutes or till vegetables are very tender. Transfer to a blender container. Cover and blend till smooth.

Return mixture to saucepan. Stir in milk and heat through. To serve, dollop each serving with a small amount of yogurt and stir slightly to swirl. If desired, sprinkle with additional nutmeg. Makes 6 servings.

OIL-FREE POPCORN:

Just pop the popcorn kernels in a heavy saucepan over medium-high heat—no oil needed. Be sure to cover the saucepan and shake constantly to keep the popcorn from scorching.

MICROWAVE-PLUS
MENU

In an ordinary day of meal preparation, you use your microwave oven whenever possible to save time in the kitchen. You may fix some foods exclusively in the microwave; for other foods you just use the microwave to speed up certain tasks.

We've done the same thing in designing this wholesome menu. It's an example of how you can use your microwave oven in addition to your other appliances to save time and energy while cooking healthful meals for your family.

MICROWAVE-PLUS

BREAKFAST

Fruit and Nut Yogurt

English muffin half with jam

Coffee or tea

LUNCH

Couscous Seafood Salad

Rusk or melba toast

Pear

Coffee or tea

DINNER

Vegetable Lasagna

Garlic Pita Triangles

Streusel-Topped Peaches

Skim milk

TOTAL

| | PER SERVING | | | | | | PERCENT U.S. RDA PER SERVING | | | | | | | |
CALORIES	PROTEIN (g)	CARBOHYDRATE (g)	FAT (g)	CHOLESTEROL (mg)	SODIUM (mg)	POTASSIUM (mg)	PROTEIN	VITAMIN A	VITAMIN C	THIAMINE	RIBOFLAVIN	NIACIN	CALCIUM	IRON
259	13	37	8	11	150	579	19	3	23	9	28	2	40	3
92	4	20	1	0	1	6	5	0	0	7	4	5	5	4
0	0	0	0	0	0	0	0	0	0	0	0	0	0	0
306	30	37	4	60	448	878	47	36	35	19	10	15	9	23
41	1	7	1	0	25	24	2	0	0	3	3	2	0	1
97	1	25	1	0	0	206	1	1	11	2	4	1	2	2
0	0	0	0	0	0	0	0	0	0	0	0	0	0	0
247	17	28	8	23	251	1066	26	186	116	21	33	16	38	30
83	3	10	3	0	34	4	4	2	0	3	3	5	1	3
121	2	21	4	0	47	225	3	12	10	5	3	5	2	4
85	8	12	0	4	126	404	13	10	4	6	20	1	30	1
1331	79	197	30	98	1082	3392	120	250	199	75	108	52	127	71

Explore the versatility of your microwave oven with this menu. Use it to thaw and cook the scallops for Couscous Seafood Salad, *melt the margarine for* Garlic Pita Triangles, *and bake the* Vegetable Lasagna *and the* Streusel-Topped Peaches.

Don't let that cold cup of coffee or tea go to waste. "Zap" it back to hot with your microwave oven. Make sure the beverage is in a nonmetal cup or mug. For 1 cup, micro-cook, uncovered, about 1½ minutes or just till steaming hot.

·QUICK RECIPE·

FRUIT and NUT YOGURT

Make your own breakfast yogurt using commercial yogurt and whatever fresh fruit you have on hand.

> **4 8-ounce cartons vanilla low-fat yogurt**
> **1 cup fresh fruit (cut-up strawberries, cut-up orange sections, blueberries, raspberries, *or* chopped apple)**
> **¼ cup chopped walnuts**

Stir together yogurt and fruit. Spoon into 4 bowls. Sprinkle with nuts. Makes 4 servings.

COUSCOUS SEAFOOD SALAD

Couscous, a wheat product native to the Middle East and North Africa, now commonly appears on American supermarket shelves and dinner tables.

> **1½ pounds fresh *or* frozen scallops**
> **⅔ cup ready-to-cook couscous**
> **1 small cucumber, quartered lengthwise and sliced**
> **1 medium carrot, shredded (½ cup)**
> **¼ cup sliced green onion**
> **⅓ cup vinegar**
> **2 tablespoons honey**
> **1 tablespoon salad oil**
> **¼ teaspoon dried tarragon, crushed**
> **⅛ teaspoon coarsely ground pepper**
> **1 6-ounce package frozen pea pods, thawed and bias-sliced**

Thaw scallops, if frozen.* Quarter any large scallops to make uniform, bite-size pieces. In a 1½-quart nonmetal casserole combine scallops and any scallop liquid. Micro-cook, covered, on 100% power (HIGH) for 4 to 6 minutes or till opaque, stirring after each minute. Drain, reserving ⅔ cup liquid. (If necessary, add water to make ⅔ cup liquid.) Cool scallops and reserved liquid.

Place couscous in a medium mixing bowl. In a 2-cup glass measure cook ⅔ cup reserved liquid on 100% power (HIGH) for 1 to 2 minutes or till boiling; pour over couscous. Let stand 5 minutes.

Stir cucumber, carrot, onion, and scallops into couscous. Combine vinegar, honey, oil, tarragon, and pepper. Pour over couscous mixture. Toss gently to coat. Cover and chill several hours. Before serving, stir in pea pods. If desired, serve on lettuce-lined plates. Makes 4 servings.

*To thaw scallops, in a 1½-quart nonmetal casserole micro-cook, uncovered, on 30% power (MEDIUM-LOW) about 11 minutes or till thawed, stirring twice.

GARLIC PITA TRIANGLES

Enjoy these toasty pitas instead of a piece of garlic bread for less than half the calories.

> **1 large whole wheat pita bread round**
> **1 tablespoon margarine**
> **⅛ teaspoon garlic powder**
> **½ teaspoon sesame seed**

Halve pita horizontally, making 2 rounds. In a custard cup micro-cook margarine, uncovered, on 100% power (HIGH) for 20 to 30 seconds or till melted. Stir in garlic powder.

Lightly spread melted margarine mixture on rough side of pita halves. Cut each pita half into 4 triangles. Sprinkle each with sesame seed. Place on a baking sheet. Bake in a 375° oven for 6 to 8 minutes or till toasted. Serve hot. Makes 8 triangles (4 servings).

VEGETABLE LASAGNA

Some brands of ricotta and mozzarella cheeses are made with whole milk and some are made partly with skim milk. Choose the latter to avoid unnecessary fat.

   4 **lasagna noodles (3 ounces)**
   1 **cup ricotta cheese**
   ½ **teaspoon dried basil, crushed**
   ¼ **teaspoon dried oregano, crushed**
   ¼ **teaspoon pepper**
  12 **cups torn fresh spinach (1 pound)** *or* **one 10-ounce package frozen chopped spinach**
   2 **cups sliced fresh mushrooms**
   ½ **cup chopped onion**
   ¼ **cup water**
  1½ **cups sodium-reduced spaghetti sauce**
   4 **ounces sliced mozzarella cheese**

Cook noodles according to package directions, *except* omit salt. Drain. Rinse with cold water and drain again. Stir together ricotta cheese, basil, oregano, and pepper.

In a Dutch oven place fresh spinach in a steamer basket over 1 inch of boiling water. Cover and steam for 2 to 3 minutes or till tender. Remove basket. (Or, cook frozen spinach according to package directions, *except* omit salt. Drain well.) In a 1-quart non-metal casserole combine mushrooms, onion, and water. Micro-cook, covered, on 100% power (HIGH) for 3 to 4 minutes or till tender, stirring once. Drain well. Stir in spaghetti sauce. Cook, covered, on 100% power (HIGH) about 3 minutes or till mixture is heated through, stirring once.

Arrange *two* lasagna noodles in a nonmetal 10x6x2-inch baking dish, cutting to fit. Spread *half* of the ricotta mixture over noodles and top with *half* of the mozzarella slices.

Top with cooked spinach and *half* of the spaghetti sauce mixture. Layer with remaining noodles, ricotta cheese mixture, mozzarella cheese, and spaghetti sauce mixture.

Cook, uncovered, on 70% power (MEDIUM-HIGH) for 13 to 15 minutes or till heated through, giving dish a half-turn after 8 minutes. Let stand 10 minutes before serving. Makes 6 servings.

NOTE: To reheat remaining portions of Vegetable Lasagna, in a nonmetal dish micro-cook, covered, on 70% power (MEDIUM-HIGH) for 3 to 4 minutes for 1 serving or 7 to 8 minutes for 2 servings or till hot.

·QUICK RECIPE·

STREUSEL-TOPPED PEACHES

Equally good with nectarines or pears.

   3 **tablespoons quick-cooking rolled oats**
   2 **tablespoons brown sugar**
   1 **tablespoon whole wheat flour** *or* **all-purpose flour**
   2 **teaspoons toasted wheat germ**
   ⅛ **teaspoon ground nutmeg**
   4 **teaspoons margarine**
   4 **medium peaches, pitted, peeled, and sliced (2 cups)**

In a small mixing bowl combine rolled oats, brown sugar, flour, wheat germ, and nutmeg. Cut in margarine till the mixture resembles coarse crumbs; set aside.

Place peaches in a 1-quart nonmetal casserole. Micro-cook, uncovered, on 100% power (HIGH) for 4 to 5 minutes or till heated through, stirring once. Sprinkle with oat mixture. Cook, uncovered, on 100% power (HIGH) for 2 to 3 minutes or till fruit is tender, giving dish a half-turn once. Serve warm. Makes 4 servings.

The recipes in this book with microwave cooking directions were tested in countertop microwave ovens that operate on 600 to 700 watts. Because microwave ovens vary with the manufacturer, micro-cooking times that appear in the recipes are approximate.

Stuffed Cornish Hen Halves (see recipe, page 103) are so special that you can serve them to company. Your guests will never suspect that they're eating a healthy entree.

MAIN DISHES

CHAPTER 3

CONTENTS

The backbone of a meal is the main dish because it provides most of the protein. When you use these main-dish recipes, you can be sure each one delivers adequate protein. At the same time, the major sources of fat and cholesterol, which are normally high in main dishes, have been reduced or eliminated.

You'll find a number of recipes in this chapter that are meatless. However, one word of warning: dishes that get their protein from eggs are often higher in cholesterol than other main dishes. For that reason, keep your intake of egg main dishes to a minimum by spacing them between several low-cholesterol entrées every few days.

	PER SERVING							PERCENT U.S. RDA PER SERVING							
	CALORIES	PROTEIN (g)	CARBOHYDRATES (g)	FAT (g)	CHOLESTEROL (mg)	SODIUM (mg)	POTASSIUM (mg)	PROTEIN	VITAMIN A	VITAMIN C	THIAMINE	RIBOFLAVIN	NIACIN	CALCIUM	IRON
Apricot-Sauced Chops (p. 92)	277	26	8	15	83	98	397	40	14	4	56	14	26	1	7
Barbecue-Sauced Pork Roast (p. 89)	288	30	11	13	93	84	648	46	12	15	64	18	31	5	14
Bean-Sauced Pasta (p. 124)	438	20	71	9	20	573	920	31	43	61	24	18	19	23	35
Beef and Apples (p. 70)	280	23	30	8	61	63	485	35	31	11	7	11	23	3	18
Beef and Barley Bake (p. 80)	240	22	30	4	49	274	841	34	104	64	48	46	60	22	105
Beef and Pasta Salad (p. 81)	175	16	18	4	24	277	396	25	46	43	9	15	11	19	11
Brandied Beef (p. 68)	228	23	11	7	61	101	495	35	86	13	8	14	23	5	19
Broccoli-Tofu Strata (p. 121)	182	13	16	8	83	237	288	20	19	51	9	17	4	29	11
Broiled Flank (p. 77)	131	19	2	5	60	150	175	30	0	0	2	9	15	1	14
Bulgur-Stuffed Salmon Steaks (p. 114)	496	31	29	28	85	201	708	47	20	16	16	22	8	24	18
Chicken and Fruit Salad (p. 106)	368	17	63	5	39	325	404	26	5	51	18	8	28	5	16
Chicken Burrito Stack-Ups (p. 104)	250	19	20	11	48	102	519	30	14	38	9	12	29	15	12
Chicken Salad for Two (p. l06)	194	23	12	6	65	114	495	36	9	33	5	13	35	10	8
Curried Beef and Cabbage (p. 76)	294	26	26	10	80	123	767	40	12	94	12	17	30	8	25
Curried Beef and Fruit (p. 79)	451	26	53	16	55	94	494	40	8	17	19	12	36	5	25
Curried Pork Stew (p. 82)	289	17	37	10	33	195	1021	25	104	71	27	13	30	5	15
Curry Chicken Kabobs (p. 103)	223	29	14	6	112	142	730	44	83	45	13	26	51	5	14
Deep-Dish Tuna Pie (p. 117)	325	24	23	15	45	229	360	36	59	8	14	15	46	17	13
Egg and Rice Skillet (p. 125)	282	15	38	9	280	273	520	23	74	223	17	18	13	17	16
Fish 'n' Shrimp Mornay (p. 108)	312	28	33	5	95	205	579	44	6	30	18	20	17	24	13
Fruit Scallop Plate (p. 109)	187	13	23	5	26	265	622	19	23	68	11	5	7	5	10
Garden Tenderloin Rolls (p. 87)	226	24	12	9	65	245	709	37	90	36	38	28	33	4	13
Gingersnap Pot Roast (p. 74)	266	31	14	9	90	124	364	47	45	18	7	15	24	3	23
Grilled Pork Burgers (p. 84)	230	23	13	9	65	263	391	36	2	19	33	17	23	4	7
Harvest Pot Pie (p. 122)	276	17	27	12	22	301	505	26	41	99	17	21	15	32	16
Healthful Joes (p. 76)	273	21	32	8	50	353	566	32	35	16	17	13	26	7	27
Healthy Cheese Soufflé (p. 125)	297	17	7	22	222	389	197	26	19	1	4	22	1	37	5
Herbed Lamb Kabobs (p. 96)	232	17	21	9	59	460	409	26	9	96	10	15	20	2	9
Honey-Ginger Chicken (p. 98)	192	27	14	3	72	169	242	41	0	4	4	6	58	2	6
Honey-Orange Beef (p. 68)	304	22	40	7	49	183	541	34	32	96	15	14	26	6	20
Hot Tuna Toss (p. 116)	290	29	32	4	58	220	461	45	26	58	15	8	69	4	17
Italian Eggplant Casserole (p. 119)	353	23	42	10	31	425	1105	35	68	116	22	26	18	51	23
Lean Irish Stew (p. 96)	233	14	30	7	39	236	837	22	159	42	13	11	22	5	12
Lean Taco Salad (p. 81)	357	32	25	15	95	353	1422	49	145	196	20	25	39	20	51
Low-Fat Moussaka (p. 97)	185	14	15	7	57	225	543	21	18	23	11	16	14	14	13
Macaroni and Cheese with Vegetables (p. 122)	306	16	32	12	37	590	429	25	34	65	14	22	8	36	8
Marinated and Grilled Leg of Lamb (p. 95)	252	32	2	12	110	78	390	49	1	10	12	20	34	2	14
Marinated Fish Fillets (p. 111)	111	15	2	5	41	90	346	23	0	10	5	3	10	1	2
Meatballs in Mushroom-Yogurt Sauce(p.75)	331	26	33	9	67	148	556	40	25	6	18	27	32	11	21
Mexicali Stew (p. 72)	283	21	33	9	44	495	768	32	91	101	11	15	21	18	30
Mexican Chops and Vegetables (p. 93)	321	26	33	11	69	373	621	40	71	105	53	20	31	6	17
Minestrone (p. 119)	333	20	59	4	7	489	1438	30	110	60	36	26	26	31	36

	PER SERVING							PERCENT U.S. RDA PER SERVING							
	CALORIES	PROTEIN (g)	CARBOHYDRATES (g)	FAT (g)	CHOLESTEROL (mg)	SODIUM (mg)	POTASSIUM (mg)	PROTEIN	VITAMIN A	VITAMIN C	THIAMINE	RIBOFLAVIN	NIACIN	CALCIUM	IRON
Mixed Fruit and Beef Stew (p. 71)	324	21	52	4	49	158	694	32	21	10	11	17	27	4	23
Mixed Seafood Étouffée (p. 109)	310	17	37	10	61	263	491	26	29	103	14	6	12	7	15
Moussaka Burgers (p. 75)	205	21	8	9	98	256	436	33	8	7	7	13	23	7	18
Mustard Beef Slices (p. 70)	276	20	32	6	47	154	337	30	3	4	15	15	25	5	18
Mustard Pork Chops (p. 92)	256	24	12	11	71	339	363	37	1	1	49	15	23	5	7
Mustard-Orange Pork Roast (p. 90)	205	21	7	9	65	178	349	32	2	37	31	14	22	2	5
Normandy Fish Stew (p. 113)	241	23	19	3	68	309	786	36	82	29	10	8	21	8	11
Onion-Tarragon Salmon Steaks (p. 114)	382	28	5	25	85	102	639	43	12	7	10	20	0	23	9
Orange-Beef Kabobs (p. 72)	299	25	33	7	61	279	560	38	56	44	15	14	31	4	19
Paprika Lamb Linguini (p. 95)	380	33	44	8	90	222	801	51	37	94	28	26	41	9	26
Parmesan Fish Fillets (p. 111)	179	25	9	4	63	249	489	39	4	9	10	10	16	13	6
Peanutty Pork Chops (p. 93)	307	27	9	18	69	262	489	41	1	26	50	13	35	2	7
Peppery Steaks with Vegetables (p. 80)	348	23	6	18	62	188	521	35	86	11	6	11	23	4	18
Pineapple Marinated Flank Steak (p. 77)	185	19	13	6	57	51	261	29	2	15	6	9	15	2	14
Pork 'n' Apples (p. 88)	272	17	24	10	52	41	408	26	55	22	26	12	19	3	7
Pork and Mushroom Lasagna (p. 84)	295	23	24	11	57	220	815	35	9	32	29	25	26	16	16
Pork Creole (p. 82)	333	25	33	11	65	345	742	38	31	65	41	17	35	4	14
Pork Roast with Mushroom Sauce (p. 90)	236	27	3	12	83	102	491	42	0	5	58	22	31	1	8
Pot Roast with Vegetables (p. 74)	269	28	15	10	75	181	757	43	117	137	11	18	26	6	26
Poultry and Pasta (p. 100)	347	27	34	11	59	289	395	41	8	11	17	19	37	17	13
Roast Turkey with Cranberry Sauce (p. 105)	185	25	13	3	74	80	379	38	0	14	7	12	26	2	9
Sauced Sirloin Steak (p. 79)	201	26	5	8	68	107	411	40	3	3	7	19	26	8	17
Saucy Fish Steaks (p. 116)	229	27	14	5	57	251	1146	42	161	93	12	12	54	11	24
Saucy Meatballs (p. 85)	320	23	33	10	52	126	616	35	14	18	37	25	33	5	19
Savory Pork and Vegetables (p. 92)	227	24	6	12	69	94	508	37	85	72	49	16	23	4	9
Sole with Cucumber Sauce (p. 113)	143	21	6	3	57	194	592	32	41	18	6	6	14	3	4
Spicy Bean Fried Rice (p. 124)	392	16	51	15	69	246	564	24	6	4	16	8	27	7	19
Stir-Fried Pork on Lettuce (p. 87)	245	23	12	12	65	316	695	36	45	24	37	30	35	4	11
Stroganoff Stir-Fry (p. 89)	307	23	29	10	52	241	593	35	7	19	34	29	28	13	12
Stuffed Cornish Hen Halves (p. 103)	310	31	30	7	86	230	467	48	22	14	15	15	67	4	13
Sweet and Sour Chicken (p. 100)	443	30	55	12	80	195	556	46	45	72	20	14	49	5	16
Tabbouleh-Stuffed Trout (p. 112)	513	50	9	29	125	205	936	77	9	21	15	28	98	1	14
Taco-Style Potato and Turkey Skillet (p. 105)	222	22	25	4	54	507	971	34	52	54	15	16	30	10	18
Tangy Barbecued Chicken (p. 98)	240	29	9	9	89	108	425	45	12	11	7	12	48	2	14
Toasted Barley and Pork Stir-Fry (p. 88)	338	22	37	11	52	363	579	34	33	44	96	74	89	35	169
Tofu and Fruit Curry (p. 120)	356	11	49	15	0	7	511	17	3	46	12	14	7	15	16
Tofu-Stuffed Tomatoes (p. 120)	262	12	12	20	0	193	413	18	36	62	11	6	5	18	18
Tomato-Seafood Stew (p. 108)	175	18	18	4	78	240	749	27	54	106	8	8	11	8	27
Tomato-Stuffed Chicken Rolls (p. 101)	217	31	6	7	84	168	296	48	7	9	6	10	60	16	8
Veal and Asparagus Stew (p. 71)	376	28	26	18	82	350	1204	44	56	212	33	38	43	7	39
Vegetable-Topped Pork (p. 85)	462	25	56	15	65	137	525	38	55	137	45	17	32	4	17

There's a good reason for partially freezing the meat before cutting it into strips for stir-frying. The meat is easier to slice when it's firm. But, don't let it get too hard. About 45 to 60 minutes in the freezer should be enough time to get the meat to the right stage—firm enough to slice.

HONEY-ORANGE BEEF

A meat and vegetable stir-fry that is delicately seasoned with curry. (Pictured on page 13.)

> 1 **pound beef top round steak**
> ½ **cup brown rice**
> ½ **cup bulgur**
> ¾ **cup orange juice**
> 1 **tablespoon honey**
> 1 **tablespoon sodium-reduced soy sauce**
> 2 **teaspoons cornstarch**
> ¼ **teaspoon ground ginger**
> ¼ **teaspoon curry powder**
> 1 **medium onion, thinly sliced and separated into rings**
> 2 **cups broccoli flowerets**
> **Nonstick spray coating**
> 1 **tablespoon cooking oil**
> ½ **cup quartered cherry tomatoes**

Partially freeze beef; bias-slice into thin bite-size strips. Set aside. In a large saucepan combine brown rice and 2¼ cups *water.* Bring to boiling. Reduce heat, then simmer, covered, for 25 minutes. Stir in bulgur. Simmer, covered, 15 to 20 minutes more or till tender. Drain if necessary. Keep warm.

For sauce, stir together orange juice, honey, soy sauce, cornstarch, ginger, and curry powder. Set aside. In a saucepan cook onion in a small amount of boiling water for 5 minutes. Add broccoli; cook 3 to 5 minutes more or till vegetables are crisp-tender. Drain. Set aside.

Spray a large skillet or wok with nonstick coating. Preheat over high heat till a drop of water sizzles. Stir-fry *half* of the beef for 2 to 3 minutes or till done. Remove beef. Add oil. Stir-fry remaining beef for 2 to 3 minutes or till done. Return all beef to skillet or wok. Stir sauce; add to skillet or wok. Cook and stir till thickened and bubbly. Cook and stir 2 minutes more. Add vegetables to skillet or wok; heat through. Stir in tomatoes. Serve with rice mixture. Makes 5 servings.

BRANDIED BEEF

Pictured on the cover.

> 1 **pound boneless beef round steak, cut ½ to ¾ inch thick**
> ¼ **cup brandy *or* apple juice**
> 2 **tablespoons vinegar**
> 1 **clove garlic, minced**
> ¼ **teaspoon dried dillweed**
> ⅛ **teaspoon ground allspice**
> ⅛ **teaspoon coarsely ground pepper**
> 2 **large carrots, bias sliced**
> 1 **9-ounce package frozen French-style green beans**
> 1 **medium onion, cut into wedges**
> 2 **teaspoons cornstarch**
> ¼ **teaspoon instant beef bouillon granules**
> **Nonstick spray coating**
> 2 **teaspoons cooking oil**

Partially freeze beef; bias-slice into thin bite-size strips. Place meat in a plastic bag; set in a bowl. For marinade, combine brandy or apple juice, vinegar, garlic, dillweed, allspice, pepper, and ⅓ cup *water;* pour over meat in bag. Close bag. Marinate meat in the refrigerator several hours or overnight, turning bag occasionally. Drain meat, reserving marinade.

In a medium saucepan combine carrots, beans, and onion. Add ½ cup *water.* Bring to boiling. Reduce heat. Simmer, covered, about 8 minutes or till vegetables are crisp-tender; stir to separate beans. Drain; keep warm. For sauce, stir together cornstarch and ¼ cup cold *water.* Stir in reserved marinade and bouillon granules. Set aside.

Pat meat dry with paper towels. Spray a 10-inch skillet with nonstick coating. Preheat over high heat till a drop of water sizzles. Stir-fry *half* of the beef for 2 to 3 minutes or till done. Remove beef. Add oil, if necessary. Stir-fry remaining beef for 2 to 3 minutes or till done. Return all beef to skillet.

Stir sauce; add to skillet. Cook and stir till thickened and bubbly. Cook and stir 2 minutes more. To serve, arrange vegetables on platter; spoon meat mixture atop. Sprinkle with pepper, if desired. Makes 4 servings.

MUSTARD BEEF SLICES

Oriental bean threads have a couple of aliases— cellophane noodles and transparent noodles.

After cooking, the white bean thread strands become translucent. They're great to use under a saucy meat mixture, such as Mustard Beef Slices.

Look for bean threads in Oriental food stores or in the supermarket along with other Oriental products.

  ¾ **pound boneless beef eye of round**
  ⅔ **cup long grain rice** *or* **2 ounces bean threads**
  1 **tablespoon all-purpose flour**
  ¼ **cup plain low-fat yogurt**
  ½ **cup water**
  2 **tablespoons dry white wine**
  1½ **teaspoons prepared mustard**
  ½ **teaspoon instant beef bouillon granules**
     Dash pepper
     Nonstick spray coating
  1 **cup sliced fresh mushrooms**
  ¼ **cup sliced green onion**
  1 **tablespoon margarine**

Partially freeze beef; bias-slice into thin bite-size strips. Cook long grain rice according to package directions, *except* omit salt and butter or margarine. (*Or,* to prepare bean threads, follow this method: Break up bean threads. Soak in warm water for 30 minutes. Drain. Add water to cover. Bring to boiling, then reduce heat and simmer, uncovered, about 2 minutes or till bean threads are transparent. Drain; keep warm.)

For sauce, stir flour into yogurt till well mixed. Stir in the water, wine, mustard, bouillon granules, and pepper. Set aside. Spray a 10-inch skillet with nonstick coating. Preheat over high heat till a drop of water sizzles. Stir-fry mushrooms and onion. Remove vegetables from skillet. Add margarine. Stir-fry beef for 2 to 3 minutes or till done.

Stir sauce; add to beef in skillet. Cook and stir till thickened and bubbly. Cook and stir 1 minute more. Return vegetables to skillet; heat through. Serve meat mixture over rice or bean threads. Makes 4 servings.

BEEF and APPLES

Remember when using a nonstick spray coating to spray it on a cool skillet—never a hot skillet.

  1 **pound beef top round steak**
  ⅔ **cup regular brown rice (optional)**
  ⅔ **cup cold water**
  3 **tablespoons frozen apple juice concentrate, thawed**
  1 **tablespoon cornstarch**
  1 **tablespoon lemon juice**
  ½ **teaspoon dried sage, crushed**
     Dash pepper
     Nonstick spray coating
  1 **tablespoon cooking oil**
  1 **small onion, sliced and separated into rings**
  1 **tart medium cooking apple, cored and coarsely chopped (1 cup)**
  1 **medium carrot, shredded (½ cup)**
  ¼ **cup raisins**

Partially freeze beef; bias-slice into thin bite-size strips. If desired, cook brown rice according to package directions, *except* omit salt and butter or margarine.

For sauce, stir together water, apple juice concentrate, cornstarch, lemon juice, sage, and pepper. Set aside.

Spray a large skillet or wok with nonstick coating. Preheat over high heat till a drop of water sizzles. Stir-fry *half* of the beef for 2 to 3 minutes or till done. Remove beef. Add oil, if necessary. Stir-fry onion with remaining beef for 2 to 3 minutes or till done. Return all beef to skillet or wok. Stir apple, carrot, and raisins into beef mixture.

Stir sauce; add to skillet or wok. Cook and stir till thickened and bubbly. Cook and stir 2 minutes more. If desired, serve meat mixture with rice. Makes 4 servings.

MIXED FRUIT and BEEF STEW

Dried fruit and wild rice make the stew special enough for company.

  Nonstick spray coating
1 pound boneless beef round steak, cut into 1-inch cubes
2 medium leeks, cut into ½-inch slices (about ¾ cup) *or* 2 small onions, cut into thin wedges
2 cups water
1½ teaspoons instant beef bouillon granules
1 8-ounce package mixed dried fruit
2 tablespoons cold water
1 tablespoon cornstarch
¼ cup dry red *or* white wine
1⅓ cups water
⅓ cup wild rice
⅓ cup brown rice

Spray a 10-inch skillet with nonstick coating. Place over medium-high heat. Quickly cook beef and leeks or onion till meat is brown. Add 2 cups water and bouillon granules. Bring to boiling. Reduce heat, then simmer, covered, for 1¼ hours.

Remove pits from prunes and cut up any large pieces of dried fruit. Stir fruit into meat mixture. Cover and simmer about 30 minutes or till meat and fruit are tender. Combine 2 tablespoons water and cornstarch; stir into stew. Cook and stir till thickened and bubbly, then cook and stir 2 minutes more. Stir in wine and heat through.

Meanwhile, in a saucepan combine 1⅓ cups water, wild rice, and brown rice. Bring to boiling. Reduce heat, then simmer, covered, without removing lid for 45 minutes. Let stand 5 minutes. Serve meat mixture spooned atop the rice. Makes 5 servings.

VEAL and ASPARAGUS STEW

Fresh asparagus is an ingredient you won't find in many stew recipes.

1 pound boneless veal
¼ cup all-purpose flour
2 tablespoons cooking oil
1 large onion, cut into wedges
1 medium green pepper, cut into strips
1 8-ounce can sodium-reduced tomato sauce
1 cup water
2 cloves garlic, minced
2 teaspoons dried marjoram, crushed
½ teaspoon sugar
½ teaspoon salt
  Dash pepper
1½ pounds asparagus, bias-sliced into 1-inch pieces
2 medium tomatoes, cut into wedges

Cut veal into bite-size cubes. Coat veal with flour. In a large saucepan cook *half* of the veal in hot oil till brown. Remove veal; set aside. Repeat with remaining veal. Return all veal to the saucepan.

Stir in onion, green pepper, tomato sauce, water, garlic, marjoram, sugar, salt, and pepper. Bring to boiling. Reduce heat, then simmer, covered, about 35 minutes or till meat is nearly tender. Stir in asparagus and tomatoes. Simmer 10 to 15 minutes more or till asparagus and meat are tender. Makes 4 servings.

A reminder: When serving your main dishes with rice, bulgur, or pasta, cook these accompaniments without salt, butter, or margarine. You'll be reducing your fat and sodium intake if you do.

MEXICALI STEW

¾ pound lean boneless beef stew meat,
    cut into 1-inch pieces
½ cup chopped onion
1 clove garlic, minced
1 teaspoon cooking oil
2 14½-ounce cans sodium-reduced
    tomatoes, cut up
1 tablespoon chili powder
1 teaspoon dried oregano, crushed
½ teaspoon ground cumin
¼ teaspoon salt
¼ teaspoon pepper
1 15-ounce can garbanzo beans
2 large carrots, cut into ½-inch pieces
1 4-ounce can green chili peppers,
    rinsed, seeded, and cut into ¾-inch
    squares
1 10-ounce package frozen whole
    kernel corn
½ cup shredded cheddar *or* Monterey
    Jack cheese (2 ounces)
2 tablespoons snipped parsley

One way to decrease fat in your diet is by careful meat shopping. Select lean cuts of meat. Then, trim off and discard any separable fat from all your meat purchases before you begin cooking.

In a large kettle or Dutch oven cook beef, onion, and garlic in hot oil till meat is brown and onion is tender. Drain off fat.

Stir in *undrained* tomatoes, chili powder, oregano, cumin, salt, and pepper. Bring to boiling. Reduce heat, then simmer, covered, for 1 hour. Stir in *undrained* garbanzo beans, carrots, and chili peppers. Return to boiling. Reduce heat, then simmer, covered, for 30 minutes more.

Stir in corn. Cook, covered, about 15 minutes or till meat and vegetables are tender. Serve in bowls with cheese and parsley sprinkled atop. Makes 6 servings.

ORANGE-BEEF KABOBS

Roll out the barbecue grill to cook these kabobs.

1 1½-pound beef round steak, cut
    1 inch thick
1 teaspoon finely shredded orange
    peel
1 cup orange juice
2 tablespoons sodium-reduced
    soy sauce
1 tablespoon cooking oil
1 teaspoon grated gingerroot
    Several dashes bottled hot pepper
    sauce
2 medium carrots, bias-sliced into
    1-inch pieces
2 medium zucchini, cut into 1-inch
    pieces
1 cup brown rice
1 tablespoon cold water
1 teaspoon cornstarch

Cut beef into 1-inch cubes. Place meat in a plastic bag; set in a bowl. For marinade, in a bowl combine orange peel, orange juice, soy sauce, oil, gingerroot, and hot pepper sauce; pour over meat in bag. Close bag. Marinate in the refrigerator for 6 to 8 hours or overnight, turning bag occasionally.

Cook carrots in a small amount of boiling water for 10 minutes. Drain. Drain meat, reserving marinade. On 6 skewers alternately thread carrots, meat, and zucchini.

Cook brown rice according to package directions, *except* omit salt and butter or margarine. In a small saucepan combine water and cornstarch. Stir in reserved marinade. Cook and stir till thickened and bubbly, then cook and stir 2 minutes more. Brush kabobs with marinade mixture. Grill over hot coals to desired doneness (allow 15 minutes for medium-rare); turn and brush kabobs often with marinade mixture. Serve with rice. Pass remaining marinade mixture. Garnish with an orange peel twist, if desired. Makes 6 servings.

GINGERSNAP POT ROAST

    1 3-pound beef chuck arm pot roast
    1 tablespoon cooking oil
    1 teaspoon instant beef bouillon
         granules
    ⅛ teaspoon ground red pepper
    1 bay leaf
    2 medium sweet potatoes, peeled and
         quartered lengthwise
    1 cup pearl onions
    ¼ cup lemon juice
    1 tablespoon brown sugar
    4 or 5 gingersnaps, crushed (¼ cup)

Cookie crumbs do double duty in the Gingersnap Pot Roast *sauce. They add both flavor and thickening. There's no need to add cornstarch or flour to thicken the sauce to its just-right consistency.*

In a Dutch oven brown beef on both sides in hot oil. Remove from heat. Drain off fat. Add bouillon granules and 1 cup *water*. Sprinkle with red pepper; add bay leaf. Return to heat. Bring to boiling. Reduce heat, then simmer, covered, for 1¼ hours. Add sweet potatoes, onions, lemon juice, and sugar. Cover and cook 30 to 45 minutes more or till meat and potatoes are tender.

Transfer meat to a platter. With a slotted spoon remove sweet potatoes and onions; place around meat on platter. Keep food warm. Remove and discard bay leaf. Measure juices; add water, if necessary, to make 1¼ cups liquid. Return liquid to Dutch oven. Stir in gingersnaps. Cook and stir till bubbly. Drizzle some sauce over roast and vegetables; pass the remainder. Makes 8 servings.

POT ROAST with VEGETABLES

    1 2-pound boneless beef round
         tip roast
    1 tablespoon cooking oil
    2 bay leaves
    2 cloves garlic, minced
    1½ teaspoons instant beef bouillon
         granules
    ¾ teaspoon dried thyme, crushed
    2 10-ounce packages frozen brussels
         sprouts
    4 medium carrots, cut into 1-inch
         pieces
    2 small onions, cut into wedges
    ¼ cup dry red wine
    2 tablespoons cornstarch

In a Dutch oven brown beef on all sides in hot oil. Remove from heat. Drain off fat. Add bay leaves, garlic, bouillon granules, thyme, 1 cup *water,* and ⅛ teaspoon *pepper.* Return to heat. Bring to boiling. Reduce heat, then simmer, covered, for 1¾ hours. Add the vegetables. Spoon juices over vegetables. Bring to boiling. Reduce heat, then simmer, covered, 25 to 30 minutes or till vegetables are tender.

Transfer meat and vegetables to a serving platter. Remove and discard bay leaves. Measure juices; add water, if necessary, to make 1½ cups liquid. Return liquid to Dutch oven. Stir in wine. Combine cornstarch and 2 tablespoons cold *water.* Add to mixture in Dutch oven. Cook and stir till thickened and bubbly, then cook and stir 2 minutes more. Serve over meat and vegetables. Makes 6 servings.

MOUSSAKA BURGERS

Hamburgers never tasted so good—and you won't even miss the bun!

- ½ **cup hot water**
- ¼ **cup bulgur**
- 1 **slightly beaten egg**
- 1 **teaspoon dried thyme, crushed**
- ½ **teaspoon ground coriander**
- ⅛ **teaspoon pepper**
  Dash salt
- 1½ **pounds lean ground beef**
- 1 **small eggplant (about 12 ounces)**
- 1 **8-ounce can tomato sauce**
- ½ **cup shredded mozzarella cheese (2 ounces)**

In a bowl combine hot water and bulgur. Let stand 30 minutes; drain off any excess liquid. Stir in egg, thyme, coriander, pepper, and salt. Add beef; mix well. Form mixture into eight ¾-inch-thick patties. Place patties on a rack in a baking pan or a broiler pan.

Peel eggplant; slice crosswise into eight ½-inch-thick slices. Place an eggplant slice atop each burger. Spread about 2 tablespoons tomato sauce on each eggplant slice, covering the surface of the eggplant.

Cover pan loosely with foil. Bake in a 350° oven for 40 to 50 minutes or till well done. Remove foil from the pan. Sprinkle eggplant-topped burgers with cheese. Return to oven. Bake, uncovered, 3 to 5 minutes more or till cheese is melted. Makes 8 servings.

MEATBALLS in MUSHROOM-YOGURT SAUCE

Spoon the delicately herbed meatballs and tangy sauce over pasta.

- ¼ **cup quick-cooking rolled oats**
- ¼ **cup water**
- ¼ **teaspoon dried thyme, crushed**
- ¼ **teaspoon dried oregano, crushed**
  Dash salt
  Dash pepper
- 1 **pound lean ground beef**
- 1 **8-ounce carton plain low-fat yogurt**
- 4 **teaspoons cornstarch**
- 5 **ounces linguine *or* fettuccine**
- 2 **cups sliced fresh mushrooms**
- ½ **cup shredded carrot**
- ⅓ **cup sliced green onion**
- ¼ **cup water**
- 1 **teaspoon sugar**
- ½ **teaspoon instant beef bouillon granules**
- 2 **tablespoons dry white wine**
  Snipped parsley

In a bowl combine oats, ¼ cup water, thyme, oregano, salt, and pepper. Add beef; mix well. Form mixture into 1-inch meatballs. Place on a rack in a large shallow baking pan. Bake in a 375° oven for 20 to 25 minutes or till no pink color remains in center of meatballs. Drain on paper towels. Stir together yogurt and cornstarch; set aside.

Meanwhile, cook pasta according to package directions, *except* omit salt. In a large saucepan cook and stir mushrooms, carrot, and green onion just till tender. Add ¼ cup water, sugar, and bouillon granules; stir to dissolve bouillon granules. Stir in yogurt mixture. Cook and stir till thickened and bubbly, then cook and stir 2 minutes more. Stir in wine and meatballs; heat through. Drain pasta. Serve meatballs and sauce over pasta. Sprinkle with parsley. Makes 5 servings.

HEALTHFUL JOES

If you want to cut the sodium in this recipe, plan to use the homemade buns from page 136. Our homemade buns have about half the sodium of regular hamburger buns.

 ¾ **pound lean ground beef**
 ½ **cup shredded carrot**
 ½ **cup chopped onion**
 1 **clove garlic, minced**
 1 **8-ounce can sodium-reduced**
  tomato sauce
 ¼ **cup water**
 2 **tablespoons toasted wheat germ**
 1 **tablespoon prepared mustard**
 1 **tablespoon vinegar**
 ½ **teaspoon sugar**
 ¼ **teaspoon pepper**
 5 **whole wheat buns, split and toasted**
  Alfalfa sprouts (optional)

In a skillet cook beef, carrot, onion, and garlic till meat is brown and onion is tender. Drain off fat. Stir in tomato sauce, water, wheat germ, mustard, vinegar, sugar, and pepper. Bring to boiling. Reduce heat, then simmer, covered, for 20 minutes. Serve spooned atop toasted whole wheat buns. Top with alfalfa sprouts, if desired. Makes 5 servings.

BUYING GROUND BEEF: *You'll undoubtedly find different types of ground beef at the meat counter. What are you supposed to use? When you're trying to cut calories and reduce fat in your diet, pick out the ground beef that's 85 to 90 percent lean. If you have to use meat with a little higher fat content, be sure to thoroughly drain off any fat that cooks out of the meat.*

CURRIED BEEF and CABBAGE

Spoon the well-seasoned ground meat mixture over tender wedges of cabbage.

 1 **pound lean ground beef**
 ¾ **cup chopped onion**
 2 **cloves garlic, minced**
 1 **tablespoon curry powder**
 2 **medium tomatoes, peeled and**
  chopped (1¼ cups)
 1 **medium apple, cored and chopped**
 ½ **cup water**
 ½ **teaspoon instant beef bouillon**
  granules
 ½ **teaspoon ground ginger**
 2 **tablespoons cold water**
 1 **tablespoon cornstarch**
 ¼ **cup raisins**
 ½ **of a small head cabbage, cored and**
  cut into 4 wedges (¾ pound)

In a large saucepan cook beef, onion, and garlic till meat is brown and onion is tender. Drain off fat. Stir in curry powder; cook for 1 minute. Stir in tomatoes, apple, ½ cup water, bouillon granules, and ginger. Bring to boiling. Reduce heat, then simmer, covered, for 5 to 10 minutes or till apple is tender.

Stir together 2 tablespoons water and cornstarch. Add to beef mixture; stir in raisins. Cook and stir till thickened and bubbly, then cook and stir 2 minutes more.

Meanwhile, cook cabbage in a small amount of boiling water for 8 to 10 minutes or till tender. Drain. To serve, place the cabbage wedges on 4 individual plates. Spoon meat mixture over cabbage. Makes 4 servings.

PINEAPPLE-MARINATED FLANK STEAK

Pineapple has a natural enzyme, bromelain, which helps tenderize the meat.

- 1 1- to 1¼-pound beef flank steak
- 1 6-ounce can frozen pineapple juice concentrate, thawed
- 1 8-ounce can pineapple slices (juice pack)
- ¼ cup sliced green onion
- 2 teaspoons margarine
- 2 teaspoons cornstarch

Score flank steak on both sides. Spread pineapple juice concentrate on both sides of steak. Place in a shallow dish. Cover and let stand 1 hour at room temperature.

Remove meat from pineapple juice concentrate, reserving the liquid; set aside ¼ cup for sauce. Place meat on an unheated rack of a broiler pan. Broil meat 3 to 4 inches from the heat for 5 minutes. Turn and broil 3 to 5 minutes more or to desired doneness, brushing occasionally with remaining liquid.

Meanwhile, drain pineapple, reserving juice. Cut pineapple into ½-inch pieces. Set aside. For sauce, cook onion in margarine till tender but not brown. Stir in cornstarch. Add reserved pineapple juice. Cook and stir till thickened and bubbly, then cook and stir 2 minutes more. Stir in pineapple pieces and reserved ¼ cup liquid; heat till bubbly. To serve, thinly slice meat diagonally across the grain. Spoon sauce atop. Makes 5 servings.

BROILED FLANK

- 1 1¼-pound beef flank steak
- 1 teaspoon instant beef bouillon granules
- ¼ cup dry sherry
- 1 teaspoon red wine vinegar
- 1 teaspoon molasses
- 2 cloves garlic, minced
- ½ teaspoon ground ginger
- ¼ teaspoon bottled hot pepper sauce

Score flank steak on both sides. Dissolve bouillon granules in ¼ cup hot *water*. For marinade, in a 12x7½x2-inch dish combine bouillon mixture, sherry, vinegar, molasses, garlic, ginger, and pepper sauce. Place steak in marinade; turn to coat. Cover; chill in refrigerator several hours, turning occasionally.

Remove meat; reserve marinade. Place meat on an unheated rack of a broiler pan. Broil 3 to 4 inches from heat for 5 minutes; brush with marinade. Turn; broil 3 to 5 minutes more or to desired doneness. Brush with marinade. Transfer to a platter. Thinly slice meat diagonally across grain. Makes 6 servings.

For tenderer flank steak, carve thin slices of meat across the grain using a diagonal cut as shown.

Perk up the serving platter of Sauced Sirloin Steak *with fresh new potatoes and brussels sprouts.*

SAUCED SIRLOIN STEAK

1 **2-pound beef top sirloin steak, cut 1½ inches thick**
1 **cup sliced fresh mushrooms**
¼ **cup shredded carrot**
¼ **cup chopped onion**
1 **tablespoon margarine**
4 **teaspoons all-purpose flour**
½ **teaspoon dried basil, crushed**
  Dash pepper
½ **cup plain low-fat yogurt**
½ **cup skim milk**

Place steak on an unheated rack of a broiler pan. Broil meat 3 inches from the heat, turning halfway through cooking. (Allow 14 to 16 minutes total time for rare, 18 to 20 minutes total time for medium, and 25 to 30 minutes total time for well-done.)

Meanwhile, for sauce, in a saucepan cook mushrooms, carrot, and onion in margarine till tender. Stir flour, basil, and pepper into yogurt; stir into mixture in saucepan. Add milk. Cook and stir till thickened and bubbly, then cook and stir 1 minute more.

Sprinkle steak with additional pepper. To serve, slice the meat diagonally across the grain into ¼-inch-thick slices. Place on a serving platter. Spoon some sauce atop. Pass remaining sauce. Makes 6 servings.

CURRIED BEEF and FRUIT

Chopped peanuts stirred into the rice lend a crunchy texture to the curry mixture.

1 **pound lean boneless beef chuck steak, cut ¾ inch thick**
1 **tablespoon cooking oil**
1 **large onion, sliced and separated into rings**
⅔ **cup water**
2 **teaspoons curry powder**
2 **teaspoons lemon juice**
1 **bay leaf**
⅛ **teaspoon salt**
  Dash pepper
1 **16-ounce can peach slices (juice pack)**
1 **tablespoon cornstarch**
1 **8-ounce can pineapple chunks (juice pack), drained**
1 **cup long grain rice**
½ **cup unsalted peanuts, coarsely chopped**

Cut beef into ¾-inch cubes. In a skillet or large saucepan brown beef in hot oil. Stir in onion, water, curry powder, lemon juice, bay leaf, salt, and pepper. Bring to boiling. Reduce heat, then simmer, covered, about 1¼ hours or till meat is tender. Remove and discard bay leaf.

Drain peaches, reserving juice. Place *half* of the peaches and all the reserved juice in a blender container or food processor bowl. Cover and process till smooth. Stir in the cornstarch. Add to beef mixture in the skillet. Cook and stir till thickened and bubbly, then cook and stir 2 minutes more. Gently stir in remaining peach slices and pineapple chunks.

Meanwhile, cook long grain rice according to package directions, *except* omit salt and butter or margarine. Stir in peanuts. Serve beef mixture atop the rice mixture. Makes 5 servings.

Read labels! That's one quick and sure way to trim calories, reduce sodium, and watch fat in your diet!

Take juice-pack fruit, for instance. It's just one product that will help you trim calories. A half-cup of pineapple chunks in syrup contains 84 calories but the same amount of pineapple in juice contains only 64 calories.

Curried Beef and Fruit uses two different fruits packed in juice—pineapple and peaches—to make its fruity sauce.

Crack whole black pepper

with a mortar and pestle till

coarsely broken. Then, rub

the pepper into both sides of

the steak pieces. The cracked

pepper will make the meat

peppery hot. And, if any

pepper falls off during

cooking, it'll spice up the

sauce that's served over

Peppery Steaks with

Vegetables.

·QUICK RECIPE·

PEPPERY STEAKS with VEGETABLES

Tailored for just two servings.

  1 **teaspoon whole black pepper**
  1 **10-ounce boneless beef top loin steak, cut ¾ inch thick**
  2 **stalks celery, bias-sliced into ½-inch pieces**
  1 **medium carrot, cut into julienne strips**
  1 **tablespoon margarine**
  1 **tablespoon cooking oil**
  ¼ **cup brandy**
  2 **tablespoons water**

Coarsely crack pepper. Cut beef into 2 portions. Rub cracked pepper into both sides of each steak portion. Let stand, covered, at room temperature for 30 minutes.

In a heavy skillet cook celery and carrot in margarine just till crisp-tender. Remove from skillet; keep warm. Add oil to the skillet. Cook steak portions in hot oil over medium-high heat to desired doneness, turning once. (Allow about 9 minutes total cooking time for medium.) Arrange meat and vegetables on a platter; keep warm.

Add brandy and water to the skillet. Bring to boiling and cook, uncovered, over medium heat about 2 minutes. Pour over meat and vegetables. Makes 2 servings.

BEEF and BARLEY BAKE

Stick this meaty casserole into the oven and forget it for two hours.

  1 **9-ounce package frozen Italian green beans**
  1 **pound beef round steak**
    Nonstick spray coating
  1 **28-ounce can tomatoes, cut up**
  1½ **cups water**
  2 **medium carrots, thinly sliced**
  1 **small onion, sliced and separated into rings**
  ¼ **cup snipped parsley**
  2 **cloves garlic, minced**
  1 **teaspoon dried basil, crushed**
  ½ **teaspoon dried thyme, crushed**
  ¼ **teaspoon dried marjoram, crushed**
    Dash pepper
  ½ **cup pearl barley**

In a colander run warm water over frozen beans to separate. Set aside. Cut meat into bite-size pieces. Spray a 10-inch skillet with nonstick coating. Quickly cook meat in skillet till brown, stirring frequently. Drain off fat.

In a 3-quart casserole stir together beef, beans, *undrained* tomatoes, water, carrots, onion, parsley, garlic, basil, thyme, marjoram, and pepper. Stir in barley.

Cover tightly and bake in a 350° oven about 2 hours or till the liquid is absorbed and beef is tender. Stir before serving. Makes 5 servings.

LEAN TACO SALAD

You'll be surprised at the generous portions—it's a meal in itself!

- ½ **pound lean ground beef**
- ½ **cup chopped onion**
- 1 **clove garlic, minced**
- 1 **8-ounce can sodium-reduced tomato sauce**
- 2 **tablespoons chopped canned green chili peppers**
- 1 **teaspoon chili powder**
- ½ **teaspoon dried oregano, crushed**
- ⅛ **teaspoon salt**
- 3 **cups torn salad greens**
- 1 **cup cauliflower flowerets**
- 1 **medium carrot, shredded**
- 1 **medium tomato, chopped**
- ¼ **cup shredded cheddar cheese (1 ounce)**

In a skillet cook beef, onion, and garlic till meat is brown and onion is tender. Drain off fat. Stir in tomato sauce, chili peppers, chili powder, oregano, and salt. Cook and stir till heated through.

Meanwhile, toss together torn greens, cauliflower, carrot, and tomato. Place in 2 individual salad bowls. Top with the hot meat mixture. Sprinkle each serving with cheese. Serve immediately. Makes 2 servings.

BEEF and PASTA SALAD

- 2 **ounces spinach noodles**
- 1 **cup cauliflower flowerets**
- ½ **of a small zucchini**
- 4 **ounces lean cooked beef, cut into thin strips (about 1 cup)**
- 1 **medium carrot, shredded**
- ½ **cup low-fat cottage cheese**
- ⅓ **cup skim milk**
- 1 **clove garlic, minced**
- ¼ **teaspoon dried oregano, crushed**
- ¼ **teaspoon dried basil, crushed**
  Dash pepper
- ¼ **cup plain low-fat yogurt**
  Lettuce leaves
- ¼ **cup grated Parmesan cheese**

Cook noodles according to package directions, *except* omit salt. Drain. Rinse with cold water and drain.

Cook cauliflower in a small amount of boiling water about 5 minutes or just till crisp-tender. Drain. Cut zucchini lengthwise into quarters, then slice. Toss together noodles, cauliflower, zucchini, beef, and carrot. Cover and chill in the refrigerator for 1 hour.

For dressing, in a blender container combine cottage cheese, milk, garlic, oregano, basil, and pepper. Cover and blend till smooth. Stir in yogurt. Cover and chill in the refrigerator for 1 hour.

Toss chilled dressing with pasta-beef mixture. Serve on lettuce. Sprinkle servings with Parmesan cheese. Makes 4 servings.

PORK CREOLE

Okra is a popular vegetable in Southern-style dishes. When sliced into gumbos and stew-type dishes, okra adds both thickening and flavor.

Your kitchen scissors can help you shortcut a variety of food preparation tasks. For example, when making Curried Pork Stew, use the scissors to cut up the tomatoes—save washing a bowl and snip the tomatoes right in the can.

Another slick trick: snip parsley in a small cup—it's neater than chopping the parsley on a board.

- 1 **pound lean boneless pork, cut into ½-inch cubes**
- 1 **teaspoon cooking oil**
- ½ **cup chopped onion**
- ¼ **cup chopped celery**
- ¼ **cup chopped green pepper**
- 1 **16-ounce can tomatoes, cut up**
- ¼ **cup water**
- 2 **tablespoons tomato paste**
- ½ **teaspoon dried oregano, crushed**
- ½ **teaspoon dried basil, crushed**
- ½ **teaspoon chili powder**
- ¼ **teaspoon garlic powder**
- ¼ **teaspoon ground red pepper**
- ⅛ **teaspoon salt**
- ⅔ **cup brown rice**
- 1 **10-ounce package frozen sliced okra**

In a large skillet cook meat in hot oil till brown. Add onion, celery, and green pepper. Cook and stir over medium heat for 5 minutes. Stir in *undrained* tomatoes, water, tomato paste, oregano, basil, chili powder, garlic powder, red pepper, and salt. Bring mixture to boiling. Reduce heat, then simmer, covered, for 45 minutes.

Meanwhile, cook brown rice according to package directions, *except* omit salt and butter or margarine. Stir okra into meat mixture. Cook, uncovered, for 10 to 12 minutes more or till okra is tender, stirring occasionally. Serve over rice. Makes 4 servings.

CURRIED PORK STEW

Leave the peel on the potatoes for this oven-baked stew. There's a concentration of nutrients in the layer right under the skin.

- ½ **pound lean boneless pork, cut into ¾-inch cubes**
- ½ **cup chopped onion**
- 1 **clove garlic, minced**
- 2 **teaspoons curry powder**
- 1 **16-ounce can tomatoes, cut up**
- 2 **medium carrots, cut into ¼-inch slices**
- 2 **medium potatoes, cut into bite-size pieces (2⅓ cups)**
- ¼ **cup water**
- 2 **tablespoons raisins**
- 1 **tablespoon quick-cooking tapioca**
- 1 **large apple, cored and cut into thin wedges**
- 2 **tablespoons snipped parsley**
- ¼ **cup unsalted peanuts**

In a skillet cook meat, onion, garlic, and curry powder over medium-high heat till onion is tender and meat is brown.

Meanwhile, in a 2-quart casserole stir together *undrained* tomatoes, carrots, potatoes, water, raisins, and tapioca. Add meat mixture to the casserole; mix well. Cover and bake in a 350° oven for 50 to 60 minutes or till meat and vegetables are nearly tender. Stir in apple and parsley. Return to oven; bake, covered, about 15 minutes more or till meat and vegetables are tender. To serve, sprinkle with nuts. Makes 4 servings.

Pieces of toasted pita bread make the perfect flavor contrast to Curried Pork Stew.

PORK and MUSHROOM LASAGNA

To judge the temperature of coals for grilling, hold your hand, palm side down, above coals at the height your food will cook. Start counting seconds, "one thousand one, one thousand two." If you need to withdraw your hand after two seconds, the coals are considered hot; after three seconds, they're medium-hot; after four seconds, they're medium; after five seconds, they're medium-slow; and after six seconds, the coals are slow.

Be sure to buy the part-skim ricotta cheese. It has fewer calories and less fat. When comparing whole milk ricotta and part-skim ricotta, there are 163 fewer calories and 23 fewer grams of fat per pound in the part-skim cheese.

- 4 **lasagna noodles**
- 1 **cup part-skim ricotta cheese**
- 2 **tablespoons skim milk**
- ½ **teaspoon dried basil, crushed**
- ¼ **teaspoon pepper**
- ¾ **pound lean ground pork**
- 2 **cups sliced fresh mushrooms**
- ¼ **cup chopped onion**
- 2 **cups sodium-reduced spaghetti sauce**
- 2 **tablespoons snipped parsley**
- ¼ **teaspoon salt**
- 1 **tablespoon grated Parmesan cheese**

Cook noodles according to package directions, *except* omit the salt; drain. Rinse and drain again. Set noodles aside. Combine ricotta, milk, basil, and pepper; set aside.

In a skillet cook pork, mushrooms, and onion till meat is brown and onion is tender. Drain well. Stir in spaghetti sauce, parsley, and salt. Cook over medium heat till heated through.

Arrange 2 of the noodles in a 10x6x2-inch baking dish. Spread half of the ricotta mixture over noodles, then add half of the mushroom mixture. Top with remaining noodles, ricotta mixture, and mushroom mixture. Sprinkle with Parmesan. Bake, covered, in a 375° oven for 30 minutes. Uncover and bake 10 minutes more. Let stand 10 minutes before serving. Makes 6 servings.

·QUICK RECIPE· GRILLED PORK BURGERS

To keep these burgers lower in fat content, we used only the egg white, skim milk instead of whole milk, and, of course, lean ground pork.

- 1 **egg white**
- ¼ **cup skim milk**
- 1 **tablespoon sodium-reduced soy sauce**
- ¼ **cup finely chopped onion**
- 3 **tablespoons fine dry bread crumbs**
- 2 **tablespoons finely chopped green pepper**
- ¼ **teaspoon ground ginger**
- 1 **pound lean ground pork**
- 1 **8-ounce can pineapple slices (juice pack), drained (4 slices)**

In a bowl combine egg white, milk, and soy sauce. Stir in onion, crumbs, green pepper, and ginger. Add meat, then mix well.

Shape meat into four 4-inch patties. Grill over *medium* coals for 8 minutes; turn. Top each patty with a pineapple ring. Grill for 6 to 8 minutes more or till meat is no longer pink and is well done. Makes 4 servings.

SAUCY MEATBALLS

1 egg white
¼ cup sliced green onion
1 8-ounce can sodium-reduced tomato sauce
¼ cup fine dry bread crumbs
¾ teaspoon dried sage, crushed
1 pound lean ground pork
5 ounces spaghetti
2 cups sliced fresh mushrooms
¼ cup sliced green onion
1 tablespoon margarine
1 tablespoon all-purpose flour
½ teaspoon dried basil, crushed
¼ teaspoon dried oregano, crushed
Dash pepper
½ cup water
2 tablespoons grated Parmesan cheese

In a mixing bowl combine egg white, ¼ cup green onion, and *2 tablespoons* of the tomato sauce. Stir in bread crumbs and sage. Add pork; mix well. Shape into 1½-inch meatballs. Place on a rack in a shallow baking pan. Bake in a 375° oven for 30 to 35 minutes or till meatballs are no longer pink.

Meanwhile, cook spaghetti according to package directions, *except* omit salt.

For sauce, cook mushrooms and ¼ cup green onion in margarine till tender. Stir in flour, basil, oregano, and pepper. Add remaining tomato sauce and water. Cook and stir till thickened and bubbly, then cook and stir 1 minute more. Spoon sauce over the meatballs. Serve over spaghetti. Sprinkle with Parmesan cheese. Makes 5 servings.

·QUICK RECIPE·
VEGETABLE-TOPPED PORK

This recipe received our taste panel's highest rating.

1 pound pork tenderloin
1 cup long grain rice (optional)
2 tablespoons margarine
1 large green pepper, cut into 1-inch pieces
½ cup chopped carrot
1 clove garlic, minced
1 cup peach nectar
1 tablespoon cornstarch
1 tablespoon brown sugar
1 tablespoon vinegar
½ teaspoon ground ginger

Cut pork into 4 pieces. Place each piece between 2 pieces of clear plastic wrap. Pound slightly to ½-inch thickness.

If desired, cook rice according to package directions, *except* omit salt and butter or margarine. In a large skillet cook tenderloin in margarine over medium-high heat about 15 minutes or till no longer pink, turning once. Transfer meat to a serving platter; keep warm. In the same skillet cook green pepper, carrot, and minced garlic in drippings till crisp-tender.

Stir together peach nectar, cornstarch, brown sugar, vinegar, and ginger. Stir into vegetable mixture in the skillet. Cook and stir till thickened and bubbly, then cook and stir 2 minutes more. Spoon mixture atop meat. Serve with rice, if desired. Makes 4 servings.

Ground pork called for in recipes is an unseasoned product that is at least 70 percent lean. When shopping for lean ground pork, check out the supermarket meat case.

If you can't find ground pork or if it doesn't look lean enough for your needs, ask the butcher to trim off the fat from a shoulder roast, then have him grind the meat for you.

Asparagus and carrots peek out of **Garden Tenderloin Rolls.**

GARDEN TENDERLOIN ROLLS

1 **10-ounce package frozen asparagus spears**
2 **medium carrots, cut into 5- to 6-inch-long julienne strips**
¾ **cup water**
1 **pound pork tenderloin**
2 **cups sliced fresh mushrooms**
½ **cup sliced green onion**
1 **tablespoon water**
½ **cup water**
¼ **cup dry sherry**
1 **tablespoon cornstarch**
1 **teaspoon instant beef bouillon granules**
¼ **teaspoon dried basil, crushed**
Dash pepper

In a large saucepan combine asparagus, carrots, and ¾ cup water. Bring to boiling. Reduce heat, then simmer, covered, for 4 to 6 minutes or just till crisp-tender. Drain.

Cut the pork into 8 pieces. Place each piece between 2 pieces of clear plastic wrap. Pound into a 4- to 5-inch circle. Sprinkle with pepper. Divide asparagus and carrots evenly among the 8 pieces of meat. Roll up jelly-roll style. Place, seam side down, in a 13x9x2-inch baking pan. Bake, covered, in a 375° oven for 15 minutes. Uncover; bake 5 to 10 minutes more or till meat is no longer pink.

Meanwhile, for sauce, in a small saucepan combine mushrooms, green onion, and 1 tablespoon water. Cook, covered, over medium heat about 5 minutes or till vegetables are tender. *Do not drain.*

Stir together ½ cup water, sherry, cornstarch, bouillon granules, basil, and pepper. Add to mushroom mixture. Cook and stir till thickened and bubbly, then cook and stir 2 minutes more. Spoon some sauce over meat rolls; pass the remaining sauce. Makes 4 servings.

STIR-FRIED PORK on LETTUCE

Serve this stir-fry over shredded lettuce or Chinese cabbage instead of the usual rice. Give it a try!

1 **pound pork tenderloin**
⅓ **cup dry sherry**
¼ **cup water**
1 **tablespoon hoisin sauce *or* catsup**
1 **teaspoon instant beef bouillon granules**
¼ **teaspoon ground ginger**
Dash garlic powder
1 **tablespoon cornstarch**
Nonstick spray coating
3 **cups sliced fresh mushrooms**
1 **medium carrot, thinly bias sliced**
½ **of a 6-ounce package frozen pea pods**
2 **teaspoons cooking oil**
4 **cups finely shredded lettuce (1 small head)**

Partially freeze pork; cut meat into ¼-inch-thick slices. For marinade, stir together sherry, water, hoisin sauce or catsup, bouillon granules, ginger, and garlic powder. Add meat and stir to coat. Let stand 15 minutes.

Drain marinade from pork; reserve marinade. Add water to marinade to make ¾ cup liquid. Combine marinade and cornstarch; set aside.

Spray a large skillet or wok with nonstick coating. Preheat over high heat till a drop of water sizzles. Stir-fry mushrooms, carrot, and pea pods for 3 to 4 minutes or just till crisp-tender. Remove vegetables from skillet or wok. Add oil. Stir-fry *half* of the pork for 3 to 4 minutes or till no longer pink. Remove pork. Stir-fry remaining pork for 3 to 4 minutes or till no longer pink. Return all pork to skillet.

Stir marinade mixture; add to skillet or wok. Cook and stir till thickened and bubbly. Cook and stir 2 minutes more. Return vegetables to skillet or wok; heat through. Serve over shredded lettuce. Makes 4 servings.

Never heard of hoisin sauce? Pronounced HOY-SIN, this thick, reddish brown paste can double as a terrific seasoning or condiment. Here are some more specifics: It's made from soybeans, flour, sugar, chili peppers, and spices and is used in Oriental recipes. Look for the seasoning sauce at the supermarket or an Oriental food shop.

TOASTED BARLEY and PORK STIR-FRY

You may be puzzled by what to use when a recipe calls for lean boneless pork. Since most pork cuts are tender, you can select from several fresh cuts.

A good choice for stewing would be a lean shoulder cut—roast or steak—which is trimmed of separable fat.

For stir-fry recipes, use lean pork shoulder or loin cuts. Remember to trim away all the fat you can.

1 **pound lean boneless pork**
1 **cup quick-cooking barley**
3 **cups water**
½ **cup water**
2 **tablespoons sodium-reduced soy sauce**
2 **tablespoons dry sherry**
2 **teaspoons cornstarch**
  Nonstick spray coating
2 **cloves garlic, minced**
½ **teaspoon finely grated gingerroot**
2 **cups shredded cabbage**
1 **large carrot, shredded**
12 **green onions, bias sliced into 1-inch pieces**
1 **tablespoon cooking oil**

Partially freeze pork; bias-slice into thin bite-size strips. Heat a 10-inch skillet over medium heat. Stir-fry barley in skillet for 6 to 8 minutes or just till toasted. Remove from heat; *carefully* add 3 cups water. Bring to boiling. Reduce heat, then simmer, covered, for 10 to 12 minutes or just till tender. Drain. Set aside.

For sauce, stir together ½ cup water, soy sauce, sherry, and cornstarch. Set aside.

Spray a large skillet or wok with nonstick coating. Preheat over high heat till a drop of water sizzles. Stir-fry garlic and gingerroot for 30 seconds. Then add cabbage and carrot to skillet or wok; stir-fry 2 minutes. Add green onions; stir-fry 1 to 2 minutes more or till vegetables are crisp-tender. Remove vegetables from skillet or wok.

Add oil. Stir-fry *half* of the pork for 3 to 4 minutes or till no longer pink. Remove pork. Stir-fry remaining pork for 3 to 4 minutes or till no longer pink. Return all pork to skillet or wok. Stir sauce; add to skillet or wok. Cook and stir till thickened and bubbly, then cook and stir 2 minutes more. Stir vegetables and barley into skillet or wok; heat through. Makes 5 servings.

·QUICK RECIPE·
PORK 'n' APPLES

Cinnamon and ginger add the perfect seasoning to apples, sweet potatoes, and pork.

1 **pound lean boneless pork**
½ **cup dry white wine**
½ **cup water**
1 **tablespoon cornstarch**
½ **teaspoon ground cinnamon**
¼ **teaspoon ground ginger**
  Nonstick spray coating
1 **large sweet potato, cut into julienne strips (1 cup)**
4 **green onions, cut into 1-inch pieces**
3 **teaspoons cooking oil**
2 **large apples, cored and cut into thin wedges**
2 **tablespoons raisins**

Partially freeze pork; bias-slice into thin bite-size strips. For sauce, stir together wine, water, cornstarch, cinnamon, and ginger. Set the mixture aside.

Spray a large skillet or wok with nonstick coating. Preheat over medium-high heat till a drop of water sizzles. Stir-fry sweet potato for 3 minutes. Add green onions and *1 teaspoon* of the oil; stir-fry 3 to 4 minutes more or till potato is tender. Remove vegetables from skillet or wok.

Add *1 teaspoon* of oil to the skillet. Stir-fry *half* of the pork for 3 to 4 minutes or till no longer pink. Remove pork. Add remaining oil and stir-fry remaining pork for 3 to 4 minutes or till no longer pink. Return all meat to skillet or wok. Add apples and raisins.

Stir sauce; add to skillet or wok. Cook and stir till thickened and bubbly. Cover and cook 2 minutes more. Return vegetables to skillet or wok; heat through. Makes 5 servings.

STROGANOFF STIR-FRY

¾ **pound lean boneless pork**
3 **ounces whole wheat noodles**
1 **8-ounce carton plain low-fat yogurt**
3 **tablespoons all-purpose flour**
¾ **cup water**
1 **tablespoon tomato paste**
1½ **teaspoons instant beef bouillon granules**
½ **teaspoon dried basil, crushed**
 Nonstick spray coating
1½ **cups sliced fresh mushrooms**
10 **green onions, sliced (about ¾ cup)**
2 **cloves garlic, minced**
2 **teaspoons cooking oil**
2 **tablespoons snipped parsley**

Partially freeze pork; bias-slice into thin bite-size strips. Cook noodles according to package directions, *except* omit salt.

Meanwhile, for sauce, thoroughly combine yogurt and flour; stir in water, tomato paste, bouillon granules, and basil. Set aside.

Spray a large skillet or wok with nonstick coating. Preheat over high heat till a drop of water sizzles. Stir-fry mushrooms, onions, and garlic about 3 minutes or till crisp-tender. Remove vegetables from skillet or wok. Add oil. Stir-fry pork over high heat for 3 to 4 minutes or till no longer pink.

Carefully add sauce mixture to meat in skillet or wok. Cook and stir till thickened and bubbly. Cook and stir 1 minute more. Stir vegetables and parsley into skillet or wok; heat through. Serve over the cooked noodles. Makes 4 servings.

BARBECUE-SAUCED PORK ROAST

Chili powder adds zip to the glaze-sauce.

1 **2½- to 3-pound pork loin center rib roast**
1 **cup water**
½ **cup chopped onion**
½ **of a 6-ounce can (⅓ cup) sodium-reduced tomato paste**
3 **tablespoons molasses**
2 **tablespoons vinegar**
2 **cloves garlic, minced**
1 **bay leaf**
1 **teaspoon dried basil, crushed**
½ **teaspoon chili powder**
¼ **teaspoon ground ginger**
¼ **teaspoon pepper**

Place meat, bone side down, in a shallow roasting pan. Insert a meat thermometer, placing bulb so it rests in the thickest portion of meat and does not rest in fat or touch bone. Roast, uncovered, in a 325° oven for 1½ to 2 hours or till the thermometer registers 170°.

Meanwhile, for sauce, in a medium saucepan bring water and onion to boiling. Reduce heat, then simmer, covered, for 5 minutes or till onion is tender. Stir in tomato paste, molasses, vinegar, garlic, bay leaf, basil, chili powder, ginger, and pepper. Bring to boiling. Reduce heat, then simmer, uncovered, about 15 minutes or till mixture is slightly thick, stirring occasionally. Spoon some sauce over roast during the last 30 minutes of roasting. Reheat remaining sauce; pass with meat. Makes 6 servings.

To make it easier to carve the Barbecue-Sauced Pork Roast, *have the butcher loosen the backbone of the roast. Then all you have to do is slice between the rib bones.*

PORK ROAST with MUSHROOM SAUCE

For gravy or sauce that's as fat-free as possible, there are two methods you can use to remove fat from drippings. The ice cube method is described in the recipe for Pork Roast with Mushroom Sauce. The other method is to chill the meat drippings in the refrigerator. Then, lift off the hardened fat.

When you have a roast with rib bones, there's no need to use a roasting rack. The rib bones serve as a rack.

1 **3-pound pork loin center rib roast**
   Coarsely ground pepper
½ **cup water**
3 **cups sliced fresh mushrooms**
   (8 ounces)
½ **cup sliced leeks *or* green onions**
1 **clove garlic, minced**
1 **tablespoon water**
1½ **teaspoons prepared horseradish**
¼ **teaspoon dried tarragon *or* thyme,**
   crushed
⅛ **teaspoon salt**
1 **tablespoon cold water**
2 **teaspoons cornstarch**

Have butcher loosen backbone of roast for easier carving. Rub pepper into roast. Place meat, bone side down, in a small shallow roasting pan. Insert a meat thermometer, placing bulb so it rests in the thickest portion of meat and does not rest in fat or touch bone. Roast, uncovered, in a 325° oven for 1¾ to 2 hours or till the thermometer registers 170°.

Remove roast from pan; cover and keep warm. Stir ½ cup water into pan to loosen drippings; strain into a 2-cup measure. Place 2 or 3 *ice cubes* in mixture, stirring to solidify fat. Remove and discard all fat and ice cubes. Add water to make ¾ cup liquid; set aside.

For sauce, in a medium saucepan cook and stir mushrooms, leeks or onions, and garlic in 1 tablespoon water over medium heat about 3 minutes or till tender. Stir in horseradish, tarragon or thyme, and salt. Add the reserved ¾ cup liquid; bring to boiling. Stir together 1 tablespoon water and cornstarch; stir into mixture. Cook and stir till thickened and bubbly, then cook and stir 2 minutes more. Serve sauce with roast. Makes 8 servings.

MUSTARD-ORANGE PORK ROAST

2 **tablespoons Dijon-style mustard**
2 **teaspoons finely shredded**
   orange peel
½ **teaspoon coarsely ground pepper**
1 **2½- to 3-pound boneless pork loin**
   roast
2 **medium oranges**
   Orange juice
4 **teaspoons cornstarch**
1 **tablespoon Dijon-style mustard**
1 **teaspoon sugar**
¼ **cup dry white wine**

Combine 2 tablespoons mustard, *1 teaspoon* orange peel, and pepper. Place meat on a rack in a shallow roasting pan. Spread mustard mixture on top and sides of roast.

Insert a meat thermometer, placing bulb so it rests in the center of the meat and does not rest in fat. Roast, uncovered, in a 325° oven for 1½ to 2 hours or till the thermometer registers 170°.

Meanwhile, for sauce, peel and section oranges over a bowl to catch juices. Add additional orange juice to make 1 cup juice.

In a saucepan stir together orange juice and cornstarch. Stir in 1 tablespoon mustard, sugar, and remaining orange peel. Cook and stir till thickened and bubbly, then cook and stir 2 minutes more. Stir in wine and orange sections. Heat through. Slice roast. Serve sauce with roast. Makes 10 to 12 servings.

APRICOT-SAUCED CHOPS

Broil chops so the fat drains away as the meat cooks.

 4 **pork loin chops, cut ¾ inch thick (about 1½ pounds total)**
 ¼ **cup sliced green onion**
 1 **tablespoon margarine**
 2 **teaspoons cornstarch**
 ¾ **cup apricot nectar**

Place chops on the unheated rack of a broiler pan. Broil 3 to 4 inches from the heat for 20 to 25 minutes or till pork is no longer pink and is well done; turn once. Meanwhile, for sauce, in a saucepan cook green onion in margarine till tender. Stir in cornstarch. Add apricot nectar all at once. Cook and stir till thickened and bubbly, then cook and stir 2 minutes more. Serve sauce atop chops. Makes 4 servings.

MUSTARD PORK CHOPS

 2 **tablespoons Dijon-style mustard**
 4 **pork loin chops, cut ½ inch thick (about 1¼ pounds total)**
 ¼ **cup fine dry bread crumbs**
 2 **tablespoons cornmeal**
 1 **tablespoon whole wheat flour**
 ⅓ **cup plain low-fat yogurt**
 1 **tablespoon chutney, chopped**

Spread mustard on all surfaces of chops. Combine bread crumbs, cornmeal, and flour. Coat chops with crumb mixture. Place chops in a 9x9x2-inch baking pan.

Bake in a 350° oven for 30 to 40 minutes or till chops are no longer pink and coating is lightly browned. Stir together yogurt and chutney; dollop atop chops. Makes 4 servings.

SAVORY PORK and VEGETABLES

The herb that flavors both the meat and vegetables is often called "summer savory." It's a member of the mint family and it adds an aromatic flavor to this and other meat and vegetable dishes.

  Nonstick spray coating
 4 **pork loin rib chops, cut ½ inch thick (about 1¼ pounds total)**
 1 **tablespoon lemon juice**
 1 **teaspoon dried savory, crushed**
 ⅛ **teaspoon ground red pepper**
 ¼ **cup water**
 1 **16-ounce package loose-pack frozen mixed broccoli, carrots, and cauliflower**
 2 **teaspoons margarine**

Spray a 10-inch skillet with nonstick coating. Sprinkle chops with lemon juice. Mix together savory and red pepper; rub both sides of chops with some of the seasoning mixture.

Heat skillet over medium heat. Add chops and cook about 10 minutes or till lightly browned, turning once. Add water. Cover and cook 10 minutes more. Remove chops.

Add vegetables to skillet. Dot with margarine. Sprinkle with remaining seasoning mixture. Place chops atop vegetables in skillet. Bring to boiling. Reduce heat, then cook, covered, over medium-low heat about 10 minutes or till meat and vegetables are tender and pork is no longer pink. To serve, place chops on platter and arrange the vegetables around the chops. Makes 4 servings.

MEXICAN CHOPS and VEGETABLES

You can substitute tomato wedges for the halved cherry tomato garnish.

> 1 **medium carrot, sliced (½ cup)**
> **Nonstick spray coating**
> 4 **pork loin chops, cut ½ inch thick**
> **(about 1¼ pounds total)**
> 1 **17-ounce can cream-style corn**
> 1½ **teaspoons chili powder**
> ¼ **teaspoon ground cumin**
> 1 **9-ounce package frozen Italian**
> **green beans**
> 1 **4-ounce can green chili peppers,**
> **rinsed, seeded, and chopped**
> 1 **stalk celery, sliced (½ cup)**
> ½ **teaspoon chili powder**
> **Dash pepper**
> **Halved cherry tomatoes (optional)**

In a small saucepan cook carrot in a small amount of boiling water, covered, for 3 to 4 minutes or till crisp-tender; drain.

Spray a 10-inch skillet with nonstick coating. Heat skillet over medium heat. Add chops and cook about 10 minutes or till lightly browned, turning once. In a bowl stir together corn, 1½ teaspoons chili powder, and cumin. Stir in beans, chili peppers, celery, and carrot. Transfer the mixture to a 12x7½x2-inch baking dish; arrange chops atop vegetable mixture. Cover with foil. Bake in a 350° oven for 35 minutes.

Sprinkle ½ teaspoon chili powder and pepper over chops. Return to oven. Bake, uncovered, for 10 to 15 minutes more or till chops are done and pork is no longer pink. Garnish with tomatoes, if desired. Makes 4 servings.

PEANUTTY PORK CHOPS

It makes no difference in this recipe whether you use creamy or chunk-style peanut butter—use whichever you have on hand.

> **Nonstick spray coating**
> 4 **pork loin rib chops, cut ½ inch thick**
> **(about 1¼ pounds total)**
> ½ **cup sliced green onion**
> ½ **cup orange juice**
> 2 **tablespoons peanut butter**
> 1 **tablespoon sodium-reduced**
> **soy sauce**
> ¼ **teaspoon ground cardamom**
> **Several dashes bottled hot**
> **pepper sauce**
> 1 **tablespoon cold water**
> 1 **teaspoon cornstarch**
> ¼ **cup chopped unsalted peanuts**
> **Snipped parsley (optional)**

Spray a large skillet with nonstick coating. Heat skillet over medium heat. Add chops and cook about 10 minutes or till lightly browned, turning once. Remove from heat. Drain off any fat. Add green onion to skillet.

In a blender container or mixer bowl combine orange juice, peanut butter, soy sauce, cardamom, and hot pepper sauce. Cover and blend or mix till smooth. Pour over chops. Cover and cook over low heat for 20 to 30 minutes or till chops are done and pork is no longer pink. Transfer chops to a platter; cover and keep warm.

For sauce, measure juices; add water, if necessary, to make ¾ cup. In a small saucepan combine water and cornstarch; stir in juices. Cook and stir till thickened and bubbly, then cook and stir 2 minutes more. Serve over chops. Sprinkle peanuts and parsley, if desired, atop. Makes 4 servings.

There is a difference between pork loin chops and loin rib chops. Loin chops include a portion of the tenderloin as well as the loin eye muscle, separated by a T-shape bone. Loin rib chops contain the loin eye muscle, but no tenderloin. Both contain a portion of the backbone.

MARINATED and GRILLED LEG of LAMB

It's easier to roll up the meat and seasonings if your butcher bones the lamb in one piece.

- 1 **5- to 6-pound leg of lamb, boned**
- ½ **cup orange juice**
- ¼ **cup cooking oil**
- ¼ **cup sliced green onion**
- 2 **tablespoons finely snipped parsley**
- 1 **clove garlic, minced**
- ½ **teaspoon dried basil, crushed**
- ½ **teaspoon dried oregano, crushed**
- ¼ **teaspoon dried tarragon, crushed**
- ¼ **teaspoon celery seed**
- 4 **artichokes, cooked (optional)**
  Baby carrots, cooked (optional)
  Yellow summer squash, cooked (optional)
- 1 **sweet red pepper, cooked (optional)**

Place lamb in a large plastic bag set in a large bowl. For marinade, in a mixing bowl combine orange juice, oil, onion, parsley, garlic, basil, oregano, tarragon, and celery seed. Pour over lamb; close bag. Marinate in the refrigerator for 4 to 6 hours or overnight, turning the bag occasionally.

Drain meat, reserving marinade. Pat excess moisture from meat with paper towels. Use a slotted spoon to remove solids from marinade. Spoon solids over meat. Starting from the wide end, tightly roll up meat jelly-roll style. Tie securely with a string.

Insert a meat thermometer near center of roll, not touching fat. In a covered grill arrange preheated coals around a drip pan; test for *medium* heat above pan. Place lamb on grill rack over drip pan but not over coals. Brush with some of the reserved marinade. Lower hood. Grill for 1½ to 2 hours or till meat thermometer registers 150°, brushing occasionally with marinade. Serve with cooked vegetables, if desired. Makes 12 servings.

PAPRIKA LAMB LINGUINE

A satisfying saucy entrée for two.

Nonstick spray coating
- 2 **lamb leg sirloin chops, cut ¾ inch thick**
- 1 **8-ounce can sodium-reduced tomatoes, cut up**
- ½ **cup chopped onion**
- ⅓ **cup chopped green pepper**
- 1 **teaspoon paprika**
- ⅛ **teaspoon salt**
- ⅛ **teaspoon pepper**
- 2 **tablespoons cold water**
- 2 **teaspoons all-purpose flour**
- 3 **ounces linguine *or* spaghetti**
- 2 **tablespoons snipped parsley**

Spray a large skillet with nonstick coating. In the skillet cook chops over medium heat about 7 minutes or till brown, turning once. Drain off fat. Add the *undrained* tomatoes, onion, green pepper, paprika, salt, and pepper. Bring to boiling; reduce the heat. Cover and simmer about 30 minutes or till meat is tender. Remove chops from skillet.

Stir together water and flour. Add to tomato mixture in skillet. Cook and stir till thick and bubbly, then cook and stir 1 minute more. Return chops to skillet; heat through.

Meanwhile, cook linguine or spaghetti according to package directions, *except* omit salt. Serve chops and tomato mixture over pasta. Sprinkle with parsley. Makes 2 servings.

Fresh artichokes complement the flavor of Marinated and Grilled Leg of Lamb. *Artichokes are abundant in spring, but you can find them year-round in many supermarkets. Before you cook artichokes, wash them, trim the stems, and remove the outer leaves. Then cut one inch off the top of each artichoke and snip off sharp leaf tips. Brush lemon juice on cut edges to prevent browning.*

Place artichokes in a Dutch oven and let simmer, covered, for 20 to 30 minutes or until a leaf pulls out easily. Pour off the water and drain them upside down on paper towels.

HERBED LAMB KABOBS

1 pound lean boneless lamb, cut into 1-inch pieces
½ cup reduced-calorie Russian salad dressing
2 tablespoons lime juice
1 clove garlic, minced
½ teaspoon dried basil, crushed
4 small fresh plums *or* peaches, pitted and quartered
1 medium green pepper, cut into 1½-inch pieces

Place lamb in a plastic bag; set in a bowl. For the marinade, in a small mixing bowl stir together salad dressing, lime juice, garlic, and basil. Pour over lamb in bag. Close the bag. Marinate in the refrigerator for 4 to 6 hours or overnight, turning bag occasionally.

Drain lamb, reserving marinade. On 4 long or 8 short skewers, alternately thread lamb, plums or peaches, and green pepper.

Place skewers on the unheated rack of a broiler pan. Broil 4 inches from the heat for 10 to 12 minutes or till meat is tender, turning once. Brush occasionally with reserved marinade. Makes 4 servings.

LEAN IRISH STEW

This popular Emerald Isle stew was originally made with goat meat instead of lamb.

1 pound lean boneless lamb, cut into ¾-inch pieces
1 tablespoon cooking oil
4 cups water
2 medium onions, cut into wedges
1 tablespoon instant beef bouillon granules
1 bay leaf
½ teaspoon dried thyme, crushed
¼ teaspoon dried basil, crushed
¼ teaspoon pepper
6 medium carrots, sliced ½ inch thick
4 medium potatoes, cut into chunks
¼ cup cold water
2 tablespoons cornstarch
Snipped parsley

In a Dutch oven brown lamb in hot oil. Drain off fat. Stir in water, onions, bouillon granules, thyme, basil, pepper, and bay leaf. Bring to boiling; reduce heat. Cover and simmer for 45 minutes. Skim off fat.

Add carrots and potatoes. Return to boiling, then reduce heat. Cover and simmer for 15 to 20 minutes or till vegetables are tender. Remove bay leaf.

Stir together water and cornstarch. Add to Dutch oven. Cook and stir till thickened and bubbly, then cook and stir 2 minutes more. Sprinkle with parsley. Makes 6 servings.

LOW-FAT MOUSSAKA

We reduced the egg yolks, used low-fat dairy products, and cut the salt so you can enjoy this rich-tasting Greek classic without guilt.

> 2 **large eggplants (2 pounds total), peeled and sliced ½ inch thick**
> 1 **pound lean ground lamb**
> 1 **large onion, chopped**
> 1 **clove garlic, minced**
> 1 **6-ounce can sodium-reduced tomato paste**
> ⅔ **cup dry red wine**
> 2 **tablespoons water**
> 1½ **teaspoons dried basil, crushed**
> 1 **teaspoon dried oregano, crushed**
> 1 **teaspoon ground cinnamon**
> ¼ **teaspoon salt**
> ⅛ **teaspoon pepper**
> 2 **tablespoons fine dry bread crumbs**
> 2 **tablespoons margarine**
> ¼ **cup all-purpose flour**
> **Dash pepper**
> 2 **cups skim milk**
> 2 **egg whites**
> 1 **egg**
> ⅓ **cup grated Parmesan cheese**
> **Ground cinnamon**

Place eggplant in a steamer basket set over boiling water. Cover and steam for 10 to 15 minutes or till tender; drain well. Set aside.

Meanwhile, in a medium skillet cook lamb, onion, and garlic till meat is brown and onion is tender; drain off fat. Stir in tomato paste, wine, water, basil, oregano, 1 teaspoon cinnamon, salt, and ⅛ teaspoon pepper. Bring to boiling; reduce heat. Cover and simmer for 10 to 15 minutes or till thick. Stir in bread crumbs; set aside.

In a medium saucepan melt margarine; stir in flour and dash pepper. Add milk all at once. Cook and stir till thickened and bubbly, then cook and stir 1 minute more. Beat together egg whites and egg. Gradually stir the thickened milk mixture into the egg mixture.

To assemble, in a 13x9x2-inch baking dish arrange *half* of the eggplant slices. Spoon tomato mixture over eggplant; top with remaining eggplant. Pour the hot milk-egg mixture over all. Sprinkle with Parmesan cheese and additional cinnamon. Bake in a 325° oven for 35 to 40 minutes or till the top layer is set. Let stand 5 minutes. Makes 10 servings.

CUTTING UP A LEG OF LAMB: A leg of lamb is the leanest portion of the lamb, making it a great choice to use in a variety of recipes. Have your butcher cut a 7- to 10-pound whole leg of lamb roughly into thirds.

The shank end is a good piece to cut into cubes or strips. Use this portion of the lamb when a recipe calls for lean boneless lamb, such as Lean Irish Stew *and* Herbed Lamb Kabobs *on the opposite page.*

Have the butcher cut the large end of the leg of lamb into four chops. Put some of them to good use in Paprika Lamb Linguine *(see recipe, page 95).*

The middle portion of the leg, or center-cut lamb roast, is a good size for small families. Roast it as you would a beef or pork roast.

To store any cuts of lamb for future use, wrap the meat in moisture- and vaporproof wrap. Then seal, label, and freeze.

HONEY-GINGER CHICKEN

TANGY BARBECUED CHICKEN

To make rice pilaf for the Honey-Ginger Chicken, spray a medium saucepan with nonstick spray coating. Cook ¼ cup sliced green onion in a saucepan till tender but not brown. Stir in 1½ cups water, ½ cup long grain rice, ¼ cup wild rice, and ¼ cup shredded carrot. Bring to boiling; reduce heat. Cover and simmer for 35 to 40 minutes or till rice is tender. Makes 4 servings.

Look for sodium-reduced soy sauce at the grocery store near the other Oriental foods.

 3   **tablespoons honey**
 1   **teaspoon finely shredded orange peel**
 1   **tablespoon orange juice**
 2   **teaspoons sodium-reduced soy sauce**
 ¼   **teaspoon coarsely ground pepper**
 ⅛   **teaspoon ground ginger**
 2   **whole medium chicken breasts, skinned and halved lengthwise**
     Rice pilaf (optional)
     Steamed asparagus spears (optional)

In a small mixing bowl stir together honey, orange peel, orange juice, soy sauce, pepper, and ginger.

Place chicken on the unheated rack of a broiler pan. Broil 4 to 5 inches from the heat about 8 minutes or till chicken is tender, turning once. Brush frequently with honey mixture during broiling. Serve with rice and asparagus, if desired. Makes 4 servings.

 1   **8-ounce can sodium-reduced tomato sauce**
 ½   **cup water**
 2   **tablespoons red wine vinegar**
 1   **teaspoon Worcestershire sauce**
     Several dashes bottled hot pepper sauce
 2   **tablespoons brown sugar**
 1   **clove garlic, minced**
 ½   **teaspoon dry mustard**
 ½   **teaspoon dried oregano, crushed**
 ½   **teaspoon chili powder**
 ¼   **teaspoon celery seed**
 1   **2½- to 3-pound broiler-fryer chicken, cut up and skinned**

For the sauce, in a small saucepan combine tomato sauce, water, vinegar, Worcestershire sauce, and hot pepper sauce. Stir in sugar, garlic, mustard, oregano, chili powder, and celery seed.

Bring to boiling, then reduce heat. Simmer, uncovered, about 10 minutes or till reduced to 1 cup, stirring occasionally.

Rinse chicken; pat dry with paper towels. Grill chicken on an uncovered grill directly over *medium* coals for 25 minutes. Turn and grill for 15 to 20 minutes more or till tender, brushing often with sauce during the last 5 to 10 minutes of grilling. Cover and chill any remaining sauce. Makes 6 servings.

SWEET and SOUR CHICKEN

"O-o-oh! That's pretty!" announced an editor when she saw this saucy stir-fry.

> ½ cup cold water
> 1 tablespoon cornstarch
> 3 tablespoons vinegar
> 2 tablespoons honey
> 1½ teaspoons sodium-reduced soy sauce
> ¼ teaspoon instant chicken bouillon granules
> ⅔ cup long grain rice
> Nonstick spray coating
> 1 clove garlic, minced
> 1 medium carrot, thinly bias sliced
> 1 small green pepper, cut into ½-inch pieces
> 3 green onions, sliced
> 1 tablespoon cooking oil
> 2 whole medium chicken breasts, skinned, boned, and cut into bite-size strips
> 1 8-ounce can pineapple chunks, drained
> 1 cup seedless red grapes, halved

Stir together the water and cornstarch. Stir in the vinegar, honey, soy sauce, and bouillon granules; set aside. Cook rice according to the package directions, *except* omit salt and butter or margarine.

Meanwhile, spray a large skillet or wok with nonstick coating. Preheat skillet over high heat. Stir-fry garlic in hot skillet for 15 seconds. Add carrot and stir-fry for 2 minutes. Add green pepper and green onion; stir-fry about 1 minute more or till vegetables are crisp-tender. Remove vegetables from skillet.

Add oil to skillet. Stir-fry *half* of the chicken in hot oil about 3 minutes or till tender; remove from skillet. Stir-fry remaining chicken about 3 minutes. Return all chicken to skillet.

Push chicken from center of skillet. Stir vinegar mixture; add to skillet. Cook and stir till thickened and bubbly. Cook and stir 2 minutes more. Stir in vegetables, pineapple, and grapes. Cover and cook about 2 minutes or till hot. Serve with rice. Makes 4 servings.

POULTRY and PASTA

Chicken and linguine in a delicately seasoned cheese sauce will satisfy three hungry people.

> 4 ounces linguine *or* spaghetti
> Nonstick spray coating
> 1 medium zucchini, halved lengthwise and cut into ¼-inch slices
> 2 teaspoons cooking oil
> 1 whole medium chicken breast, skinned, boned, and cut into bite-size pieces
> 1 clove garlic, minced
> ½ teaspoon dried basil, crushed
> ⅛ teaspoon pepper
> ½ cup skim milk
> 1 teaspoon all-purpose flour
> 4 cherry tomatoes, halved
> 3 tablespoons grated Parmesan cheese

In a large saucepan cook pasta according to package directions, *except* omit salt; drain. Meanwhile, spray a large skillet with nonstick coating. Add zucchini and cook over medium-high heat for 2 to 3 minutes or till crisp-tender. Remove from skillet. Add oil to the hot skillet. Add chicken, garlic, basil, and pepper; cook and stir about 2 minutes or till chicken is tender.

In a small bowl combine milk and flour; add to the skillet. Cook and stir till thickened and bubbly. Cook and stir 1 minute more.

To serve, gently toss together chicken mixture, pasta, zucchini, tomatoes, and Parmesan cheese. Makes 3 servings.

TOMATO-STUFFED CHICKEN ROLLS

2 whole medium chicken breasts,
    skinned, halved lengthwise,
    and boned
1 slice Swiss cheese, cut into
    fourths (1½ ounces)
1 small tomato, peeled, seeded, and
    chopped
½ teaspoon dried basil, crushed
1 tablespoon skim milk *or* water
¼ cup fine dry bread crumbs
1 tablespoon grated Parmesan cheese
1 tablespoon snipped parsley

Place 1 piece of chicken, boned side up, between 2 pieces of clear plastic wrap. Working from the center to the edges, pound with a meat mallet to ¼-inch thickness. Repeat with remaining chicken.

Place a piece of cheese and some of the tomato on a piece of chicken. Sprinkle with some of the basil. Fold in sides of chicken; roll up jelly-roll style, gently pressing all edges together to seal.

Place chicken rolls, seam side down, in a 10x6x2-inch baking dish. Brush tops with milk or water. In a small mixing bowl stir together bread crumbs, Parmesan, and parsley. Sprinkle over chicken. Bake, uncovered, in a 350° oven for 40 to 45 minutes or till chicken is tender. Makes 4 servings.

STUFFING THE CHICKEN ROLLS: *After you pound the chicken breasts to ¼-inch thickness, place 1 piece of cheese and one-fourth of the tomato on each piece of the chicken. Sprinkle each with some basil. To form the chicken rolls, fold in the sides of the chicken. Then roll up the chicken and filling jelly-roll style, gently pressing all edges together to seal. Place the chicken rolls, seam side down, in a baking dish.*

A lemony apple juice mixture is brushed on the Stuffed Cornish Hen Halves.

STUFFED CORNISH HEN HALVES

1⅓ cups water
¼ cup sliced green onion
1 tablespoon margarine
1 teaspoon instant chicken bouillon
   granules
¼ teaspoon ground sage
⅓ cup wild rice
⅓ cup long grain rice
¼ cup shredded carrot
2 tablespoons snipped parsley
2 1- to 1½-pound Cornish game hens,
   split lengthwise
¼ cup frozen apple juice concentrate,
   thawed
1 teaspoon lemon juice

In a medium saucepan combine water, green onion, margarine, bouillon granules, and sage. Bring to boiling. Stir in wild rice; reduce heat. Cover and simmer for 30 minutes. Stir in long grain rice, carrot, and parsley. Cover and simmer about 20 minutes more or till rice is done and liquid is absorbed.

In a shallow baking dish spoon rice mixture into 4 mounds. Place hens on rice mounds; cover loosely with foil. Roast in a 375° oven for 30 minutes.

Meanwhile, in a small bowl stir together apple juice concentrate and lemon juice. Uncover hens and roast about 35 minutes more or till drumsticks can be twisted easily in sockets. Brush during the last 15 minutes with apple juice mixture. Garnish with green onion tops, if desired. Makes 4 servings.

CURRY CHICKEN KABOBS

These skewers are jam-packed with tender chicken and colorful fresh vegetables.

1½ pounds chicken thighs *or* whole
   breasts, skinned and boned
4 boiling *or* frozen small whole onions
2 medium carrots, bias sliced into
   1-inch pieces
1 small zucchini, cut into 1-inch pieces
8 fresh medium mushrooms
½ cup orange juice
1 clove garlic, minced
2 teaspoons curry powder
1 teaspoon cornstarch

Cut chicken into 1-inch pieces; set aside. In a medium saucepan cook onions, carrots, and zucchini, covered, in a small amount of boiling water for 8 minutes. Add mushrooms and cook about 2 minutes more or just till tender. Drain and set aside.

For sauce, in a small saucepan stir together orange juice, garlic, curry powder, and cornstarch. Cook and stir till thickened and bubbly. Cook and stir 2 minutes more.

On 4 small skewers alternately thread onion, carrots, zucchini, and mushrooms. On 4 more small skewers thread chicken pieces. Grill the chicken on an uncovered grill over *medium-hot* coals for 15 to 20 minutes or till tender, turning and brushing with sauce after 10 minutes. Grill the vegetables with chicken the last 5 to 6 minutes or till heated through, turning and brushing vegetables with sauce after 3 minutes. Makes 4 servings.

Curry powder really isn't a single spice—it's a blend of up to 20 different spices. And you'll find that no two blends are exactly alike. When cooking with curry powder, you'll get the most well-rounded flavor by cooking it in a sauce as we did with the Curry Chicken Kabobs.

CHICKEN BURRITO STACK-UPS

High-fat avocados usually are off limits, but this recipe divides a small one among six servings for a tasty, yet harmless splurge.

6 5-inch tortillas
2 cups chopped cooked chicken
2 medium tomatoes, peeled and chopped
1 4-ounce can chopped green chili peppers, drained
2 tablespoons sliced green onion
1 tablespoon lemon juice
Dash bottled hot pepper sauce
2 cups shredded lettuce
½ cup shredded mozzarella cheese (2 ounces)
1 small avocado, halved, seeded, peeled, and thinly sliced

Place tortillas on a large baking sheet. Heat in a 350° oven for 10 to 15 minutes or till crisp and light brown.

In a mixing bowl stir together chicken, tomatoes, chili peppers, onion, lemon juice, and hot pepper sauce.

To assemble the stacks, place tortillas on individual serving plates; top each of the 6 tortillas with chicken mixture, lettuce, and cheese. Garnish each stack with avocado slices. Makes 6 servings.

ASSEMBLING CHICKEN BURRITO STACK-UPS: *To make the stacks, place the baked tortillas on individual serving plates. Top each of the six tortillas with about ½ cup chicken mixture, ⅓ cup shredded lettuce, and about 1 tablespoon mozzarella cheese. For the finishing touch, arrange avocado slices on each stack.*

TACO-STYLE POTATO and TURKEY SKILLET

Don't be heavy-handed measuring the chili powder if you're watching your sodium intake.

    4 medium potatoes, peeled and
       quartered
    ¼ teaspoon salt
    3 to 4 tablespoons skim milk
    1 pound ground raw turkey
    ½ cup shredded carrot
    ½ cup chopped onion
    1 cup water
    1 6-ounce can tomato paste
    2 teaspoons chili powder
    ¼ teaspoon salt
    ¼ teaspoon dried oregano, crushed
    ⅛ teaspoon garlic powder
       Fews dashes bottled hot pepper
       sauce
    1 10-ounce package frozen cut green
       beans
    ¼ cup shredded cheddar cheese
       (1 ounce)

In a medium saucepan cook potatoes, covered, in a small amount of boiling water about 20 minutes or till tender; drain.

Add ¼ teaspoon salt to potatoes; mash potatoes. Gradually beat in enough milk to make light and fluffy. Cover and keep warm.

In a large skillet cook turkey, carrot, and onion till turkey is brown and vegetables are nearly tender. Drain off fat, if necessary. Stir in water, tomato paste, chili powder, ¼ teaspoon salt, oregano, garlic powder, and hot pepper sauce. Add green beans, stirring to break up. Bring to boiling; reduce heat. Cover and simmer for 5 to 8 minutes or till beans are crisp-tender.

Spoon potatoes on turkey mixture. Sprinkle with cheese. Cover and cook 2 to 3 minutes or till cheese melts. Makes 6 servings.

ROAST TURKEY with CRANBERRY SAUCE

A delicious and healthful change of pace from traditional turkey and stuffing. And much easier!

    1 3- to 3½-pound fresh *or* frozen breast
       of turkey
    ½ teaspoon finely shredded orange
       peel
    ⅔ cup orange juice
    ½ cup sugar
    3 cups cranberries

If using frozen turkey, thaw. Place turkey, skin side up, on a rack in a shallow roasting pan. Cover loosely with foil. Roast in a 325° oven for 1½ to 2 hours or till tender. Uncover the last 45 minutes of roasting. Baste occasionally with pan juices, if desired.

Meanwhile, for the sauce, in a medium saucepan combine orange peel, orange juice, and sugar. Bring to boiling, stirring to dissolve sugar. Add cranberries; return to boiling. Reduce heat. Simmer, uncovered, over medium-low heat for 7 to 8 minutes or till cranberries pop and sauce thickens slightly. Serve warm with turkey. Makes 12 servings.

CHICKEN SALAD
for TWO

This curry-spiked salad looks extra yummy when spooned over tomato slices and green pepper rings.

- ⅓ cup plain low-fat yogurt
- ¼ cup chopped celery
- 3 tablespoons finely chopped green onion
- ½ teaspoon curry powder
- ¼ teaspoon sugar
  Dash pepper
- 1 cup chopped cooked chicken
- ½ of an 8-ounce can water chestnuts, drained and chopped (½ cup)
- 1 small tomato, sliced
- 1 small green pepper, sliced into rings
  Lettuce leaves

In a small mixing bowl stir together yogurt, celery, onion, curry powder, sugar, and pepper. Stir in chicken and water chestnuts; cover and chill.

To serve, arrange tomato slices and green pepper rings on 2 lettuce-lined plates. Top with chicken mixture. Makes 2 servings.

LEAN POULTRY CHOICES: *Chicken and turkey are good choices for healthful eating, especially if you heed these simple fat-fighting hints:*

Reduce fat in poultry by about 10 percent by removing the skin and pockets of fat under the skin.

Be choosy about the type of meat you eat. Light meat, such as the breast, is leaner than dark meat, such as thighs and legs.

CHICKEN and
FRUIT SALAD

- 1 cup long grain rice
- 1 8-ounce can pineapple chunks (juice pack)
- ¼ cup packed brown sugar
- 4 teaspoons cornstarch
- ¼ teaspoon garlic powder
- ¼ teaspoon ground ginger
- ½ cup unsweetened pineapple juice
- ⅓ cup water
- ¼ cup red wine vinegar
- 2 5½-ounce cans chunk-style chicken, drained and chilled
- 1 medium apple, cored and chopped
- ½ cup chopped green pepper
- ½ cup seedless red grapes, halved
  Lettuce leaves

Cook rice according to package directions, *except* omit salt and butter or margarine. Cover and chill.

Meanwhile, drain pineapple, reserving juice. Cover and chill pineapple. In a small saucepan combine brown sugar, cornstarch, garlic powder, and ginger. Stir in reserved pineapple juice, the ½ cup pineapple juice, water, and vinegar. Cook and stir till thickened and bubbly. Cook and stir 2 minutes more. Cover surface with clear plastic wrap; chill.

Just before serving, toss together rice, pineapple, chicken, apple, green pepper, and grapes. Add cornstarch mixture, tossing to coat. Serve on 5 lettuce-lined salad plates. Makes 5 servings.

The rich-flavored cheese coating makes the Parmesan Fish Fillets *taste almost like they're fried.*

PARMESAN FISH FILLETS

Individual frozen fish fillets are an excellent choice for this dish because they're easy to handle.

**4 fresh *or* frozen fish fillets
  (1 pound total)**
1 beaten egg white
2 tablespoons water
**½ cup finely crushed sodium-reduced
  wheat wafers**
3 tablespoons grated Parmesan cheese
**2 tablespoons finely snipped parsley
  Nonstick spray coating**

Thaw fish, if frozen. Pat dry with paper towels. In a small mixing bowl stir together egg white and water. In another mixing bowl stir together crushed wheat wafers, Parmesan cheese, and parsley. Dip fish into egg white mixture, then into cracker mixture to coat.

Spray a large skillet with nonstick coating. Cook crumb-coated fish in the hot skillet for 6 to 8 minutes or till fish flakes easily with a fork, turning once. Makes 4 servings.

MARINATED FISH FILLETS

Compared to most nuts, pine nuts and almonds are relatively low in fat.

**1 11½-ounce package (4 portions)
  frozen fish portions**
½ cup water
**3 tablespoons frozen pineapple-
  orange juice concentrate**
**1 tablespoon cooking oil
  Dash salt**
**1 tablespoon pine nuts *or* slivered
  almonds, toasted**

Thaw fish; pat dry with paper towels. Place fish in a shallow baking dish. For marinade, in a small mixing bowl stir together water, juice concentrate, oil, and salt. Pour over fish in dish. Cover and refrigerate for 3 to 24 hours.

Remove fish from the baking dish, reserving marinade. Place fish on the unheated rack of a broiler pan. Broil 4 inches from the heat for 4 to 7 minutes or till fish flakes easily with a fork, brushing frequently with reserved marinade and turning once. Sprinkle with pine nuts or almonds. Makes 4 servings.

LOW-FAT FISH AND SEAFOOD: *Some fish are lower in fat than others. When selecting fish, keep these guidelines in mind.*

Cod, haddock, halibut, flounder, sole, red snapper, and orange roughie all qualify for lean dining. They contain less than one gram of fat per ounce.

Other fish, such as sardines, salmon, lake trout, and mackerel, are oily throughout the meat, so choose them less frequently. Tuna canned in oil is high in fat, but if you opt for fresh or the canned water-pack sodium-reduced type, you'll be better off.

Shrimp and lobster are a mixed blessing since they are lower in fat but higher in cholesterol than most fish and seafood.

TABBOULEH-STUFFED TROUT

Tabbouleh is a popular Middle Eastern salad that uses bulgur as the main ingredient.

> 4 **8-ounce fresh** *or* **frozen pan-dressed trout with head and tail (backbone removed)**
> ¼ **cup bulgur**
> 1 **cup hot water**
> 1 **large tomato, peeled, seeded, and chopped**
> 2 **tablespoons finely snipped parsley**
> 1 **tablespoon finely chopped green onion**
> 1 **tablespoon lemon juice**
> 1 **tablespoon cooking oil**
> ½ . **teaspoon dried mint, crushed**
> ⅛ **teaspoon salt**
>   **Nonstick spray coating**
>   **Fresh mint leaves (optional)**
>   **Lemon slices (optional)**

Thaw fish, if frozen. Rinse and pat dry with paper towels. For stuffing, soak bulgur in hot water for 30 minutes; drain. Combine bulgur, tomato, parsley, onion, lemon juice, oil, dried mint, and salt. Toss to mix well.

Spray a 15x10x1-inch baking pan with non-stick coating. Place trout in baking pan. Spoon bulgur mixture into the cavity of each trout; brush lightly with additional oil.

Bake fish, uncovered, in a 400° oven for 20 to 25 minutes or till fish flakes easily with a fork. Carefully transfer fish to a warm serving platter. Garnish with mint leaves and lemon slices, if desired. Makes 4 servings.

STUFFING THE TROUT: *To eliminate transferring the stuffed trout, you can stuff it right in the baking pan. Start by spraying the baking pan with nonstick coating. Place the trout in the baking pan. Then spoon about ¼ cup of the bulgur mixture into the cavity of each fish. With a pastry brush, lightly brush the surface of the fish with oil to keep it from drying out during baking.*

SOLE with CUCUMBER SAUCE

4 fresh *or* frozen sole *or* other fish fillets (1 pound total)
1 medium cucumber
1 medium carrot, cut into julienne strips
1 tablespoon margarine, melted
¼ cup sliced green onion
¾ teaspoon instant chicken bouillon granules
¼ teaspoon dried dillweed
2 teaspoons cornstarch
2 tablespoons dry white wine

Thaw fish, if frozen. Pat dry with paper towels. Peel and halve cucumber crosswise. Cut *half* of the cucumber into 12 sticks. Remove seeds and coarsely shred remaining cucumber (should have about ½ cup shredded).

In a small saucepan cook cucumber sticks and carrot strips in a small amount of boiling water, covered, about 5 minutes or till crisp-tender. Drain.

Divide cucumber and carrot sticks evenly among the 4 fillets. Roll fillets around vegetables, starting from the short end. Place, seam side down, in a 10x6x2-inch baking dish. Brush tops with melted margarine. Bake, uncovered, in a 400° oven for 20 to 25 minutes or till fish flakes easily with a fork.

Meanwhile, for sauce, in a small saucepan combine shredded cucumber, green onion, bouillon granules, dillweed, and ¼ cup *water*. Bring to boiling; reduce heat. Stir together cornstarch and 2 tablespoons *cold water*; stir into mixture in saucepan. Cook and stir till thickened and bubbly. Cook and stir 2 minutes more. Stir in wine. Transfer cooked fish to a warm serving platter. Pour sauce over. Garnish with additional cucumber slices, if desired. Makes 4 servings.

NORMANDY FISH STEW

Normandy-style cooking (à la Normandie) is a French cooking method in which fish is simmered in white wine.

1 pound fresh *or* frozen haddock *or* other fish fillets
1½ cups sliced leek *or* chopped onion
1 tablespoon margarine
1¼ cups water
1 cup dry white wine
6 whole tiny new potatoes, quartered
2 carrots, sliced ¼ inch thick
2 teaspoons instant chicken bouillon granules
1 bay leaf
½ teaspoon fennel seed, crushed
¼ teaspoon pepper
¼ cup cold water
1 tablespoon cornstarch

Thaw the fish, if frozen. Pat dry with paper towels. Cut the fish into 1-inch cubes; set aside. In a large saucepan cook the leek or onion in margarine till tender. Carefully add 1¼ cups water, wine, potatoes, carrots, bouillon granules, bay leaf, fennel, and pepper. Bring to boiling; reduce heat. Cover and simmer for 15 to 20 minutes or till vegetables are almost tender. Remove bay leaf.

Stir together ¼ cup water and cornstarch; add to mixture in saucepan. Cook and stir till thick and bubbly. Cook and stir 2 minutes more. Add fish cubes. Return to boiling; reduce heat. Cover and simmer for 3 to 5 minutes or till fish flakes easily with a fork. Makes 4 servings.

BULGUR-STUFFED SALMON STEAKS

Look for bulgur (precooked cracked wheat) in the cereal section of a supermarket or health food store.

4 **fresh** *or* **frozen salmon** *or* **halibut steaks, cut 1 inch thick (1¼ to 1½ pounds total)**
1 **cup bulgur**
2 **cups hot water**
¼ **cup snipped parsley**
2 **tablespoons sliced green onion**
1 **teaspoon ground coriander**
⅛ **teaspoon salt**
⅛ **teaspoon pepper**
2 **tablespoons margarine, melted**
1 **tablespoon lemon juice**
  Wilted romaine (optional)
  Strips of lemon peel (optional)

Thaw fish, if frozen. Pat dry with paper towels. In a small mixing bowl combine bulgur and water. Let stand for 30 minutes; drain well. Stir together bulgur, parsley, green onion, coriander, salt, and pepper; set aside. Stir together melted margarine and lemon juice.

Reserve *1 tablespoon* of the margarine mixture. Add remaining margarine mixture to bulgur mixture; toss to coat. Spoon *half* of the bulgur mixture onto the bottom of a 3-quart casserole. Place salmon on top of mixture in casserole. Spoon remaining bulgur mixture into the center cavity of each salmon steak.

Cover loosely with foil and bake in a 375° oven for 15 minutes; brush fish with remaining margarine mixture. Continue baking, covered, for 5 to 10 minutes more or till fish flakes easily with a fork. Serve with romaine and garnish with lemon peel, if desired. Makes 4 servings.

To wilt the romaine for Bulgur-Stuffed Salmon Steaks, rinse one medium bunch romaine in cool water. Tear into bite-size pieces. In a large saucepan cook the romaine, covered, in just the water that clings to the leaves. Reduce the heat when steam forms; cover and cook about 1 minute or till the romaine is wilted.

ONION-TARRAGON SALMON STEAKS

You can cut down on fat even further by removing the skin of the salmon before the fish is cooked.

4 **fresh** *or* **frozen salmon steaks, cut 1 inch thick (about 1¼ pounds total)**
2 **medium onions, sliced and separated into rings**
1 **tablespoon margarine**
½ **cup dry white wine**
¼ **teaspoon dried tarragon, crushed**

Thaw salmon, if frozen. Pat dry with paper towels. In a large skillet cook onions in margarine till tender. Remove from skillet.

Place salmon steaks in skillet; top with cooked onions. Stir together wine and tarragon; pour over salmon. Bring to boiling; reduce heat. Cover and simmer for 10 to 12 minutes or till salmon flakes easily with a fork. With a slotted spoon transfer salmon and onions to a serving platter. Makes 4 servings.

·QUICK RECIPE·
HOT TUNA TOSS

½ **cup sliced green onion**
1 **tablespoon margarine**
1⅔ **cups water**
¾ **cup long grain rice**
½ **cup chopped green pepper**
¼ **cup shredded carrot**
1½ **teaspoons instant chicken bouillon granules**
½ **teaspoon dried thyme, crushed**
2 **6½-ounce cans sodium-reduced tuna (water pack), drained and broken into chunks**
1 **large tomato, peeled, seeded, and chopped**

In a medium saucepan cook green onion in margarine till tender. Stir in water, rice, green pepper, carrot, bouillon granules, and thyme. Bring to boiling; reduce heat. Cover and simmer for 15 minutes. Remove from heat.

Carefully stir tuna and tomato into rice mixture in saucepan. Cover and let stand for 5 to 8 minutes or till rice has absorbed all the liquid and tuna is heated through. Serve immediately. Makes 4 servings.

SODIUM-REDUCED PRODUCTS AND SALT: *It's no mistake! Some of the recipes, such as Vegetable-Sauced Fish Steaks, contain a sodium-reduced product (such as sodium-reduced tomato sauce) and some salt. We discovered that by using sodium-reduced products and keeping the amount of added salt to a minimum, the recipe ends up lower in total sodium than if a regular product (such as tomato sauce) were used with no added salt.*

SAUCY FISH STEAKS

A zesty tomato and spinach mixture is served with the poached fish steaks.

4 **¾-inch-thick fresh *or* frozen red snapper fillets *or* halibut steaks**
½ **cup chopped onion**
½ **cup chopped carrot**
½ **cup chopped green pepper**
2 **cloves garlic, minced**
1 **tablespoon cooking oil**
1 **8-ounce can sodium-reduced tomato sauce**
½ **cup dry white wine**
1 **teaspoon dried basil, crushed**
½ **teaspoon ground cumin**
¼ **teaspoon salt**
¼ **teaspoon pepper**
1 **10-ounce package frozen chopped spinach, thawed and well drained**
1 **medium tomato, peeled, seeded, and chopped**
1 **cup water**
2 **tablespoons snipped parsley**

Thaw fish, if frozen. Pat fish dry with paper towels. In a large saucepan cook onion, carrot, green pepper, and garlic in hot oil till tender. Stir in tomato sauce, wine, basil, cumin, salt, and pepper. Bring to boiling; reduce heat. Cover and simmer for 15 minutes. Stir in spinach and tomato. Cover and simmer for 2 to 3 minutes more or till heated through.

Meanwhile, in a large skillet bring water to boiling. Add fish. Return to boiling; reduce heat. Cover and simmer for 7 to 10 minutes or till fish flakes easily with a fork. Spoon spinach mixture onto a platter. Top with fish; sprinkle with parsley. Makes 4 servings.

DEEP-DISH TUNA PIE

A custom-made, wholesome version of a pot pie.

¼ **cup margarine**
¾ **cup all-purpose flour**
 2 **to 3 tablespoons cold water**
¼ **cup finely chopped onion**
 2 **tablespoons margarine**
 2 **tablespoons all-purpose flour**
⅛ **teaspoon pepper**
 1 **cup skim milk**
 1 **10-ounce package frozen mixed**
    vegetables
½ **cup shredded process Swiss cheese**
 2 **6½-ounce cans sodium-reduced**
    tuna (water pack), drained
    Skim milk
 1 **teaspoon yellow cornmeal**

In a mixing bowl cut ¼ cup margarine into ¾ cup flour till pieces are the size of small peas. Sprinkle *1 tablespoon* of the water over part of the mixture; gently toss with a fork. Push to side of bowl. Repeat till all is moistened. Form dough into a ball. On a lightly floured surface roll dough into a 9-inch circle; cover.

In a large saucepan cook the onion in 2 tablespoons margarine till tender. Stir in the 2 tablespoons flour and the pepper. Add 1 cup milk. Cook and stir till thickened and bubbly. Add vegetables and cheese. Cook and stir till cheese melts. Fold in tuna.

Spoon the tuna mixture into an 8x1½-inch round baking dish. Cut slits in pastry. Place pastry over dish; crimp edges. Brush with additional milk; sprinkle with cornmeal. Bake in a 400° oven for 25 to 30 minutes or till crust is light brown. Makes 6 servings.

ASSEMBLING THE DEEP-DISH TUNA PIE: *When you roll out the pastry, start from the center and work toward the edges. Cut vents in the top of the pastry to allow steam to escape during baking. Then gently lift the pastry and place it over the tuna mixture in the baking dish, being careful not to tear the pastry.*

Crusty French bread or baguettes are a low-fat bread choice to serve with the **Minestrone.**

MINESTRONE

Minestrone comes from the Italian word "minestra," meaning a soup with a combination of many vegetables and pasta.

  9 **cups water**
  1 **cup dry navy beans**
  7 **cups water**
  1 **cup chopped onion**
  2 **medium carrots, bias sliced**
  1 **bay leaf**
  1 **28-ounce can sodium-reduced tomatoes, cut up**
  2 **cloves garlic, minced**
  2 **teaspoons dried basil, crushed**
  1 **teaspoon sugar**
  ½ **teaspoon salt**
  2 **ounces spaghetti, broken into 2-inch pieces (½ cup)**
  2 **cups sliced fresh mushrooms**
  1 **medium zucchini, sliced**
  ⅓ **cup grated Parmesan cheese**

In a Dutch oven combine 9 cups water and beans. Bring to boiling; reduce heat. Simmer, uncovered, for 2 minutes. Remove from heat. Cover; let stand 1 hour. (Or, soak beans in water overnight.) Drain beans; rinse.

In the Dutch oven combine rinsed beans, 7 cups water, onion, carrots, and bay leaf. Bring to boiling; reduce heat. Cover and simmer for 60 to 70 minutes or till beans are tender; drain, reserving 3 cups liquid.

Return bean mixture to Dutch oven. Add *undrained* tomatoes, garlic, basil, sugar, and salt. Stir in reserved bean liquid. Bring to boiling. Stir in spaghetti; reduce heat. Cover and simmer for 20 minutes. Stir in mushrooms and zucchini; cover and simmer for 10 to 15 minutes more or till vegetables and spaghetti are tender. Remove bay leaf. Spoon into 4 serving bowls. Sprinkle each serving with some of the Parmesan cheese. Makes 4 servings.

ITALIAN EGGPLANT CASSEROLE

Try whole wheat spaghetti for added flavor and fiber.

  4 **ounces spaghetti, broken into 2-inch pieces (1 cup)**
  1 **large eggplant, peeled and cut into ½-inch cubes (6 cups)**
  1 **medium onion, chopped**
  1 **medium carrot, chopped**
  1 **medium green pepper, chopped**
  1 **small zucchini, chopped**
  1 **14½-ounce can sodium-reduced tomatoes**
  1 **6-ounce can sodium-reduced tomato paste**
  ½ **cup dry white wine**
  2 **cloves garlic, minced**
  1½ **teaspoons dried basil, crushed**
  1 **teaspoon dried oregano, crushed**
  ¼ **teaspoon salt**
  ¼ **teaspoon pepper**
  3 **cups shredded mozzarella cheese (12 ounces)**

Cook spaghetti according to package directions, *except* omit salt; drain. Meanwhile, in a steamer basket place eggplant, onion, carrot, green pepper, and zucchini. In a Dutch oven place filled basket over, but not touching, boiling water. Cover; reduce heat. Steam for 5 to 7 minutes or till vegetables are crisp-tender; remove vegetables from Dutch oven.

In a large mixing bowl stir together steamed vegetables, *undrained* tomatoes, tomato paste, wine, garlic, basil, oregano, salt, and pepper. Spread *2 cups* tomato mixture on the bottom of a 12x7½x2-inch baking dish. Top with cooked spaghetti; sprinkle with *half* of the cheese. Spoon remaining tomato mixture over top; sprinkle with remaining cheese. Bake, uncovered, in a 350° oven for 30 to 35 minutes or till bubbly. Makes 6 servings.

TOFU and FRUIT CURRY

Shred frozen and thawed tofu just like a block of cheese. Simply rub the block of tofu against the surface of a hand shredder, using the large holes.

Tofu (soybean curd) contains as much protein as chicken and almost as much as beef, is low in calories and fat, and contains no cholesterol.

- 1 **medium orange, peeled**
  Orange juice
- 2 **teaspoons curry powder**
- 1 **teaspoon grated gingerroot**
- 1 **tablespoon cooking oil**
- 8 **ounces tofu (bean curd), drained
  and cut into bite-size pieces**
- 1 **medium apple, cored and sliced**
- ½ **cup seedless green grapes, halved**
- ⅔ **cup quick-cooking couscous**
- ⅔ **cup boiling water**
- 2 **tablespoons cold water**
- 1 **teaspoon cornstarch**
- ½ **cup sliced almonds, toasted**
- 1 **medium banana, sliced**
- ¼ **cup raisins**

Section orange over a small mixing bowl to catch juice; add enough additional orange juice to juice in bowl to make ½ cup. Set orange sections and juice aside. In a large skillet cook curry powder and gingerroot in oil over medium heat for 30 seconds. Add tofu. Cook and stir for 3 minutes. Stir in apple, grapes, and orange juice. Bring to boiling; reduce heat. Cover and simmer about 5 minutes or till apple is tender.

Meanwhile, combine couscous and ⅔ cup boiling water. Cover and let stand for 3 to 4 minutes or till water is absorbed.

Stir together 2 tablespoons water and cornstarch. Add to tofu mixture in skillet. Cook and stir till thickened and bubbly. Cook and stir 2 minutes more. Stir in almonds and orange sections; heat through. Serve with couscous, banana, and raisins. Makes 4 servings.

TOFU-STUFFED TOMATOES

Freezing and thawing tofu changes the texture to that of cooked chicken.

- 1 **pound tofu (bean curd), frozen**
- ⅓ **cup broken walnuts**
- ¼ **cup finely chopped celery**
- ¼ **cup finely chopped green pepper**
- ¼ **cup shredded carrot**
- 1 **tablespoon finely chopped onion**
- ½ **cup reduced-calorie mayonnaise
  or salad dressing**
- 1 **tablespoon lemon juice**
- ⅛ **teaspoon pepper**
- 4 **medium tomatoes
  Lettuce leaves
  Coarsely ground pepper (optional)**

Thaw tofu overnight in the refrigerator. Squeeze out excess liquid; pat dry with paper towels. Coarsely shred tofu.

In a mixing bowl combine tofu, walnuts, celery, green pepper, carrot, and onion. Stir together mayonnaise, lemon juice, and pepper; pour over tofu mixture, tossing to coat.

Core tomatoes. Place tomatoes, cored end down, on a cutting surface. Cut each tomato into 6 wedges, cutting to, but not through, the cored end of the tomato. Spread the tomato wedges apart slightly.

Place each tomato on a lettuce-lined salad plate. Spoon the tofu mixture into each tomato cup. Sprinkle lightly with coarsely ground pepper, if desired. Makes 4 servings.

BROCCOLI-TOFU STRATA

1½ cups broccoli flowerets *or* one
　　10-ounce package frozen chopped
　　broccoli
½ cup chopped onion
6 slices day-old rye *or* whole wheat
　　bread, cubed (4½ cups)
1 cup shredded Monterey Jack cheese
　　(4 ounces)
12 ounces tofu (bean curd), drained
　　and cut up
2 cups skim milk
2 eggs
⅛ teaspoon ground red pepper

In a medium saucepan cook broccoli and on-ion, covered, in a small amount of boiling water for 5 to 7 minutes or till crisp-tender; drain. Arrange bread cubes and broccoli mix-ture in the bottom of an 8x8x2-inch baking dish; sprinkle with cheese.

In a blender container or food processor bowl place tofu, skim milk, eggs, and ground red pepper. Cover and blend on low speed till smooth. Pour over bread-broccoli mixture. Cover and chill several hours or overnight.

Bake, uncovered, in a 325° oven for 50 to 55 minutes or till a knife inserted near the center comes out clean. Let stand 10 minutes before serving. Makes 8 servings.

PREPARING THE STRATA: *Before you make strata out of tofu, blend the tofu into a smooth liquid. You can do this by placing the tofu in a blender container or food processor bowl with the skim milk, eggs, and ground red pepper. Cover and blend on low speed till the mixture is smooth. Then pour the blended mixture over the bread-broccoli mixture and chill it, covered, for several hours. Chilling gives the bread a chance to absorb the liquid from the blended mixture, which helps bind the strata during baking.*

MACARONI and CHEESE with VEGETABLES

A classic family feast with a new twist—broccoli.

6 ounces elbow macaroni (1½ cups)
1 small onion, cut into thin wedges
2 cups skim milk
2 tablespoons cornstarch
⅛ teaspoon pepper
2 cups shredded American cheese
(8 ounces)
1 10-ounce package frozen chopped
broccoli, thawed and drained
2 medium tomatoes, sliced

Cook macaroni according to package directions, *except* omit salt. Add onion during the last 5 minutes of cooking; drain.

For sauce, in a large saucepan combine milk, cornstarch, and pepper. Cook and stir till thickened and bubbly. Add cheese; stir till cheese melts. Stir in macaroni and broccoli.

Spoon macaroni mixture into a 12x7½x2-inch baking dish. Arrange tomato slices over mixture. Bake, uncovered, in a 350° oven for 30 to 35 minutes or till heated through. Let stand 10 minutes. Makes 6 servings.

LIGHT AND LEAN DAIRY CHOICES: *Dairy foods often are a major source of protein in meatless main dishes. Unfortunately, many of these foods also contain a significant amount of fat and calories. By making smart choices, you can still enjoy dairy foods without tipping the fat and calorie scales.*

Among the healthy choices are skim milk, low-fat or dry cottage cheese, low-fat yogurt, Neufchâtel cheese, and hard cheeses that are low in milk fat. Read the package label to find out what type of milk was used.

HARVEST POT PIE

The bulk of the protein comes from the Monterey Jack and cottage cheeses.

1½ cups sliced and halved zucchini
1 cup sliced fresh mushrooms
1 small parsnip, peeled and cubed
1 cup frozen whole kernel corn
¾ cup chopped green pepper
1 clove garlic, minced
1 cup frozen peas
1 8-ounce can sodium-reduced tomato
sauce
1 teaspoon sugar
1 teaspoon dried oregano, crushed
1 teaspoon chili powder
½ teaspoon dried basil, crushed
2 cups shredded Monterey Jack cheese
(8 ounces)
1 tablespoon all-purpose flour
2 tablespoons shortening
½ cup all-purpose flour
⅓ cup cream-style cottage cheese,
sieved

In a large saucepan cook zucchini, mushrooms, parsnip, corn, green pepper, and garlic, covered, in a small amount of boiling water about 4 minutes or till parsnip is crisp-tender; drain.

Stir peas, tomato sauce, sugar, oregano, chili powder, and basil into vegetable mixture in the saucepan. Bring to boiling; reduce heat. Simmer, uncovered, for 2 minutes. Toss Monterey Jack cheese with 1 tablespoon flour; stir into vegetable mixture. Spoon mixture into an 8x1½-inch round baking dish or a 1½-quart casserole.

For pastry, cut shortening into the ½ cup flour till pieces are the size of small peas. Add cottage cheese; stir with a fork till moistened. If necessary, stir in a little water. Form dough into a ball. On a lightly floured surface roll dough into an 8-inch circle. Cut into 6 wedges; prick with a fork. Arrange pastry wedges on top of the hot vegetable mixture. Bake in a 375° oven for 25 to 30 minutes or till pastry is light brown. Makes 6 servings.

You'll find a bounty of saucy vegetables in Harvest Pot Pie.

123

BEAN-SAUCED PASTA

Rinsing the canned kidney and garbanzo beans helps wash away some of the sodium.

   1 16-ounce can tomatoes,
    cut up
1½ cups water
   1 6-ounce can sodium-reduced tomato
    paste
   1 large onion, chopped
   2 cloves garlic, minced
   1 teaspoon sugar
   1 teaspoon instant beef bouillon
    granules
   1 teaspoon dried oregano, crushed
   ½ teaspoon dried basil, crushed
   ⅛ teaspoon ground red pepper
   ⅛ teaspoon pepper
   1 15-ounce can red kidney beans,
    drained and rinsed
   1 15-ounce can garbanzo beans,
    drained and rinsed
   ¼ cup snipped parsley
  10 ounces linguine *or*
    fettuccine, broken into small
    pieces
   1 cup shredded cheddar cheese

For sauce, in a large saucepan combine *un-drained* tomatoes, water, tomato paste, onion, garlic, sugar, bouillon granules, oregano, basil, ground red pepper, and pepper. Bring to boiling; reduce heat. Simmer, uncovered, for 30 minutes.

In a small mixing bowl slightly mash *half* of the kidney beans with a fork or potato masher. Add mashed and whole kidney beans and garbanzo beans to the sauce. Heat through. Stir in parsley.

Meanwhile, cook pasta according to package directions, *except* omit salt; drain. Serve sauce over hot pasta. Sprinkle with cheddar cheese. Makes 6 servings.

SPICY BEAN FRIED RICE

Chilling the cooked rice helps prevent it from sticking to the surface of the skillet.

   ¾ cup regular brown rice
    Nonstick spray coating
   1 beaten egg
   ½ cup chopped onion
   1 clove garlic, minced
   1 teaspoon chili powder
   ½ teaspoon ground cumin
   1 tablespoon cooking oil
   1 15-ounce can red kidney beans,
    drained and rinsed
   4 teaspoons sodium-reduced soy sauce
    Several dashes bottled hot pepper
    sauce
   ½ cup unsalted dry roasted peanuts

Cook rice according to package directions, *except* omit salt and butter or margarine. Chill. Spray a large skillet with nonstick coating; add egg. Cook egg without stirring till set. Invert skillet over a cutting board to remove cooked egg; cut into short, narrow strips.

In the same skillet cook onion, garlic, chili powder, and cumin in oil till onion is tender. Add rice; cook and stir for 3 minutes. Stir in beans, soy sauce, and bottled hot pepper sauce. Cook and stir till heated through. Toss with nuts and cooked egg. Makes 4 servings.

EGG and RICE SKILLET

Make the depressions in the rice mixture with the back of a large spoon.

- **1 10-ounce package frozen chopped broccoli**
- **1⅔ cups water**
- **¾ cup regular brown rice**
- **½ cup chopped onion**
- **1 clove garlic, minced**
- **¼ teaspoon ground red pepper**
- **1 7½-ounce can tomatoes, cut up**
- **1 medium sweet red pepper *or* green pepper, chopped**
- **¼ cup grated Parmesan cheese**
- **¼ teaspoon dried thyme, crushed**
- **4 eggs**

Cook broccoli according to package directions; drain. Meanwhile, in a 10-inch skillet stir together water, rice, onion, garlic, and ground red pepper. Bring to boiling; reduce heat. Cover and simmer for 30 minutes. Stir in broccoli, *undrained* tomatoes, red or green pepper, *half* of the Parmesan cheese, and the thyme. Return to a simmer.

Make 4 depressions in the top of the rice mixture. Carefully break eggs into depressions. Cover and cook over medium heat for 10 to 15 minutes more or till eggs are set and rice is tender. Sprinkle with remaining Parmesan cheese. Makes 4 servings.

HEALTHY CHEESE SOUFFLÉ

We cut the fat and cholesterol from a classic cheese soufflé by more than 20 percent.

- **3 tablespoons margarine**
- **3 tablespoons cornstarch**
- **⅛ teaspoon pepper**
- **1½ cups skim milk**
- **2 cups shredded cheddar cheese (8 ounces)**
- **4 egg yolks**
- **6 egg whites**

Attach a foil collar to a 2-quart soufflé dish. For collar, measure enough foil to go around dish plus a 2- to 3-inch overlap. Fold foil into thirds lengthwise. Lightly grease one side. With greased side in, position foil around dish, letting collar extend 2 inches above top of dish; fasten with tape. Set aside.

In a saucepan melt margarine; stir in cornstarch and pepper. Add milk all at once. Cook and stir till thick and bubbly. Cook and stir 2 minutes more. Remove from heat. Add cheese, stirring till cheese melts.

In a small mixer bowl beat egg yolks about 5 minutes or till thick and lemon colored. *Slowly* add cheese mixture to yolks, stirring constantly. Cool slightly.

Wash beaters thoroughly. In a large mixer bowl beat egg whites till stiff peaks form (tips stand straight). Gradually pour cheese-yolk mixture over beaten whites, folding to combine. Pour into soufflé dish.

Bake in a 300° oven for 55 to 60 minutes or till a knife inserted near the center comes out clean. Gently peel off the collar; serve soufflé immediately. Makes 6 servings.

Soufflés are light and airy, so serve them right after they come out of the oven before they fall. It's better to wait for the soufflé because the soufflé won't wait for you.

To serve, insert two forks, back to back, and gently pull the soufflé apart. Cut into servings this way. Then use a large spoon to transfer the soufflé to individual plates.

Orange-Glazed Pea Pods (see recipe, page 154) is one of the many side dishes that is low in fat, cholesterol, calories, and sodium, but high in vitamins.

SIDE DISHES

CHAPTER 4

Breads, vegetables, and salads take a supporting role in a meal, yet they can greatly affect your total nutrition picture. For instance, overuse of baking soda or powder, commercial salad dressings, and salty seasonings can send sodium counts soaring. The recipes you'll find in this chapter reduce or eliminate these sodium sources without sacrificing quality. They also meet the challenge of holding down cholesterol in baked goods by replacing traditionally used whole eggs with egg whites in many instances.

Some side dishes are typically served with a "side" of their own, such as butter with bread or dressing with salad. This chapter closes with healthy stand-ins for these indulgences.

CONTENTS

	PER SERVING						PERCENT U.S. RDA PER SERVING							
	CALORIES	PROTEIN (g)	CARBOHYDRATES (g)	FAT (g)	CHOLESTEROL (mg)	SODIUM (mg)	POTASSIUM (mg)	PROTEIN	VITAMIN A	VITAMIN C	THIAMINE	RIBOFLAVIN	NIACIN	CALCIUM	IRON
Acorn Squash Puree (p. 152)	174	2	31	6	0	104	656	4	131	37	6	11	5	5	7
Apple Biscuit Spirals (p. 140)	140	2	18	6	0	122	52	4	5	1	7	5	5	4	5
Apricot Fruit Salad (p. 167)	90	2	14	3	11	60	194	3	32	8	2	3	2	2	2
Armenian Flat Breads (p. 130)	200	5	34	5	0	70	58	8	0	0	20	12	13	1	12
Baked Cottage Potatoes (p. 149)	166	6	28	4	5	145	660	9	3	43	8	5	11	10	6
Banana Bread (p. 144)	161	2	25	6	0	63	91	4	0	2	6	4	4	1	4
Basil-Garlic Dressing (p. 170)	32	0	1	3	0	0	15	0	0	0	0	0	0	0	1
Blue Cheese Spread (p. 169)	28	2	1	2	5	53	25	3	4	4	0	1	0	3	2
Broccoli-Pasta Toss (p. 146)	168	6	24	5	3	72	168	10	22	49	11	8	6	9	7
Brussels Sprout Toss (p. 149)	71	3	5	5	0	44	241	5	10	96	4	6	3	3	4
Buttermilk Salad Dressing (p. 170)	36	1	2	3	1	69	43	1	2	2	1	2	0	3	1
California Gazpacho (p. 154)	37	1	7	0	0	74	364	2	22	68	5	3	5	1	6
Chinese Coleslaw (p. 160)	57	1	9	2	0	80	214	2	15	43	3	3	2	4	5
Cinnamon Bread (p. 138)	136	4	26	2	0	61	63	6	2	0	11	9	7	2	6
Citrus Waffles with Blueberry Sauce (p. 143)	386	9	57	15	1	112	474	13	4	26	18	20	11	9	9
Coffee Cake Muffins (p. 141)	182	4	21	10	0	113	96	6	1	0	9	6	4	5	6
Creamy Garlic Dressing (p. 171)	24	1	2	1	2	29	41	2	0	0	0	2	0	4	0
Creamy Zucchini-Carrot Mold (p. 164)	68	4	12	1	3	40	238	6	26	48	3	7	1	9	2
Cucumber-Blue Cheese Dressing (p. 171)	34	2	3	2	5	80	65	3	1	1	1	3	0	6	1
Cucumber Sauté (p. 152)	42	2	4	2	0	36	241	2	5	15	3	9	7	2	6
Curried Bulgur Salad (p. 162)	162	6	26	5	2	40	406	9	52	12	8	8	11	11	9
Curried Fruit and Pasta Salad (p. 161)	166	3	34	3	1	60	278	5	3	38	11	6	4	5	5
Dill Vegetable Tabbouleh (p. 162)	82	2	16	1	0	49	125	3	4	33	5	2	5	1	6
Dilled Brussels Sprouts and Cauliflower (p. 159)	105	2	5	9	0	123	216	3	8	95	4	4	2	2	4
Dilly Salad Dressing (p. 171)	33	1	2	2	1	66	38	1	1	0	1	2	0	3	0
Double Apricot Coffee Cake (p. 145)	243	4	39	8	0	116	213	6	19	1	11	9	8	4	10
Double-Banana Salad (p. 165)	91	4	19	1	2	80	340	5	29	41	5	5	3	3	3
Flaming Spinach Salad (p. 157)	62	2	6	2	0	32	296	3	64	70	5	6	2	5	9
Flat Onion Bread (p. 135)	134	3	22	4	0	70	78	5	0	4	12	9	8	1	7
Fruited Spinach Salad (p. 156)	85	2	11	4	0	33	298	3	77	54	5	6	2	5	8
Garden Potpourri (p. 161)	38	2	7	0	1	26	297	4	26	101	4	7	4	6	4
Garlic Soup (p. 154)	76	2	10	4	0	52	254	3	9	30	4	3	3	3	4
Gingered Ambrosia Salad (p. 165)	49	1	11	1	0	2	138	1	1	46	4	1	1	2	1
Gingered Carrots (p. 151)	47	1	11	0	0	35	323	2	161	36	4	2	3	3	3
Golden Cabbage Toss (p. 160)	103	3	17	3	1	26	351	5	43	69	13	5	4	7	5
Greek-Style Salad (p. 157)	69	2	4	6	4	54	208	2	19	29	3	5	2	6	5
Green Bean and Pasta Salad (p. 161)	100	3	16	3	2	14	178	4	26	9	7	6	4	4	6
Hamburger Buns (p. 136)	208	6	35	5	0	115	94	9	1	0	18	14	12	3	10
Horseradish Dressing (p. 170)	43	1	2	3	1	72	57	2	2	1	1	3	0	4	0
Indonesian Rice Salad (p. 162)	137	3	27	3	0	90	253	4	2	46	9	2	6	2	3
Ladder Coffee Cakes (p. 138)	145	4	24	4	0	93	72	6	3	0	12	9	7	2	6
Lemon-Dill Potatoes (p. 149)	92	2	13	4	0	47	314	3	3	22	4	2	6	1	3

	PER SERVING						PERCENT U.S. RDA PER SERVING							
	CALORIES	PROTEIN (g)	CARBOHYDRATES (g)	FAT (g)	CHOLESTEROL (mg)	SODIUM (mg)	POTASSIUM (mg)	PROTEIN	VITAMIN A	VITAMIN C	THIAMINE	RIBOFLAVIN	NIACIN	CALCIUM	IRON
Lemony Gingered Beets (p. 148)	40	1	9	0	0	45	257	2	0	15	1	2	2	1	3
Molasses-Rye Bread (p. 136)	94	3	18	1	0	69	80	4	0	0	9	5	5	1	6
Onion Biscuits (p. 140)	190	3	21	10	0	69	60	5	1	1	11	7	7	6	6
Onion-Sesame Spread (p. 169)	44	2	1	4	11	58	26	3	3	1	1	2	0	1	1
Orange Oatmeal Scones (p. 141)	125	3	16	6	0	106	49	4	4	2	8	4	3	3	4
Orange-Glazed Pea Pods (p. 154)	60	2	11	2	0	5	125	3	3	42	7	5	3	3	4
Orange-Strawberry Salad Mold (p. 165)	62	3	12	1	1	18	246	5	2	77	5	5	1	5	1
Peach Butter (p. 168)	30	0	8	0	0	0	51	0	3	3	0	1	1	0	0
Peanut Butter and Apple Spread (p. 168)	51	2	2	4	0	52	65	4	0	1	1	1	6	1	1
Pear-Nut Loaf (p. 144)	96	2	11	5	0	46	43	3	0	1	6	4	3	1	4
Pepper and Garlic Spread (p. 169)	38	2	1	3	11	58	24	2	3	0	0	2	0	1	1
Pepper Cheese Braids (p. 132)	77	3	14	1	3	54	28	4	1	2	7	6	5	3	4
Pineapple Toss (p. 156)	75	1	9	5	0	91	160	1	5	24	4	2	1	2	2
Romaine Stir-Fry (p. 149)	19	2	4	0	0	24	221	3	29	90	4	7	2	6	4
Saucy Succotash (p. 151)	93	5	18	1	1	67	281	8	10	59	6	5	6	6	8
Sourdough Double Wheat Bread (p. 133)	116	4	23	1	0	45	61	5	0	0	12	6	8	1	7
Sourdough Orange-Wheat Muffins (p. 143)	177	4	31	4	0	92	76	7	0	5	15	9	10	3	8
Sourdough Starter (1 cup) (p. 133)	244	7	51	1	0	2	94	11	0	0	29	20	20	1	17
Spaghetti Squash Vinaigrette (p. 159)	123	2	15	7	0	13	462	3	115	71	4	7	4	4	6
Special Spaetzle (p. 148)	136	6	25	1	35	34	87	9	2	0	14	12	8	4	8
Spiced Pear Coffee Cake (p. 137)	183	4	33	4	0	111	126	7	3	3	13	11	8	3	8
Spicy Squash Bread (p. 144)	140	2	26	4	0	42	89	3	10	3	6	4	4	1	4
Squash with Vegetable Sauce (p. 153)	119	4	28	1	0	118	911	6	183	98	10	14	9	9	11
Steamed Greens and Zucchini (p. 153)	24	2	5	0	0	39	290	3	48	63	4	6	3	6	7
Stewed Corn and Tomatoes (p. 146)	100	4	23	1	0	38	394	6	16	57	11	8	9	2	6
Struesel Coffee Cake (p. 145)	207	4	28	9	0	112	98	6	1	1	12	9	7	5	7
Sunflower-Herb Salad Dressing (p. 171)	46	3	3	3	2	24	123	4	1	1	7	4	1	7	3
Sweet Peppers and Beans (p. 152)	64	2	8	3	0	37	223	3	61	209	6	5	3	3	5
Swiss Rye Bread (p. 135)	130	5	23	2	4	36	92	7	1	0	11	8	6	6	7
Swiss Vegetable-Pasta Platter (p. 146)	116	7	16	3	9	57	305	11	49	49	8	12	6	18	5
Tangy Sesame Slaw (p. 160)	55	1	8	2	0	20	201	2	55	77	3	2	2	2	3
Tomato Fans (p. 164)	81	6	8	3	10	92	333	9	22	37	5	8	4	13	5
Tossed Ensalada Supreme (p. 156)	104	4	12	5	1	135	513	6	37	112	7	12	7	14	8
Triticale-Rice Pilaf (p. 151)	101	3	21	1	0	51	105	5	0	3	9	5	8	1	5
Tropical Fruit Platter (p. 167)	589	10	123	11	5	74	2032	15	98	325	17	34	16	24	14
Wheat Italian Bread (p. 130)	88	3	15	2	0	73	65	5	0	0	14	7	6	1	7
Whole Wheat Buns (p. 136)	203	6	34	5	0	115	121	9	1	0	17	12	11	4	9
Yogurt-Fruit Toss (p. 167)	73	2	17	1	1	17	273	3	1	52	3	6	2	5	2

What makes the breads in this book better for you than standard homemade or store-bought breads? First of all, we reduced the salt to a minimum, sometimes to one-fourth of the typical amount. Some salt, however, is necessary for good texture and palatable flavor in yeast breads. Also, we cut the sodium in quick breads by using the least amount of baking soda or baking powder possible.

To decrease cholesterol in the breads, we usually substituted egg whites for whole eggs, when appropriate, to avoid the cholesterol-rich egg yolks.

WHEAT ITALIAN BREAD

Wheat germ adds protein, iron, and B vitamins to the bread. Sprinkle extra wheat germ on the baking sheet for a crisp bottom crust. (Pictured on page 13.)

> 2 **to 2½ cups all-purpose flour**
> 1 **package active dry yeast**
> 1 **cup warm water (115° to 120°)**
> 1 **tablespoon cooking oil**
> 1 **teaspoon sugar**
> ½ **teaspoon salt**
> ¾ **cup toasted wheat germ**
> **Nonstick spray coating**
> **Toasted wheat germ**

In a large mixer bowl combine *1 cup* of the flour and the yeast. Combine water, cooking oil, sugar, and salt and add to flour mixture. Beat with an electric mixer on low speed for ½ minute, scraping sides of bowl constantly. Beat on high speed for 3 minutes.

With a spoon, stir in wheat germ and as much of the remaining flour as you can. On a lightly floured surface, knead in enough of the remaining flour to make a moderately stiff dough that is smooth and elastic (6 to 8 minutes total). Place in a lightly greased bowl and turn once to grease surface. Cover and let rise in a warm place till double (1 to 1¼ hours).

Punch down. Shape into a large loaf about 15 inches long, tapering the ends. Spray a baking sheet with nonstick coating and sprinkle with additional wheat germ. Place loaf on prepared baking sheet. Cover and let rise till nearly double (about 45 minutes).

With a sharp knife, make 3 or 4 diagonal slashes about ¼ inch deep across the top of the loaf. Bake in a 375° oven for 35 to 40 minutes or till done. Cool on a wire rack. Makes 1 loaf (15 servings).

ARMENIAN FLAT BREADS

> 5½ **to 6 cups all-purpose flour**
> 1 **package active dry yeast**
> 2 **cups water**
> ¼ **cup shortening**
> 1 **tablespoon sugar**
> ½ **teaspoon salt**
> ¼ **cup sesame seed, toasted**
> **Nonstick spray coating**

In a large mixer bowl combine *2 cups* of the flour and the yeast. In a medium saucepan heat water, shortening, sugar, and salt just till warm (115° to 120°) and shortening is almost melted, stirring constantly. Add to flour mixture. Beat with an electric mixer on low speed for ½ minute, scraping sides of bowl constantly. Beat on high speed for 3 minutes.

Using a spoon, stir in *half* of the sesame seed and as much of the remaining flour as you can. On a lightly floured surface, knead in enough of the remaining flour to make a moderately stiff dough that is smooth and elastic (6 to 8 minutes total). Shape into a ball. Place in a greased bowl and turn once to grease surface. Cover and let rise in a warm place till double (about 1 hour). Punch down. Divide into 16 portions and shape into balls. Cover and let rest 10 minutes.

On a lightly floured surface, roll 4 of the balls into 7-inch rounds. Place remaining balls in the refrigerator till ready to use. Spray 2 baking sheets with nonstick coating. Place 2 rounds of dough on each baking sheet. Brush each round lightly with cold water. Sprinkle with some of the remaining sesame seed and, if desired, poppy seed or crushed dried oregano. With a fork, prick the entire surface of each round. *Do not allow to rise.*

Bake in a 350° oven for 20 to 25 minutes or till lightly browned and crisp. Cool on a wire rack. Repeat rolling and baking remaining dough. Makes 16 flat breads (16 servings).

PEPPER CHEESE BRAIDS

Flecks of jalapeño peppers in the cheese give these savory braids a delightful bite.

4¼ **to 4¾ cups all-purpose flour**
 2 **tablespoons sugar**
 1 **package active dry yeast**
½ **teaspoon salt**
1½ **cups warm water (115° to 120°)**
 1 **cup shredded Monterey Jack cheese with jalapeño peppers (4 ounces)**
 2 **egg whites**
   Nonstick spray coating

To braid dough, line up three ropes of dough about 1 inch apart on a baking sheet sprayed with nonstick coating. Start working from the center to avoid stretching the dough and making a lopsided loaf.

For one half of the loaf, alternately bring one of the outside ropes over the middle one. Continue braiding loosely to allow the dough room to expand without cracking or losing its shape. Pinch the end and tuck under the braid. Repeat, braiding the second half of the loaf, except *alternately bring the outside ropes* under *the middle one.*

In a large mixer bowl stir together *2 cups* of the flour, sugar, yeast, and salt. Add warm water, shredded cheese, and egg whites. Beat with an electric mixer on low speed for ½ minute, scraping the sides of the bowl constantly. Beat on high speed for 3 minutes. With a spoon, stir in as much of the remaining flour as you can.

On a lightly floured surface, knead in enough of the remaining flour to make a moderately stiff dough that is smooth and elastic (6 to 8 minutes total). Shape into a ball. Place in a lightly greased bowl and turn once to grease surface. Cover and let rise in a warm place till double (about 1½ hours).

Punch dough down. Divide the dough into 6 portions. Cover and let rest 10 minutes. Spray 2 baking sheets with nonstick coating. Roll each portion of dough into a rope 15 inches long. Using 3 ropes for each, shape the ropes into 2 braids on the prepared baking sheets.

Cover and let rise till nearly double (35 to 45 minutes). Bake in a 375° oven about 20 minutes or till done. Cool on wire racks. Makes 2 loaves (32 servings).

SOURDOUGH DOUBLE WHEAT BREAD

Cracked wheat and whole wheat flour add fiber and chewy, whole grain texture to these loaves.

- 1 cup Sourdough Starter
- 1 cup cracked wheat
- 2 cups boiling water
- 1 package active dry yeast
- 1½ cups warm water (110° to 115°)
- 2 cups whole wheat flour
- 2 tablespoons sugar
- 2 tablespoons cooking oil
- ¾ teaspoon salt
- 5¼ to 5¾ cups all-purpose flour
  Nonstick spray coating

Bring Sourdough Starter to room temperature. Soak cracked wheat in the 2 cups boiling water for 5 minutes. Drain well. In a large mixing bowl dissolve yeast in the 1½ cups warm water. With a spoon, stir in the whole wheat flour, sugar, cooking oil, salt, Sourdough Starter, and cracked wheat. Stir in as much of the all-purpose flour as you can.

On a lightly floured surface, knead in enough of the remaining all-purpose flour to make a moderately stiff dough that is smooth and elastic (6 to 8 minutes total). Shape into a ball. Place in a lightly greased bowl and turn once to grease surface. Cover and let rise in a warm place till double (1 to 1½ hours).

Punch down. Divide in half. Cover and let rest 10 minutes. Spray two 9x5x3-inch loaf pans with nonstick coating. Shape dough into 2 loaves. Place in prepared pans. Cover and let rise till nearly double (45 minutes to 1 hour). Bake in a 375° oven for 35 to 40 minutes or till done; cover with foil after 25 minutes, if necessary, to prevent overbrowning. Remove from pans. Cool on wire racks. Makes 2 loaves (36 servings).

SOURDOUGH STARTER

Use this starter in yeast breads such as Sourdough Double Wheat Bread and in quick breads such as Sourdough Orange-Wheat Muffins on page 143.

- 1 package active dry yeast
- 2½ cups warm water (110° to 115°)
- 2 cups all-purpose flour
- 1 tablespoon sugar *or* honey

In a large mixing bowl dissolve yeast in ½ *cup* of the warm water. Stir in remaining water, flour, and sugar or honey. Beat till smooth. Cover with cheesecloth. Let stand at room temperature for 5 to 10 days or till bubbly. Stir 2 or 3 times a day. (A warmer room hastens fermentation.)

To store, transfer Starter to a jar and cover with cheesecloth; refrigerate. *Do not cover jar tightly with a metal lid.* Before use, stir Starter. Bring desired amount to room temperature.

To replenish Starter after using, stir ¾ cup all-purpose *flour*, ¾ cup *water*, and 1 teaspoon *sugar or honey* into remaining amount. Cover; let stand at room temperature at least 1 day or till bubbly. Refrigerate for later use. If Starter isn't used within 10 days, stir in 1 teaspoon *sugar or honey*. Repeat every 10 days until used.

THE HISTORY OF SOURDOUGH: *Since colonial days, Americans have been saving a portion of the "soured" dough from one batch of bread to leaven the next. Westward pioneers and prospectors used sourdough in loaves and even in their flapjacks and biscuits. With the invention of commercial yeast, however, sourdough became unnecessary and declined in use.*

Today, sourdough bread, with its distinctive tang, is regaining popularity. Usually yeast is added to the dough along with the starter to speed the rising process.

FLAT ONION BREAD

Great for a crisp snack! (Pictured on page 131.)

- 1½ **to 2 cups all-purpose flour**
- 1 **package active dry yeast**
- ¼ **teaspoon salt**
- ⅔ **cup warm water (115° to 120°)**
- 2 **tablespoons cooking oil**
- 1 **teaspoon sugar**
- 2 **medium onions, very thinly sliced and separated into rings**
- 2 **tablespoons yellow cornmeal Nonstick spray coating**

In a small mixer bowl combine *¾ cup* of the flour, yeast, and salt. Stir together water and *1 tablespoon* of the cooking oil. Add to flour mixture. Beat with an electric mixer on low speed for ½ minute, scraping sides of bowl constantly. Beat on high speed for 3 minutes. Using a spoon, stir in as much of the remaining flour as you can. On a lightly floured surface, knead in enough of the remaining flour to make a moderately stiff dough that is smooth and elastic (6 to 8 minutes total). Shape into a ball. Place in a lightly greased bowl and turn once. Cover and let rise in a warm place till double (about 1 hour).

Punch down. Divide dough in half and shape into 2 balls. Cover and let rest 10 minutes. Meanwhile, in a medium skillet combine remaining oil and the sugar. Add onions. Cover and cook over medium heat for 3 to 5 minutes or till translucent, stirring occasionally. Uncover, then cook and stir just till beginning to brown. Drain on paper towels.

Place 1 ball of dough on a surface sprinkled with *1 tablespoon* of the cornmeal. Roll the dough and stretch with your hands. Continue rolling and stretching to form a 12-inch round. (If necessary, allow dough to rest a few minutes between periods of rolling and stretching.) Be sure edges are not thicker than the rest of the dough.

Spray a baking sheet or pizza pan with nonstick coating. Transfer dough to pan. With a fork, prick the entire surface of the round. Arrange *half* of the onion rings over the round. Bake in a 450° oven for 12 to 13 minutes or till golden. Cool on a wire rack. Repeat with remaining cornmeal, dough, and onion rings. To serve, break each round into 4 pieces. Makes 2 rounds (8 servings).

SWISS RYE BREAD

- 3¼ **to 3¾ cups all-purpose flour**
- 2 **packages active dry yeast**
- 1½ **teaspoons caraway seed**
- 2 **cups warm water (115° to 120°)**
- ¼ **cup packed brown sugar**
- 1 **tablespoon cooking oil**
- ¼ **teaspoon salt**
- 1 **cup shredded process Swiss cheese (4 ounces)**
- 2½ **cups rye flour Nonstick spray coating**

In a large mixer bowl combine *2 cups* of the all-purpose flour, yeast, and caraway seed. Stir together water, brown sugar, oil, and salt. Add to flour mixture. Add cheese. Beat with an electric mixer on low speed for ½ minute, scraping sides of bowl constantly. Beat on high speed for 3 minutes. With a spoon, stir in rye flour and as much of the remaining all-purpose flour as you can.

On a lightly floured surface, knead in enough of the remaining all-purpose flour to make a moderately stiff dough that is smooth and elastic (6 to 8 minutes total). (Dough will be sticky.) Place in a greased bowl and turn once to grease surface. Cover and let rise in a warm place till double (1 to 1½ hours).

Punch down. Divide in half. Cover and let rest 10 minutes. Spray 2 baking sheets with nonstick coating. Shape dough into two 5½-inch round loaves. Place on the prepared baking sheets. Cover and let rise till nearly double (30 to 40 minutes). Bake in a 350° oven for 35 to 40 minutes or till done. Cool on wire racks. Makes 2 loaves (24 servings).

TESTING FOR

DONENESS:

The technique for telling if yeast loaves have baked long enough is right at your fingertips. Tap the top of the baked loaf with your finger. If the bread is properly baked, you will hear a hollow sound. Another test for doneness is to gently push the loaf away from the side of the pan with a metal spatula. If the sides of the loaf are golden brown, the bread is done. Remove the loaf from the pan or baking sheet to cool on a wire rack.

QUICK-RISING YEAST:

*To speed up the rising time
in any bread recipe calling
for active dry yeast, try
quick-rising active dry
yeast. This highly active
strain of yeast can make
dough rise up to 50 percent
faster! Use it in your
favorite recipes just like
regular yeast, but check the
dough after half of the usual
rising time to see if it has
nearly doubled in size.*

MOLASSES-RYE BREAD

The taste panel that was served this bread rated it outstanding for its looks, taste, and texture.

    1¾ to 2¼ cups all-purpose flour
    1   package active dry yeast
    1   cup warm water (115° to 120°)
    2   tablespoons molasses
    1   tablespoon cooking oil
    ½   teaspoon salt
    ¾   cup rye flour
    ½   cup yellow cornmeal
        Nonstick spray coating

In a large mixer bowl combine *1½ cups* of the all-purpose flour and yeast. Combine water, molasses, oil, and salt. Add to flour mixture. Beat with an electric mixer on low speed for ½ minute, scraping sides of bowl. Beat on high speed for 3 minutes. Using a spoon, stir in rye flour, cornmeal, and as much of the remaining all-purpose flour as you can.

On a lightly floured surface, knead in enough of the remaining all-purpose flour to make a moderately stiff dough that is smooth and elastic (6 to 8 minutes total). Shape into a ball. Place in a lightly greased bowl and turn once to grease surface. Cover and let rise in a warm place till double (about 1 hour).

Punch down. Turn out onto a lightly floured surface. Cover and let rest 10 minutes. Spray an 8x4x2-inch loaf pan with nonstick coating. Shape dough into a loaf. Place in the loaf pan. Cover and let rise till nearly double (about 30 minutes). Bake in a 375° oven for 30 to 35 minutes or till done. Remove from pan. Cool on a wire rack. Makes 1 loaf (16 servings).

HAMBURGER BUNS

These buns have about half the sodium of regular hamburger buns and next to no cholesterol!

    3¾ to 4¼ cups all-purpose flour
    1   package active dry yeast
    1   cup skim milk
    ¼   cup sugar
    ¼   cup shortening
    ½   teaspoon salt
    3   egg whites
        Nonstick spray coating

In a large mixer bowl combine *2 cups* of the flour and the yeast. In a medium saucepan heat the milk, sugar, shortening, and salt just till warm (115° to 120°) and shortening is almost melted, stirring constantly. Add to flour mixture; add egg whites. Beat with an electric mixer on low speed for ½ minute, scraping sides of bowl constantly. Beat on high speed for 3 minutes.

Using a spoon, stir in as much of the remaining flour as you can. On a lightly floured surface, knead in enough of the remaining flour to make a moderately stiff dough that is smooth and elastic (6 to 8 minutes total). Shape into a ball. Place in a lightly greased bowl and turn once to grease the surface. Cover and let rise in a warm place till double (40 to 60 minutes).

Punch down. Divide dough into 12 portions. Cover and let rest 10 minutes. Spray a large baking sheet with nonstick coating. Shape each portion into an even ball, folding edges under. Flatten each into a 3½-inch circle. Place on prepared baking sheet. Cover and let rise till nearly double (25 to 30 minutes). Bake in a 375° oven for 10 to 15 minutes or till golden. Remove from baking sheet. Cool on wire racks. Makes 12 servings.

WHOLE WHEAT BUNS: Prepare Hamburger Buns as directed above, *except* after beating for 3 minutes, stir in 1 cup *whole wheat flour* instead of 1 cup of the all-purpose flour.

SPICED PEAR COFFEE CAKE

2 to 2½ **cups all-purpose flour**
1 **package active dry yeast**
½ **cup skim milk**
3 **tablespoons sugar**
3 **tablespoons margarine**
¼ **teaspoon salt**
2 **egg whites**
2 **tablespoons raisins**
2 **medium pears, cored and finely chopped (about 1½ cups)**
1 **tablespoon all-purpose flour**
1 **tablespoon sugar**
¼ **teaspoon finely shredded lemon peel**
1 **teaspoon lemon juice**
½ **teaspoon ground cinnamon**
  Dash ground cloves
  Nonstick spray coating
1 **tablespoon sugar**
¼ **teaspoon ground cinnamon**

In a small mixer bowl combine *1 cup* of the flour and the yeast. In a small saucepan heat milk, 3 tablespoons sugar, margarine, and salt just till warm (115° to 120°) and margarine is almost melted, stirring constantly. Add to flour mixture; add egg whites. Beat with an electric mixer on low speed for ½ minute, scraping bowl. Beat on high speed for 3 minutes. Using a spoon, stir in as much of the remaining 2 to 2½ cups flour as you can.

On a lightly floured surface, knead in enough of the remaining 2 to 2½ cups flour to make a moderately stiff dough that is smooth and elastic (6 to 8 minutes total). Shape into a ball. Place in a lightly greased bowl and turn once to grease surface. Cover and let rise in a warm place till double (about 1 hour). Punch down. Cover and let rest 10 minutes. Meanwhile, in

a small mixing bowl pour ½ cup *boiling water* over raisins. Let stand 5 minutes. Drain.

On a lightly floured surface, roll the dough into a 15x10-inch rectangle. Toss together raisins, pears, 1 tablespoon flour, 1 tablespoon sugar, lemon peel, lemon juice, ½ teaspoon cinnamon, and cloves. Spread over dough. Roll up jelly-roll style, beginning with the long side. Seal edge.

Spray a baking sheet with nonstick coating. Place dough on baking sheet; curve into a ring. Seal ends together. Cut slits in dough. Turn slices to 1 side. Cover; let rise till nearly double (about 40 minutes).

Brush top of dough with water. Combine 1 tablespoon sugar and ¼ teaspoon cinnamon. Sprinkle over dough. Bake in a 350° oven for 20 to 30 minutes or till light brown. Cool on a wire rack. Makes 1 coffee cake (10 servings).

To make petals in the filled ring of dough, use kitchen shears to cut slits in the dough about 1 inch apart, cutting to within ½ inch of the center. Twist each slice slightly to one side, making all the petals lie in the same direction.

LADDER COFFEE CAKES

Wrap and freeze one coffee cake for a later treat.

>   2 to 2½ **cups all-purpose flour**
>   2 **tablespoons unsalted sunflower nuts,**
>   **chopped**
>   1 **package active dry yeast**
>   ½ **cup skim milk**
>   3 **tablespoons sugar**
>   3 **tablespoons margarine**
>   2 **egg whites**
>   ½ **teaspoon finely shredded orange**
>   **peel**
>   **Nonstick spray coating**
>   ½ **cup low-calorie orange marmalade**

In a large mixer bowl combine *1 cup* of the flour, sunflower nuts, and yeast. In a small saucepan heat milk, sugar, margarine, and ¼ teaspoon *salt* just till warm (115° to 120°), stirring constantly. Add to flour mixture; add egg whites and peel. Beat with an electric mixer on low speed for ½ minute. Beat on high speed for 3 minutes. Using a spoon, stir in as much of the remaining flour as you can.

On a floured surface, knead in enough of the remaining flour to make a moderately soft dough that is smooth and elastic (3 to 5 minutes total). Shape into a ball. Place in a lightly greased bowl and turn once to grease surface. Cover and let rise in a warm place till double (about 45 minutes). Punch down. Cover and let rest 10 minutes. Divide dough in half.

Spray a baking sheet with nonstick coating. On the baking sheet roll *half* of the dough into a 10-inch square. Spread *half* of the marmalade down the center third of the dough. With kitchen shears, snip sides toward center into strips 1 inch wide and 3 inches long. Fold strips over marmalade, alternating sides in a V-shape pattern. Repeat with the remaining dough and marmalade. Cover and let rise till nearly double (30 to 40 minutes). Bake in a 350° oven for 20 to 25 minutes or till golden. Cool. Makes 2 coffee cakes (12 servings).

CINNAMON BREAD

>   3½ to 4 **cups all-purpose flour**
>   1 **package active dry yeast**
>   1 **cup skim milk**
>   2 **tablespoons sugar**
>   2 **tablespoons margarine**
>   3 **egg whites**
>   ¼ **cup sugar**
>   1 **teaspoon ground cinnamon**
>   **Nonstick spray coating**
>   ½ **cup sifted powdered sugar**
>   ¼ **teaspoon vanilla**
>   **Skim milk (about 2 teaspoons)**

In a large mixer bowl combine *1½ cups* of the flour and the yeast. In a small saucepan heat the milk, 2 tablespoons sugar, margarine, and ¼ teaspoon *salt* just till warm (115° to 120°) and margarine is almost melted, stirring constantly. Add to flour mixture; add egg whites. Beat with an electric mixer on low speed for ½ minute, scraping sides of bowl. Beat on high speed for 3 minutes. With a spoon, stir in as much of the remaining flour as you can.

Turn out onto a lightly floured surface. Knead in enough of the remaining flour to make a moderately stiff dough that is smooth and elastic (6 to 8 minutes total). Shape into a ball. Place in a lightly greased bowl and turn once to grease surface. Cover and let rise in a warm place till double (1 to 1¼ hours).

Punch down. Cover and let rest 10 minutes. Roll into a 15x7-inch rectangle; brush lightly with water. Combine ¼ cup sugar and cinnamon; sprinkle over dough. Starting at the short end, roll up jelly-roll style. Moisten and seal edge and ends. Spray a 9x5x3-inch loaf pan with nonstick coating. Place roll, seam side down, in prepared pan. Cover and let rise till nearly double (35 to 40 minutes).

Bake in a 375° oven for 35 to 40 minutes or till done, covering with foil after 25 minutes to prevent overbrowning. Remove from pan. Cool for 20 minutes. Combine powdered sugar and vanilla. Stir in enough milk to make of drizzling consistency. Drizzle over warm loaf. Makes 1 loaf (18 servings).

APPLE BISCUIT SPIRALS

To make spirals out of the apple-filled strips, hold a strip at both ends. Carefully twist the strip in opposite directions twice. Place on the prepared baking sheet and press down both ends of the spiral. Repeat with the remaining strips.

2 **cups all-purpose flour**
2 **tablespoons sugar**
2 **teaspoons baking powder**
½ **cup margarine**
2 **slightly beaten egg whites**
⅓ **cup skim milk**
3 **tablespoons brown sugar**
¼ **teaspoon ground allspice**
1 **small apple, cored and finely chopped (⅔ cup)**
2 **teaspoons lemon juice**
   Nonstick spray coating

In a large mixing bowl stir together flour, sugar, and baking powder. Cut in margarine till mixture resembles coarse crumbs. Make a well in the center. Combine egg whites and milk; add all at once to flour mixture. Stir just till dough clings together. On a lightly floured surface, knead gently for 12 to 15 strokes.

Roll dough into a 15x8-inch rectangle. Mix brown sugar and allspice. Combine apple and lemon juice. Brush dough lightly with water; sprinkle with sugar mixture. Sprinkle apple lengthwise on *half* of the dough. Fold dough over apple to make a 15x4-inch rectangle. Cut into fifteen 4x1-inch strips.

Spray a baking sheet with nonstick coating. Twist strips. Place on baking sheet, pressing ends down. Bake in a 450° oven about 10 minutes or till golden. Remove at once. Serve warm. Makes 15 biscuits (15 servings).

NOTE: You may reheat spirals in a microwave or a conventional oven. In a microwave oven, place 1 spiral on a paper plate and micro-cook on high (100%) power for 15 to 20 seconds if refrigerated (25 to 30 seconds for 2 spirals) and 25 to 30 seconds if frozen (35 to 40 seconds for 2 spirals). In a conventional oven, wrap 1 or more in foil and heat in a 300° oven for 7 to 9 minutes if refrigerated and 18 to 20 minutes if frozen.

ONION BISCUITS

2 **cups all-purpose flour**
¼ **cup sliced green onion**
2 **teaspoons baking powder**
2 **teaspoons sugar**
½ **teaspoon dried basil, crushed**
½ **cup shortening**
⅔ **cup skim milk**

Stir together flour, onion, baking powder, sugar, basil, and ¼ teaspoon *salt*. Cut in shortening till the mixture resembles coarse crumbs. Make a well in the center. Add milk all at once. Stir just till dough clings together. On a lightly floured surface, knead gently for 10 to 12 strokes. Roll or pat ½ inch thick. Cut with a floured 2½-inch biscuit cutter. Place on an ungreased baking sheet. Bake in a 450° oven for 10 to 12 minutes or till golden. Serve warm. Makes 12 biscuits (12 servings).

·QUICK RECIPE·
ORANGE-OATMEAL SCONES

For a golden crust, brush these biscuitlike wedges with skim milk before baking.

- 1 **cup all-purpose flour**
- 3 **tablespoons sugar**
- 1½ **teaspoons baking powder**
- 1 **teaspoon finely shredded orange peel**
- ⅓ **cup margarine**
- 1 **cup quick-cooking rolled oats**
- 2 **slightly beaten egg whites**
- 2 **tablespoons orange juice**
  Nonstick spray coating
  Skim milk (optional)

In a mixing bowl stir together flour, sugar, baking powder, and finely shredded orange peel. Cut in margarine till mixture resembles coarse crumbs. Stir in oats. Combine egg whites and orange juice and stir into oat mixture (dough will be sticky).

On a lightly floured surface, roll or pat dough into a 7-inch circle. With a floured knife cut the circle into 12 wedges. Spray a baking sheet with nonstick coating. Place the wedges on the prepared baking sheet. Brush tops with milk, if desired. Bake in a 400° oven for 12 to 15 minutes or till golden brown. Serve warm. Makes 12 scones (12 servings).

COFFEE CAKE MUFFINS

Keep the batter and streusel topping in the refrigerator for up to seven days for freshly baked muffins any day of the week.

- 1¼ **cups all-purpose flour**
- ⅔ **cup quick-cooking rolled oats**
- ¼ **cup packed brown sugar**
- 1½ **teaspoons baking powder**
- ½ **teaspoon pumpkin pie spice**
- ¼ **teaspoon salt**
- 2 **slightly beaten egg whites**
- ⅔ **cup skim milk**
- ⅓ **cup cooking oil**
- ⅓ **cup chopped walnuts**
- 2 **tablespoons chopped walnuts**
- 2 **tablespoons all-purpose flour**
- 1 **tablespoon brown sugar**
- 1 **tablespoon margarine**
  Nonstick spray coating

In a medium mixing bowl stir together 1¼ cups flour, oats, ¼ cup brown sugar, baking powder, pumpkin pie spice, and salt. Make a well in the center. Combine egg whites, milk, and oil. Add all at once to the flour mixture. Stir just till moistened (batter should be lumpy). Fold in ⅓ cup chopped walnuts. Transfer to an airtight container. Cover and store in the refrigerator for up to 7 days.

Mix 2 tablespoons chopped walnuts, 2 tablespoons flour, and 1 tablespoon brown sugar. Cut in margarine. Place in an airtight container and store in the refrigerator.

To bake, spray muffin cups with nonstick coating. Without stirring batter, fill muffin cups ⅔ full. Sprinkle about 1 teaspoon of the nut mixture over each muffin. Bake in a 400° oven for 20 to 25 minutes or till brown. Remove from muffin pan. Serve warm. Makes 12 muffins (12 servings).

SOURDOUGH ORANGE-WHEAT MUFFINS

Sourdough starter gives these muffins the texture of sweet yeast rolls. Simply stir the starter into the batter—no rising needed.

- ⅓ **cup Sourdough Starter (see recipe, page 133)**
- 1¼ **cups all-purpose flour**
- ½ **cup whole wheat flour**
- ¼ **cup sugar**
- 1½ **teaspoons baking powder**
- ¼ **teaspoon salt**
- 2 **slightly beaten egg whites**
- 1 **teaspoon finely shredded orange peel**
- ⅓ **cup orange juice**
- 3 **tablespoons cooking oil**
  Nonstick spray coating

Bring Sourdough Starter to room temperature. In a large mixing bowl stir together all-purpose flour, whole wheat flour, sugar, baking powder, and salt. Make a well in the center. Combine egg whites, orange peel, orange juice, oil, and Sourdough Starter. Add all at once to flour mixture. Stir just till moistened (batter should be lumpy).

Spray muffin cups with nonstick coating. Fill ⅔ full. Bake in a 400° oven for 15 to 20 minutes or till golden. Remove from pan. Serve warm. Makes 12 muffins.

CITRUS WAFFLES with BLUEBERRY SAUCE

- **Blueberry Sauce**
- ¾ **cup all-purpose flour**
- ½ **teaspoon finely shredded orange peel**
  Dash salt
- ¾ **cup skim milk**
- 3 **tablespoons cooking oil**
- 2 **egg whites**
- 2 **small bananas, sliced**

Prepare Blueberry Sauce and set aside. In a medium mixing bowl stir together flour, orange peel, and salt. Combine milk and oil. Add to flour mixture all at once. Stir till mixture is combined but still slightly lumpy.

In a small mixer bowl beat egg whites till stiff peaks form. Gently fold beaten egg whites into the flour-milk mixture, leaving a few fluffs of egg white. *Do not overmix.*

Pour the batter onto the grids of a preheated, lightly greased waffle baker. Close lid quickly; *do not open* during baking. Bake till steam stops escaping from sides of baker.

Use a fork to help lift the baked waffle off the grids. To keep baked waffles warm for serving, arrange in a single layer on a wire rack placed on a baking sheet; place in a warm oven. Serve waffles topped with bananas and Blueberry Sauce. Makes 3 waffles (3 servings).

BLUEBERRY SAUCE: In a small saucepan combine 2 tablespoons *sugar* and 1 teaspoon *cornstarch*. Stir in 2 tablespoons *orange juice* till well mixed. Add ⅔ cup fresh or frozen *blueberries*. Cook and stir till thickened and bubbly, then cook and stir 2 minutes more. Remove from heat. Slightly crush the blueberries.

With a little substitution, you can make different flavored waffles following the recipe for Citrus Waffles at left.

To make Wheat Germ Waffles, prepare Citrus Waffles as directed, except *omit orange peel and stir 2 tablespoons of toasted* wheat germ *into the flour mixture. Serve with low-calorie syrup or preserves.*

To make Cinnamon Waffles, prepare Citrus Waffles as directed, except *omit orange peel and stir ½ teaspoon ground* cinnamon *into the flour mixture. Serve with warm applesauce.*

PEAR-NUT LOAF

1½ **cups all-purpose flour**
1 **teaspoon ground cinnamon**
½ **teaspoon baking soda**
¼ **teaspoon baking powder**
¼ **teaspoon ground nutmeg**
2 **egg whites**
1 **cup sugar**
¾ **cup finely shredded pear**
3 **tablespoons cooking oil**
½ **teaspoon finely shredded orange peel**
½ **cup chopped walnuts**
Nonstick spray coating

Stir together flour, cinnamon, soda, baking powder, and nutmeg. In a large mixing bowl beat together egg whites, sugar, and pear. Add oil and orange peel and mix well.

Stir flour mixture into pear mixture. Gently fold in nuts. Spray an 8x4x2-inch loaf pan with nonstick coating. Transfer batter to prepared pan. Bake in a 350° oven for 55 to 60 minutes or till done. Cool in pan for 10 minutes. Remove from pan and cool thoroughly on a wire rack. Makes 1 loaf (16 servings).

SPICY SQUASH BREAD

Use buttercup, butternut, banana, or acorn squash.

1½ **cups chopped, peeled winter squash**
¼ **cup cooking oil**
1½ **cups all-purpose flour**
1 **teaspoon ground cinnamon**
½ **teaspoon baking soda**
½ **teaspoon ground nutmeg**
⅛ **teaspoon ground cloves**
2 **slightly beaten egg whites**
1 **cup sugar**
⅓ **cup raisins**
Nonstick spray coating

Place squash in a medium saucepan with about ½ inch of water. Cook, covered, about 20 minutes or till tender. Drain. Place squash and cooking oil in a blender container or a food processor bowl. Cover and blend or process till smooth.

Stir together flour, cinnamon, baking soda, nutmeg, and cloves. In a medium mixing bowl stir together egg whites, sugar, and squash mixture. Stir in flour mixture. Gently fold in raisins.

Spray an 8x4x2-inch loaf pan with nonstick coating. Transfer batter to prepared pan. Bake in a 350° oven for 55 to 60 minutes or till done. Cool in the pan for 10 minutes. Remove from pan and cool thoroughly on a wire rack. Makes 1 loaf (16 servings).

BANANA BREAD

1½ **cups all-purpose flour**
½ **teaspoon baking soda**
½ **teaspoon ground cinnamon**
¼ **teaspoon baking powder**
¼ **teaspoon ground nutmeg**
⅛ **teaspoon salt**
2 **egg whites**
1 **cup sugar**
1 **cup mashed ripe banana**
¼ **cup cooking oil**
½ **cup chopped walnuts**
Nonstick spray coating

Stir together flour, baking soda, cinnamon, baking powder, nutmeg, and salt. In a medium mixing bowl beat together egg whites, sugar, and banana. Add oil and mix well. Stir flour mixture into banana mixture. Gently fold in chopped walnuts.

Spray an 8x4x2-inch loaf pan with nonstick coating. Transfer batter to prepared pan. Bake in a 350° oven for 50 to 60 minutes or till done. Cool in pan for 10 minutes. Remove from pan and cool thoroughly on a wire rack. Makes 1 loaf (16 servings).

QUICK BREAD

KNOW-HOW:

To check the doneness of a quick bread loaf, stick a wooden toothpick into the baked loaf near the center. If the bread is done, the toothpick will come out clean. If there is batter on the toothpick when you pull it out, return the loaf to the oven till it tests done.

You'll find it easier to slice a loaf of quick bread the day after you bake it. Cool the loaf, tightly wrap it in clear plastic wrap or foil, and keep the loaf overnight at room temperature before you slice.

DOUBLE APRICOT COFFEE CAKE

¾ cup finely snipped dried apricots (4 ounces)
½ cup water
1 5½-ounce can (⅔ cup) apricot nectar
⅓ cup cooking oil
2 cups all-purpose flour
½ cup sugar
1 package active dry yeast
1½ teaspoons baking powder
½ teaspoon ground cinnamon
¼ teaspoon salt
2 slightly beaten egg whites
Nonstick spray coating
½ cup regular *or* quick-cooking rolled oats
¼ cup packed brown sugar
2 tablespoons margarine, melted

In a saucepan combine apricots and water and bring to a full boil. Remove from heat. Stir in apricot nectar and oil. Cool about 25 minutes or till still warm (115° to 120°).

Meanwhile, stir together flour, sugar, yeast, baking powder, cinnamon, and salt till well mixed. Add apricot mixture and egg whites. Stir just till combined. Spray an 11x7x1½-inch baking pan with nonstick coating. Transfer batter to prepared pan.

Combine oats and brown sugar. Stir in margarine. Sprinkle over batter. Bake in a 350° oven for 25 to 30 minutes or till brown. Serve warm. Makes 1 coffee cake (12 servings).

STREUSEL COFFEE CAKE

2 cups all-purpose flour
⅓ cup sugar
1 package active dry yeast
1½ teaspoons baking powder
1 teaspoon finely shredded orange peel
¼ teaspoon ground nutmeg
¼ teaspoon salt
¾ cup skim milk
⅓ cup cooking oil
2 slightly beaten egg whites
¼ cup broken pecans
Nonstick spray coating
¼ cup packed brown sugar
1 tablespoon all-purpose flour
1 tablespoon margarine, softened
⅛ teaspoon ground nutmeg

In a large mixing bowl combine the 2 cups flour, sugar, yeast, baking powder, peel, ¼ teaspoon nutmeg, and salt. In a saucepan combine milk and oil. Heat to 115° to 120°. Add to flour mixture along with egg whites. Stir just till combined. Fold in nuts.

Spray an 11x7x1½-inch baking pan with non-stick coating. Spoon batter into the pan. Combine brown sugar, 1 tablespoon flour, softened margarine, and ⅛ teaspoon nutmeg. Sprinkle over batter. Bake in a 350° oven for 25 to 30 minutes or till brown. Serve warm. Makes 1 coffee cake (12 servings).

STEWED CORN and TOMATOES

Slit the corn kernels to release their milky juice.

COOK THE PASTA

WITHOUT SALT:

Make it a rule to cook pasta

without the salt specified on

most package directions. The

sauce, cheese, or seasonings

you usually toss with the

pasta provide ample flavor.

 6 **fresh ears of corn**
 3 **large tomatoes, peeled and chopped**
 ¾ **cup finely chopped onion**
 ½ **cup finely chopped green pepper**
 1 **teaspoon sugar**
 ¾ **teaspoon dried basil, crushed**
 ⅛ **teaspoon salt**
 ⅛ **teaspoon pepper**

Score corn down each row of kernels. Cut corn off cob. Scrape cob to remove corn liquid. (You should have about 3 cups total.) In a large saucepan combine corn, tomatoes, onion, green pepper, sugar, basil, salt, and pepper. Bring to boiling; reduce heat. Cover and simmer 15 to 20 minutes or till vegetables are tender; stir occasionally. Makes 8 servings.

SWISS VEGETABLE-PASTA PLATTER

Try this recipe with whole wheat pasta. Besides extra fiber, it adds a slightly nutty flavor to the dish.

 2 **ounces linguine *or* fettuccine**
 ½ **cup sliced carrots**
 2 **cups broccoli flowerets**
 2 **cups sliced zucchini**
 1 **cup skim milk**
 2 **tablespoons all-purpose flour**
 ¾ **teaspoon dried basil, crushed**
 ⅛ **teaspoon pepper**
 ½ **cup shredded process Swiss cheese**

In a large saucepan cook pasta according to package directions, *except* omit salt. Drain. Meanwhile, in a medium saucepan cook carrots, covered, in a small amount of boiling water for 5 minutes. Add broccoli and zucchini and cook for 3 to 5 minutes more or till crisp-tender. Drain.

For sauce, in a small saucepan combine milk, flour, basil, and pepper. Cook and stir till thickened and bubbly. Cook and stir 1 minute more. Stir in cheese till melted. On a large platter combine pasta and vegetables. Pour sauce over and toss gently to coat. Serves 6.

·QUICK RECIPE·

BROCCOLI-PASTA TOSS

Save on cleanup! Cook the broccoli and pasta in the same saucepan, then toss with the other ingredients. Pictured on the cover.

 2 **cups broccoli flowerets**
 4 **ounces fettuccine *or* linguine, broken up**
 1 **tablespoon olive oil *or* cooking oil**
 3 **tablespoons grated Parmesan cheese**
 1 **teaspoon sesame seed, toasted**
 ⅛ **teaspoon garlic powder**
 ⅛ **teaspoon pepper**

In a large saucepan cook broccoli and pasta in a large amount of boiling water for 6 to 8 minutes or just till tender, stirring once or twice to prevent pasta from sticking. Drain. Add oil to pasta-vegetable mixture and toss. Add Parmesan cheese, sesame seed, garlic powder, and pepper. Toss gently to coat. Serve immediately. Makes 4 servings.

·QUICK RECIPE·
SPECIAL SPAETZLE

By omitting salt and substituting two egg whites for one of the eggs, we've cut the sodium, fat, cholesterol, and calories of classic spaetzle (SHPETS luh).

2 cups all-purpose flour
2 slightly beaten egg whites
1 beaten egg
¾ cup skim milk

To form spaetzle, pour the batter into a colander with 3/16-inch or larger holes.

Holding the colander over a kettle of boiling water, use a rubber scraper to press the

batter through the holes so irregular droplets fall into the water. If the batter is too

thick to go through the holes, stir in more skim milk.

Place flour in a medium mixing bowl. Make a well in the center. In a small mixing bowl combine egg whites, egg, and milk. Pour liquids all at once into the flour well. Mix well.

In a Dutch oven bring a large amount of water to boiling. Pour batter into a colander with large holes or a spaetzle maker. Hold colander over boiling water. Press batter through holes in colander so it falls into the water.

Cook and stir for 5 minutes. Remove cooked spaetzle with a slotted spoon. Drain well. Makes 8 servings.

LEMONY
GINGERED BEETS

If your beets come with nice tops, save them for use in a tossed salad or as a cooked green vegetable. They're an excellent source of vitamin A.

1 pound beets, peeled and sliced
2 teaspoons sugar
¾ teaspoon cornstarch
¼ cup water
½ teaspoon finely shredded lemon peel
1 tablespoon lemon juice
⅛ teaspoon ground ginger

In a large saucepan cook the beets, covered, in boiling water for 20 to 30 minutes or till beets are tender. Drain.

Meanwhile, in a small saucepan stir together sugar and cornstarch. Stir in water, lemon peel, lemon juice, and ginger. Cook and stir till thick and bubbly. Cook and stir 2 minutes more. In a serving bowl stir together beets and lemon mixture. Serve warm. Makes 6 servings.

BAKED COTTAGE POTATOES

Enjoy crispy potatoes without frying!

    Nonstick spray coating
 4 medium potatoes, thinly sliced
 1 small onion, thinly sliced
 2 teaspoons margarine, melted
 ¼ cup grated Parmesan cheese
 ½ teaspoon dried basil, crushed
 ⅛ teaspoon coarsely ground pepper

Spray a 13x9x2-inch baking pan with nonstick coating. Arrange potatoes in a thin layer in the pan. Arrange onion slices over the potatoes. Brush with melted margarine. Stir together cheese, basil, and pepper. Sprinkle over potato mixture. Bake, uncovered, in a 450° oven about 25 minutes or till potatoes are brown and crisp. Makes 4 servings.

·QUICK RECIPE·

ROMAINE STIR-FRY

A salad green co-stars with broccoli in this stir-fry.

    Nonstick spray coating
 3 cups broccoli flowerets
 2 tablespoons water
 ½ teaspoon sugar
 ¼ teaspoon instant chicken bouillon
     granules
 2 cups sliced romaine

Spray a large skillet or wok with nonstick coating. Preheat over high heat till a drop of water sizzles. Stir-fry broccoli for 4 minutes. Stir in water, sugar, and bouillon granules. Cover and simmer for 4 minutes. Stir in romaine. Stir-fry about 3 minutes or till vegetables are tender. Makes 6 servings.

·QUICK RECIPE·

LEMON-DILL POTATOES

 1 pound whole tiny new potatoes
     (about 18)
 2 tablespoons margarine, melted
 1 tablespoon lemon juice
 ¼ teaspoon dried dillweed

Remove a narrow strip of peel from around the center of each potato. In a large saucepan cook potatoes, covered, in boiling water for 12 to 14 minutes or till tender. Drain. Place in a serving bowl. Combine margarine, lemon juice, and dillweed. Drizzle over potatoes. Makes 6 servings.

·QUICK RECIPE·

BRUSSELS SPROUTS TOSS

 2 cups brussels sprouts *or*
     one 10-ounce package
     frozen brussels sprouts
 1 tablespoon margarine
 2 tablespoons slivered
     almonds
 ¼ teaspoon aniseed, crushed

Halve brussels sprouts. If using fresh brussels sprouts, cook, covered, in boiling water for 10 to 15 minutes or till crisp-tender. If using frozen brussels sprouts, cook according to package directions, *except* omit salt. Drain. Transfer to a serving bowl and keep warm.

Meanwhile, in a small skillet melt margarine over medium heat. Add almonds and aniseed. Cook and stir for 2 to 3 minutes or till almonds are lightly toasted. Spoon over brussels sprouts. Toss to coat. Makes 4 servings.

Instead of plain cooked rice and sliced carrots, serve Triticale-Rice Pilaf *and* Gingered Carrots.

·QUICK RECIPE·

SAUCY SUCCOTASH

Adding chili peppers and hot pepper sauce makes this yogurt-sauced succotash delightfully spicy.

  1 **10-ounce package frozen baby lima beans**
  1 **10-ounce package frozen whole kernel corn**
  ½ **cup plain low-fat yogurt**
  2 **teaspoons cornstarch**
  1 **4-ounce can green chili peppers, rinsed, seeded, and chopped**
  ¼ **cup skim milk**
     Several dashes bottled hot pepper sauce
  ¼ **cup snipped parsley**

In a large saucepan cook beans and corn according to package directions for the beans, *except* omit salt. Drain and return to saucepan.

Combine yogurt and cornstarch. Stir in green chili peppers, milk, and hot pepper sauce. Stir into bean mixture in the saucepan. Cook and stir till thickened and bubbly. Cook and stir 2 minutes more. Stir in parsley. Serves 8.

TRITICALE-RICE PILAF

Cross wheat with rye and you get a grain called triticale. Look for the berries in health food stores.

 2¾ **cups water**
  ¾ **teaspoon instant chicken bouillon granules**
  ½ **cup triticale berries**
  ½ **cup brown rice**
  ½ **cup chopped onion**
  ½ **teaspoon ground nutmeg**
  1 **cup thinly sliced fresh mushrooms**
     Nonstick spray coating (optional)
  1 **orange slice, halved (optional)**

In a medium saucepan bring water and bouillon granules to boiling. Stir in triticale berries. Return to boiling; reduce heat. Cover and simmer for 1 hour.

Stir in brown rice, onion, and nutmeg. Return to boiling; reduce heat. Cover and simmer for 35 minutes. Add mushrooms. Cover and simmer 5 to 10 minutes more or till rice and berries are tender. Drain off excess liquid, if necessary.

Spoon rice mixture into a serving bowl. (Or, if desired, spray a 3½-cup ring mold with nonstick coating. Press rice mixture into the ring mold. Unmold onto a platter.) Garnish with orange slice, if desired. Makes 6 servings.

·QUICK RECIPE·

GINGERED CARROTS

Orange juice concentrate gives this single-serving side dish a refreshing tang.

  1 **large carrot, bias sliced (about ⅔ cup)**
  2 **teaspoons frozen orange juice concentrate**
     Several dashes ground ginger
  1 **teaspoon snipped parsley**

In a small saucepan cook carrot, covered, in a small amount of boiling water about 4 minutes or till crisp-tender; drain well.

Stir in orange juice concentrate and ginger. Cook over low heat 1 minute more, stirring occasionally. Stir in parsley. Makes 1 serving.

·QUICK RECIPE·

CUCUMBER SAUTÉ

Usually confined to the salad bowl, cucumbers make a delicious cooked vegetable too. In this recipe, sauté cucumbers with mushrooms and season with dill.

- 2 cups sliced fresh mushrooms
- ¼ cup chopped onion
- 1 clove garlic, minced
- 1 tablespoon margarine
- 2 medium cucumbers, thinly sliced (about 3 cups)
- 1 tablespoon snipped fresh dill *or* 1 teaspoon dried dillweed

In a 10-inch skillet cook mushrooms, onion, and garlic in margarine till tender. Add cucumber slices. Cook and stir about 5 minutes or till cucumbers are crisp-tender and liquid is almost evaporated. Stir in fresh dill or dried dillweed. Makes 5 servings.

·QUICK RECIPE·

SWEET PEPPERS and BEANS

If sweet red peppers aren't available, use sweet yellow or green bell peppers.

- 1 9-ounce package frozen cut green beans
- ¼ cup chopped onion
- 2 sweet red peppers, cut into 1-inch squares
- 1 tablespoon sesame seed, toasted
- 1 tablespoon margarine
- ¼ teaspoon dried thyme, crushed

In a medium saucepan cook beans and onion in ½ inch of boiling water for 2 minutes. Add pepper squares and cook 3 to 4 minutes more or till vegetables are crisp-tender. Drain. Toss with sesame seed, margarine, and thyme. Makes 5 servings.

ACORN SQUASH PUREE

This is a new way to serve winter squash. Try it as a side dish to broiled pork or lamb chops.

- 2 small acorn squash, halved and seeded (1 pound each)
- 2 tablespoons brown sugar
- 2 tablespoons margarine
- 1 tablespoon hazelnut liqueur *or* skim milk
  Dash salt
  Dash pepper

Place squash, cut side down, in a baking pan. Bake, uncovered, in a 350° oven for 45 to 60 minutes or till tender. Using a spoon, scoop squash out of shells into a small mixer bowl. Discard shells.

Add brown sugar, margarine, hazelnut liqueur or milk, salt, and pepper to squash in the mixer bowl. Beat with an electric mixer till smooth and well mixed. Transfer to a saucepan and heat through.

Place *half* of the squash mixture in a pastry bag fitted with a large star tip. With a hot pad wrapped around the pastry bag to protect your hands, pipe mixture in rows or stars onto a serving plate. Repeat with remaining mixture. (Or spoon mixture into a serving dish.) Makes 4 servings.

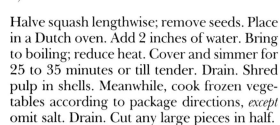

·QUICK RECIPE·
STEAMED GREENS and ZUCCHINI

Ideal as a bed for roasted poultry or poached fish.

  3 **tablespoons water**
  ½ **teaspoon sugar**
  ¼ **teaspoon instant chicken bouillon
     granules**
  ¼ **teaspoon dried basil, crushed**
  2 **cups cabbage cut into 1-inch chunks**
  1 **medium zucchini, chopped**
  2 **cups torn fresh spinach**

In a skillet combine water, sugar, bouillon, and basil. Bring to boiling. Add cabbage and zucchini. Return to boiling; reduce heat. Cover and simmer for 3 minutes. Add spinach; cook for 1 to 2 minutes more or till spinach is wilted, stirring occasionally. Makes 4 servings.

SQUASH with VEGETABLE SAUCE

  1 **3-pound spaghetti squash**
  ½ **of a 20-ounce package (3 cups) loose-
     pack frozen mixed cauliflower,
     broccoli, and carrots**
  2 **tablespoons snipped parsley**
  2 **teaspoons cornstarch**
  1 **teaspoon sugar**
  ½ **teaspoon dried basil, crushed**
  ¼ **teaspoon salt**
  ¼ **teaspoon dried thyme, crushed**
  ⅛ **teaspoon pepper**
  1 **16-ounce can sodium-reduced
     tomatoes, cut up**
  2 **tablespoons dry red wine**

Halve squash lengthwise; remove seeds. Place in a Dutch oven. Add 2 inches of water. Bring to boiling; reduce heat. Cover and simmer for 25 to 35 minutes or till tender. Drain. Shred pulp in shells. Meanwhile, cook frozen vegetables according to package directions, *except* omit salt. Drain. Cut any large pieces in half.

In a medium saucepan combine parsley, cornstarch, sugar, basil, salt, thyme, and pepper. Stir in *undrained* tomatoes and wine. Cook and stir till thickened and bubbly. Cook and stir 2 minutes more. Stir in vegetables; heat through. Spoon over squash in shells. Makes 6 servings.

To shred the cooked squash into spaghetti-like strands, steady a squash half with one hand, protecting your hand from the hot shell with a hot pad or thick towel. Using a fork, pull the squash pulp away from the shell but do not remove the shredded pulp. To serve, pour the vegetable sauce over the shredded squash. Place the filled shells on a platter and serve right from the shells.

GARLIC SOUP

Even with ten cloves of garlic, this soup has a mild, sweet flavor. The long, slow cooking of the onions and garlic is the secret to the flavor.

  2 **large onions, sliced**
 10 **cloves garlic, peeled and thinly sliced (about 1 bulb)**
  1 **tablespoon cooking oil**
  2 **medium tomatoes, peeled, seeded, and chopped**
 ¼ **teaspoon dried oregano, crushed**
 1½ **cups water**
 ½ **teaspoon instant beef bouillon granules**

In a medium saucepan cook onions and garlic in hot oil over medium-low heat for 15 to 20 minutes or till onions begin to brown, stirring occasionally. Stir in tomatoes and oregano. Cover and cook over low heat for 30 minutes, stirring occasionally.

Stir in water and bouillon granules. Bring to boiling; reduce heat. Simmer, uncovered, for 10 minutes. Makes 4 servings.

CALIFORNIA GAZPACHO

This gazpacho gives you one-fourth the sodium of regular gazpacho without sacrificing flavor.

  4 **large tomatoes, peeled and coarsely chopped**
  1 **small cucumber, chopped**
  1 **medium green pepper, chopped**
  1 **small onion, finely chopped**
  1 **clove garlic, minced**
  3 **cups sodium-reduced tomato juice**
 ¼ **cup wine vinegar**
 1½ **teaspoons instant chicken bouillon granules**
 ½ **teaspoon pepper**
    Few dashes bottled hot pepper sauce

In a large mixing bowl combine tomatoes, cucumber, green pepper, onion, and garlic. Stir in tomato juice, wine vinegar, bouillon granules, pepper, and hot pepper sauce. Cover and chill several hours. Makes 10 servings.

·QUICK RECIPE·

ORANGE-GLAZED PEA PODS

To remove the ends and strings from the pea pods, simply snap off the tip of the pod with your fingers and pull the string down the length of the pod.

  8 **ounces fresh pea pods**
  1 **tablespoon sugar**
  1 **teaspoon cornstarch**
 ½ **teaspoon finely shredded orange peel**
 ¼ **cup orange juice**
  2 **tablespoons sliced almonds, toasted**

Rinse pea pods. Remove ends and strings. Cut pea pods in half diagonally. In a small saucepan cook pea pods, covered, in a small amount of boiling water for 3 minutes. Drain. Cover and set aside.

In a small saucepan combine sugar and cornstarch. Stir in orange peel and juice. Cook and stir till thickened and bubbly. Cook and stir 2 minutes more. Pour over hot pea pods, stirring to coat. Transfer to a serving dish. Sprinkle sliced almonds on top. Serve immediately. Makes 4 servings.

Orange-Glazed Pea Pods *are a worthy accompaniment to broiled chicken breasts, lamb chops, or lean steak.*

WASHING FRESH

SPINACH:

Because spinach leaves grow

close to the ground, they

often collect small amounts

of grit, especially in the folds

near the center vein. To

remove the grit easily, place

a bunch of leaves in a bowl

of cool water, swishing them

around with your hands to

loosen the particles. Lift out

the leaves, discard the sandy

water, and repeat several

times until no grit appears.

Drain the leaves well or pat

them dry with paper towels

before using.

·QUICK RECIPE·

FRUITED SPINACH SALAD

A delicious honey and poppy seed dressing unites the fruit and greens.

- ¼ **cup white wine vinegar**
- 3 **tablespoons salad oil**
- 2 **tablespoons honey**
- 1 **teaspoon poppy seed**
- ½ **teaspoon dry mustard**
- 8 **cups torn spinach**
- 1 **medium papaya, seeded, peeled, and cubed,** *or* **2 medium pears, cored, peeled, and cubed**
- 1½ **cups seedless grapes, halved**

For dressing, in a screw-top jar combine vinegar, salad oil, honey, poppy seed, and dry mustard. Cover and shake well to mix.

In a large salad bowl combine spinach, papaya or pears, and grapes. Shake dressing again and pour over salad. Toss to coat. Serve immediately. Makes 10 servings.

·QUICK RECIPE·

TOSSED ENSALADA SUPREME

Jicama (HICK-ah-mah), a popular vegetable in Mexican cooking, looks like a turnip and tastes a lot like a water chestnut.

- 4 **cups torn leaf lettuce**
- 1 **cup cubed, peeled jicama**
- 1 **small zucchini, cut into julienne strips**
- 2 **medium tomatoes, cut into wedges**
- ½ **cup skim milk**

- ¼ **cup plain low-fat yogurt**
- ¼ **cup reduced-calorie mayonnaise** *or* **salad dressing**
- ½ **of a 4-ounce can whole green chili peppers, rinsed, seeded, and chopped**
- 1 **tablespoon snipped cilantro** *or* **parsley**

In a salad bowl toss together lettuce, jicama, and zucchini. Arrange tomato wedges around the edge of the bowl. Stir together milk, yogurt, mayonnaise or salad dressing, and chili peppers. Spoon into the center of the lettuce mixture. Sprinkle with cilantro or parsley. Toss before serving. Makes 4 servings.

·QUICK RECIPE·

PINEAPPLE TOSS

Toss this refreshing salad with a simple dressing made from just two ingredients.

- 3 **cups torn salad greens**
- 1 **cup shredded green** *or* **red cabbage**
- 1 **8-ounce can pineapple tidbits (juice pack)**
- ¼ **cup reduced-calorie mayonnaise** *or* **salad dressing**

In a salad bowl combine greens and cabbage. Drain pineapple, reserving *2 tablespoons* of the juice. Add pineapple to greens and cabbage.

In a small bowl stir together mayonnaise and reserved pineapple juice. Pour over salad and toss to coat. Makes 4 servings.

GREEK-STYLE SALAD

- **4 cups torn romaine**
- **1 medium tomato, cut into wedges**
- **1 small cucumber, sliced**
- **¼ cup sliced green onion**
- **3 tablespoons finely crumbled feta cheese**
- **2 tablespoons snipped parsley**
- **3 tablespoons white wine vinegar**
- **2 tablespoons olive oil *or* salad oil**
- **1 tablespoon lemon juice**
- **¼ teaspoon dried oregano, crushed**

In a salad bowl combine romaine, tomato, cucumber, green onion, cheese, and parsley. Cover and chill. For dressing, in a screw-top jar combine vinegar, oil, lemon juice, and oregano. Cover and shake well to mix. Chill. To serve, shake dressing again and pour over salad. Toss to coat. Makes 6 servings.

FLAMING SPINACH SALAD

If you heat the brandy in a ladle, have someone else ignite the brandy so you don't have to set down the ladle to light a match.

- **6 cups torn spinach (8 ounces)**
- **1½ cups cauliflower flowerets**
- **8 cherry tomatoes, halved**
- **2 tablespoons sliced green onion**
- **1 clove garlic, minced**
- **1 tablespoon cooking oil**
- **1 tablespoon brown sugar**
- **1 tablespoon vinegar**
- **¼ teaspoon dried thyme, crushed**
- **2 tablespoons brandy**

In a large salad bowl combine spinach, cauliflower, and tomatoes. In a small skillet cook onion and garlic in hot oil till tender. Stir in brown sugar, vinegar, and thyme. Cook and stir till bubbly. Pour over spinach mixture and toss to coat.

Pour brandy into a ladle or small saucepan. Heat till brandy almost simmers. *Do not boil.* Quickly ignite the brandy with a long match. Pour the flaming brandy over the spinach mixture. When the flame dies, toss to coat. Serve immediately. Makes 6 servings.

Flame a salad! It's an unusual idea that will wow your dinner guests. First warm the brandy in a ladle over a burner just till hot. Do not allow it to boil or the alcohol needed to ignite the brandy will evaporate. Quickly bring the ladle to the table and, using a long match, ignite the brandy. While it is still flaming, pour the brandy over the salad. When the flame dies, toss the brandy with the salad.

DILLED BRUSSELS SPROUTS and CAULIFLOWER

Save any remaining marinade for a dressing on another salad.

- 2 **cups brussels sprouts** *or* **one 10-ounce package frozen brussels sprouts**
- 1 **cup cauliflower flowerets**
- ¼ **cup olive oil** *or* **salad oil**
- 3 **tablespoons vinegar**
- 1 **tablespoon lemon juice**
- 1 **teaspoon dried dillweed**
- 1 **2-ounce jar sliced pimiento, drained**
  Lettuce leaves (optional)

Cook fresh brussels sprouts and cauliflower in a small amount of boiling water for 8 to 10 minutes or till crisp-tender. (Or, cook frozen brussels sprouts according to package directions, *except* omit salt.) Drain. Halve any large pieces. Place in a mixing bowl.

In a small saucepan combine olive or salad oil, vinegar, lemon juice, and dillweed. Bring just to boiling. Pour over brussels sprouts and cauliflower. Cool. Cover and chill at least 2 hours, stirring occasionally.

Stir in sliced pimiento. If desired, line salad plates with lettuce leaves. With a slotted spoon, lift the vegetable mixture onto salad plates. Makes 6 servings.

SPAGHETTI SQUASH VINAIGRETTE

Cut the squash in half lengthwise, from end to end. Save the unused half to replace spaghetti noodles in your next pasta dinner.

- ½ **of a 2-pound spaghetti squash**
- ½ **cup thinly bias-sliced carrots**
- ⅓ **cup chopped sweet red** *or* **green pepper**
- ¼ **cup sliced green onion**
- ¼ **teaspoon finely shredded lemon peel**
- 2 **tablespoons lemon juice**
- 2 **tablespoons olive oil** *or* **salad oil**
- ½ **teaspoon dried oregano, crushed**
- ⅛ **teaspoon garlic powder**
  Dash pepper
  Leaf lettuce

Remove seeds from squash half. Place squash in a large saucepan with 2 inches of water. Bring to boiling; reduce heat. Cover and simmer for 25 to 35 minutes or till tender. Drain. Using a fork, scrape pulp into spaghetti-like strands. Transfer strands to a large mixing bowl, reserving squash shell. Cover and refrigerate shell. In a small saucepan cook carrots in a small amount of boiling water for 8 to 10 minutes or till crisp-tender. Drain.

Stir carrots, chopped pepper, and green onion into spaghetti squash in bowl. In a screw-top jar combine lemon peel, lemon juice, oil, oregano, garlic powder, and pepper. Cover and shake well to mix. Pour over vegetables and stir to coat. Cover and refrigerate several hours or overnight, stirring occasionally.

To serve, line the reserved squash shell with lettuce or place squash shell in a lettuce-lined bowl. Mound the chilled vegetable mixture into the shell. Makes 4 servings.

When olive oil is chilled in the refrigerator, the low temperature causes the oil to solidify. You may notice this happening with chilled salad mixtures that use olive oil in the dressing, such as the salads on this page. To allow the olive oil to return to its liquid state, simply remove the salad from the refrigerator about 15 minutes before serving.

Raw cabbage has a lot going for it as a salad ingredient. Along with its characteristic taste and crunch, it contributes valuable nutrients. Cabbage ranks with citrus fruits as a major source of vitamin C and also is rich in minerals. There's good news for waist-watchers, too. One cup of shredded cabbage costs you only 17 calories. In addition, raw cabbage provides excellent roughage for the digestive system and acts as a good cleanser for your teeth and gums.

·QUICK RECIPE·
CHINESE COLESLAW

The leaves of Chinese cabbage have a more delicate texture than common cabbage and form a head similar in shape to romaine.

    4 cups shredded Chinese cabbage
    1 8¼-ounce can crushed pineapple
       (juice pack), drained
    1 8-ounce can sliced water chestnuts,
       drained
    1 cup snipped parsley
    ¼ cup chopped green onion
    ¼ cup reduced-calorie mayonnaise *or*
       salad dressing
    1 tablespoon prepared mustard
    1 teaspoon grated gingerroot *or*
       ½ teaspoon ground ginger

In a large bowl combine cabbage, pineapple, water chestnuts, parsley, and onion. Cover and chill. For dressing, in a small bowl combine mayonnaise or salad dressing, mustard, and gingerroot or ground ginger. Cover and chill. To serve, spoon dressing over cabbage mixture and toss to coat. Makes 8 servings.

·QUICK RECIPE·
TANGY SESAME SLAW

Sesame oil is a full-flavored oil that gives an unmistakable sesame flavor to salad dressings and stir-fried foods. Look for it in Oriental markets.

    2 tablespoons water
    1 tablespoon lemon juice
    1 tablespoon red wine vinegar
    1 tablespoon honey
    2 teaspoons sesame oil
    1 teaspoon cornstarch
    2 cups finely shredded cabbage
    2 medium carrots, shredded
    1 medium green pepper, chopped
    1 tablespoon sesame seed, toasted

For dressing, in a small saucepan combine water, lemon juice, vinegar, honey, sesame oil, and cornstarch. Cook and stir till thickened and bubbly. Cook and stir 2 minutes more. Cover and chill.

In a bowl combine cabbage, carrots, green pepper, and sesame seed. Pour dressing over salad and toss to coat. Makes 6 servings.

·QUICK RECIPE·
GOLDEN CABBAGE TOSS

Toss this fruit-and-nut slaw with a simple, delicious dressing of orange yogurt.

    3 cups shredded cabbage
    2 medium oranges, peeled and
       sectioned
    1 cup shredded carrot
    ¼ cup raisins
    ¼ cup unsalted sunflower nuts
    ⅓ cup orange low-fat yogurt

In a bowl combine cabbage, orange sections, carrot, raisins, and sunflower nuts. Spoon yogurt over cabbage mixture and toss to coat. Makes 6 servings.

GARDEN POTPOURRI

Serve this crunchy vegetable slaw over pepper rings.

- 1½ **cups shredded zucchini**
- ⅓ **cup shredded carrot**
- ⅓ **cup sliced radishes**
- ⅓ **cup chopped cucumber**
- 2 **tablespoons sliced green onion**
- ⅓ **cup plain low-fat yogurt**
- 1 **teaspoon sugar**
- ¼ **teaspoon celery seed**
- ⅛ **teaspoon garlic powder**
  Dash pepper
- 1 **medium green pepper**

In a mixing bowl combine zucchini, carrot, radishes, cucumber, and green onion. For dressing, in a small bowl stir together yogurt, sugar, celery seed, garlic powder, and pepper. Cover and chill vegetable mixture and dressing separately at least 1 hour.

To serve, cut top from green pepper and discard top, seeds, and membranes. Thinly slice pepper into rings and arrange on 4 salad plates. Toss together vegetable mixture and dressing and spoon over pepper rings. Makes 4 servings.

GREEN BEAN and PASTA SALAD

Reduced-calorie Italian salad dressing makes an easy and zesty marinade for the vegetables and pasta.

- 1 **9-ounce package frozen Italian green beans *or* cut green beans**
- ½ **cup corkscrew macaroni**
- ½ **cup reduced-calorie Italian salad dressing**
- ¼ **cup shredded carrot**
  Lettuce leaves

Cook beans according to package directions, *except* omit salt. Drain. Cook macaroni according to package directions, *except* omit salt. Drain. Rinse with cold water; drain.

In a medium mixing bowl toss together beans, macaroni, salad dressing, and carrot. Cover and chill for several hours or overnight, stirring occasionally. Serve on lettuce-lined salad plates. Makes 4 servings.

CURRIED FRUIT and PASTA SALAD

If you can't find farfalle, or bow tie pasta, in your grocery store, substitute whole wheat macaroni or any other medium-size pasta.

- 4 **ounces farfalle *or* whole wheat macaroni (1 cup)**
- 1 **orange, peeled and sectioned**
- 1 **8-ounce can pineapple tidbits (juice pack), drained**
- ½ **cup red seedless grapes, halved**
- ¼ **cup raisins**
- ¼ **cup buttermilk**
- 2 **tablespoons reduced-calorie mayonnaise *or* salad dressing**
- 1 **teaspoon sugar**
- 1 **teaspoon curry powder**

Cook farfalle or whole wheat macaroni according to package directions, *except* omit salt. Drain. Rinse with cold water; drain.

In a medium bowl combine cooked farfalle or macaroni, orange sections, pineapple tidbits, grapes, and raisins. For dressing, in a small bowl stir together buttermilk, mayonnaise or salad dressing, sugar, and curry powder. Spoon over fruit mixture and toss to coat. Cover and chill. Makes 4 servings.

After draining cooked pasta for cold salads, rinse with cold water and drain again. Not only does a cold-water rinse cool the pasta to speed chilling, it also helps keep the pasta from sticking together so you can easily mix in other ingredients.

DILL VEGETABLE TABBOULEH

Bulgur refers to coarsely ground wheat kernels that have been precooked in processing. Like other whole wheat products, it is a good source of the B vitamins and protein. When prepared, bulgur becomes tender but retains the shape of the kernel pieces. It has a chewy texture and a flavor similar to wild rice.

- ¾ **cup bulgur**
- ½ **cup chopped green pepper**
- 3 **tablespoons white wine vinegar**
- 2 **tablespoons thinly sliced green onion**
- 1½ **teaspoons salad oil**
- 1½ **teaspoons snipped fresh dill** *or*
- ½ **teaspoon dried dillweed**
- ⅛ **teaspoon salt**
- 1 **medium tomato, peeled, seeded, and chopped**

Place bulgur in a bowl. Add 1½ cups *boiling water* and let stand for 1 hour. Drain well. Stir in green pepper, vinegar, onion, oil, dill or dillweed, and salt. Cover and chill several hours. Before serving, stir in tomato. If desired, serve on lettuce-lined plates with lemon wedges. Makes 6 servings.

CURRIED BULGUR SALAD

Use firm lettuce, such as romaine or iceberg, that will stay crisp when tossed with the bulgur and dressing.

- ½ **cup bulgur**
- ½ **cup raisins**
- 1 **cup shredded carrot**
- 1 **8-ounce carton plain low-fat yogurt**
- ¾ **teaspoon curry powder**
  Dash ground cinnamon
- 3 **cups torn romaine** *or* **iceberg lettuce**
- ⅓ **cup unsalted peanuts**

In a bowl combine bulgur and raisins. Add 1 cup *boiling water* and let stand for 1 hour. Drain well. Stir in carrot. Cover and chill at least 2 hours. Before serving, combine yogurt, curry powder, and cinnamon. Combine bulgur mixture, yogurt mixture, lettuce, and peanuts. Toss to coat. Makes 6 servings.

INDONESIAN RICE SALAD

Brown rice is the same grain as white rice but with the fiber-rich bran layers intact. Bran contributes a nutty flavor and chewy texture to brown rice.

- 1⅔ **cups water**
- ⅔ **cup brown rice**
- 1 **clove garlic, minced**
- ½ **teaspoon grated gingerroot**
- ⅓ **cup orange juice**
- 1 **tablespoon salad oil**
- 1 **tablespoon lemon juice**
- 1 **tablespoon dry sherry**
- 2 **teaspoons sodium-reduced soy sauce**
- 1 **medium orange, peeled, sectioned, and cut up**
- ½ **cup sliced bamboo shoots** *or* **thinly sliced water chestnuts**
- ¼ **cup raisins**
- ¼ **cup chopped green** *or* **sweet red pepper**
- 2 **tablespoons sliced green onion**

In a medium saucepan combine water, brown rice, garlic, and gingerroot. Bring to boiling; reduce heat. Cover and simmer about 40 minutes or till rice is tender and water is absorbed. Cool slightly.

For dressing, in a screw-top jar combine orange juice, salad oil, lemon juice, dry sherry, and soy sauce. Cover and shake well to mix.

In a mixing bowl combine rice mixture, orange pieces, bamboo shoots or water chestnuts, raisins, green or red pepper, and green onion. Shake dressing again and pour over rice mixture. Toss to coat. Cover and chill several hours or overnight. Makes 6 servings.

TOMATO FANS

Drape these ricotta-filled tomatoes with a creamy mustard-yogurt sauce.

> 4 **medium tomatoes**
> ½ **cup ricotta cheese**
> 1 **tablespoon snipped chives**
> 1 **tablespoon skim milk**
>   **Dash pepper**
> ¼ **cup plain low-fat yogurt**
> 1 **teaspoon Dijon-style mustard**
> ¼ **teaspoon sugar**
> 4 **lettuce leaves**

To make tomato fans, place each cored tomato, stem end down, on a cutting board.

Cut it into four equal slices, cutting to, but not through, the base of the tomato.

Gently spread the slices apart to allow enough room for the ricotta cheese filling.

Using about two tablespoons of filling for each tomato, spoon equal amounts of the

filling between the slices.

Core the tomatoes. With stem end down, cut each into 4 equal slices, cutting to, but not through, the base of the tomato. Pull slices apart slightly. For filling, combine ricotta cheese, chives, milk, and pepper. Using about 2 tablespoons of filling for each tomato, divide filling evenly among the slices.

Stir together yogurt, mustard, and sugar. Place each tomato on an individual lettuce-lined salad plate. Drizzle with the yogurt mixture. Makes 4 servings.

CREAMY ZUCCHINI-CARROT MOLD

Apple juice adds a pleasing sweetness.

> 1 **envelope unflavored gelatin**
> 1¼ **cups apple juice**
> 1 **8-ounce carton plain low-fat yogurt**
> ½ **cup shredded zucchini**
> ½ **cup shredded carrot**

In a medium saucepan soften gelatin in ½ *cup* of the apple juice for 5 minutes. Heat and stir the gelatin mixture till the gelatin is dissolved. Remove from heat. Stir in remaining apple juice and yogurt. Chill till partially set (the consistency of unbeaten egg whites). Fold in zucchini and carrot. Pour into a 2½- to 3-cup mold. Chill till firm. Unmold onto a serving plate. Makes 5 servings.

GINGERED AMBROSIA SALAD

Easy, pretty, and refreshing as the tropics!

- **1 8-ounce can pineapple chunks (juice pack)**
- **1 11-ounce can mandarin orange sections, drained**
- **1 kiwi fruit, peeled, halved lengthwise, and sliced**
- **1 teaspoon grated gingerroot**
- **2 tablespoons flaked *or* shredded coconut, toasted**
- **Mint leaves (optional)**

Drain pineapple chunks, reserving *3 tablespoons* of the juice. In a bowl combine reserved juice, pineapple, drained oranges, kiwi fruit, and gingerroot. Toss gently till well combined. Cover and chill for several hours or overnight. Before serving, sprinkle with toasted coconut. Garnish with fresh mint leaves, if desired. Makes 6 servings.

·QUICK RECIPE·

DOUBLE-BANANA SALAD

One-fourth of a cantaloupe yields about one cup of cubed melon.

- **⅓ cup cream-style cottage cheese**
- **1 ripe large banana, sliced**
- **1 teaspoon honey**
- **½ teaspoon lemon juice**
- **1 cup cubcd cantaloupc**
- **1 8-ounce can pineapple chunks (juice pack), drained**
- **Lettuce leaves**
- **¼ teaspoon poppy seed**

For dressing, in a blender container combine cottage cheese, *half* of the banana slices, and honey. Cover and blend till smooth.

Toss together remaining banana slices and lemon juice. Arrange banana slices, cantaloupe, and pineapple on 4 lettuce-lined salad plates. Top each serving with about 2 tablespoons of dressing. Sprinkle with poppy seed. Makes 4 servings.

ORANGE-STRAWBERRY SALAD MOLD

To unmold this salad, dip the mold just to the rim in warm water for a few seconds. Tilt to ease the salad away from the sides of the mold and let in air. Then invert the salad onto a plate.

- **2 envelopes unflavored gelatin**
- **3 cups orange juice**
- **1 8-ounce carton orange low-fat yogurt**
- **2 cups sliced strawberries**

In a small saucepan soften gelatin in *1 cup* of orange juice for 5 minutes. Heat and stir the gelatin mixture till the gelatin is dissolved.

In a medium mixing bowl combine remaining orange juice and yogurt. Gradually stir in gelatin mixture. Chill till partially set (consistency of unbeaten egg whites). Fold in sliced strawberries. Pour into a 6-cup mold. Chill at least 4 hours or till firm. Unmold onto a serving plate. Makes 10 servings.

TROPICAL FRUIT PLATTER

- ⅓ cup plain low-fat yogurt
- ⅓ cup frozen whipped dessert topping, thawed
- ½ teaspoon finely shredded orange *or* lemon peel
- 2 tablespoons orange juice
- 1 teaspoon sugar
- 1 tablespoon water
- 2 teaspoons lemon juice
- 2 medium bananas, bias sliced
  Salad greens
- 2 kiwi fruit, peeled and sliced
- 1 medium mango, seeded, peeled, and sliced
- ¼ cup red raspberries *or* pomegranate seeds

For dressing, stir together yogurt, dessert topping, orange or lemon peel, orange juice, and sugar. Cover and chill for 1 hour.

In a bowl combine water and lemon juice. Add bananas and toss. Line a platter with salad greens. Arrange bananas, kiwi fruit, and mango over greens. Scatter raspberries or pomegranate seeds on top. Serve dressing with fruit. Makes 6 servings.

·QUICK RECIPE·

APRICOT FRUIT SALAD

Chill the unopened can of apricots several hours before serving so they'll be refreshingly cold.

- 1 16-ounce can unpeeled apricot halves (juice pack), chilled
- ½ cup halved seedless green grapes
  Lettuce leaves
- 2 ounces Neufchâtel cheese, softened
- ¼ teaspoon ground ginger
  Ground nutmeg

Drain apricots, reserving *1 tablespoon* of the juice. Cut apricot halves in half to form quarters. Arrange apricots and grapes on 4 individual lettuce-lined salad plates. Stir together Neufchâtel cheese and ginger. Gradually stir in reserved apricot juice to make of drizzling consistency. Drizzle over fruit. Sprinkle with nutmeg. Makes 4 servings.

YOGURT-FRUIT TOSS

- ½ cup plain low-fat yogurt
- 1 tablespoon brown sugar
- ¼ teaspoon ground cinnamon
- ¼ teaspoon poppy seed
- 2 cups strawberries, halved
- 1 cup seedless grapes
- 1 ripe medium banana, sliced

Stir together yogurt, brown sugar, cinnamon, and poppy seed. In a medium mixing bowl combine strawberries, grapes, and banana slices. Pour yogurt mixture over fruit and toss gently to coat. Cover and chill. Toss again before serving. Makes 6 servings.

PEACH BUTTER

This spicy peach spread has a consistency similar to apple butter.

- **3 cups peeled, sliced fresh peaches** *or* **nectarines**
- **½ cup sugar**
- **¼ teaspoon ground cinnamon**
- **¼ teaspoon ground nutmeg**
- **Dash ground cloves**

Place peaches or nectarines in a blender container or a food processor bowl. Cover and blend or process till smooth, stopping to scrape sides of container as necessary. Pour into an 8x8x2-inch baking pan. Stir in sugar, cinnamon, nutmeg, and cloves.

Bake the peach mixture, uncovered, in a 300° oven about 2 hours or till thickened, stirring every 20 minutes. Serve warm or cold on toast, pancakes, or muffins. Store, covered, in refrigerator. Makes 1¼ cups (20 servings).

NOTE: For long-term storage, place the Peach Butter in a clean jar or in a moisture- and vaporproof container, leaving ½ inch between the surface of the Peach Butter and the rim of the container. Seal, label, and freeze for up to 1 year.

·QUICK RECIPE·

PEANUT BUTTER and APPLE SPREAD

A creamy spread with about half the calories of straight peanut butter.

- **½ cup creamy peanut butter**
- **¼ cup plain low-fat yogurt**
- **¼ cup unsweetened applesauce**

Stir together peanut butter, yogurt, and applesauce till well combined. Serve on toast, muffins, or waffles. Store, covered, in the refrigerator. Makes 1 cup (16 servings).

·QUICK RECIPE·
PEPPER and GARLIC SPREAD

Perk up a plain roast beef or chicken sandwich with this peppy spread.

- **1 8-ounce package Neufchâtel cheese, softened**
- **2 tablespoons skim milk**
- **1½ teaspoons cracked black pepper**
- **2 cloves garlic, minced**

In a small mixer bowl combine softened Neufchâtel cheese and skim milk. Beat with an electric mixer on medium speed till fluffy. Add cracked black pepper and minced garlic and beat till well mixed. Serve on crackers or bread. Store, covered, in the refrigerator. Makes 1 cup (16 servings).

·QUICK RECIPE·
BLUE CHEESE SPREAD

For the true blue-cheese lover.

- **4 ounces tofu (fresh bean curd)**
- **¼ of an 8-ounce package Neufchâtel cheese, softened**
- **¼ cup crumbled blue cheese (1 ounce)**
- **¼ cup snipped parsley**
- **1 tablespoon warm water**
- **⅛ teaspoon onion powder**

Press excess water from tofu; cut up. In a blender container or a food processor bowl combine tofu, Neufchâtel cheese, blue cheese, parsley, water, and onion powder. Cover; blend or process till smooth. Serve on crackers or bread. Store, covered, in the refrigerator. Makes ¾ cup (12 servings).

ONION-SESAME SPREAD

Chill the spread several hours to enhance the sesame and onion flavors.

- **3 tablespoons chopped green onion**
- **1 8-ounce package Neufchâtel cheese, softened**
- **2 tablespoons sesame seed, toasted**
- **2 tablespoons skim milk**

In a small saucepan cook onion in a small amount of boiling water for 2 to 3 minutes or till tender. Drain.

In a small mixer bowl combine onion, Neufchâtel cheese, sesame seed, and milk. Beat with an electric mixer on medium speed till fluffy. Cover and refrigerate several hours or overnight. Serve on bread, biscuits, or crackers. Store, covered, in the refrigerator. Makes 1 cup (16 servings).

HORSERADISH DRESSING

Transform this dressing into a vegetable dip by decreasing the milk to ½ cup.

- ½ **cup reduced-calorie mayonnaise** *or* **salad dressing**
- ½ **cup plain low-fat yogurt**
- 2 **tablespoons snipped chives**
- 1 **tablespoon prepared horseradish**
- 1 **teaspoon poppy seed**
- ¾ **cup skim milk**

In a bowl stir together mayonnaise or salad dressing, yogurt, chives, horseradish, and poppy seed. Stir in skim milk. Cover and chill. Makes 1½ cups (12 servings).

BUTTERMILK SALAD DRESSING

- 1 **cup buttermilk**
- ½ **cup reduced-calorie mayonnaise** *or* **salad dressing**
- ¼ **cup plain low-fat yogurt**
- 2 **tablespoons snipped parsley**
- 2 **teaspoons snipped chives**
- 1 **teaspoon sugar**
- ¼ **teaspoon dried oregano, crushed**
- ¼ **teaspoon dried basil, crushed**
- ¼ **teaspoon dried marjoram, crushed**
- ⅛ **teaspoon pepper**
  Dash garlic powder

In a bowl stir together buttermilk, mayonnaise or salad dressing, yogurt, snipped parsley, chives, sugar, oregano, basil, marjoram, pepper, and garlic powder. Cover and chill. Makes 1¾ cups (14 servings).

BASIL-GARLIC DRESSING

- ¼ **cup vinegar**
- 3 **tablespoons water**
- 2 **tablespoons olive oil** *or* **salad oil**
- 1½ **teaspoons snipped fresh basil** *or*
  ½ **teaspoon dried basil, crushed**
- 1 **teaspoon finely chopped green onion**
- 2 **cloves garlic, minced**

In a screw-top jar combine vinegar, water, oil, basil, onion, and garlic. Cover and shake till well combined. Chill. Shake again before serving. Makes ½ cup (8 servings).

SUNFLOWER-HERB SALAD DRESSING

¼ cup unsalted sunflower nuts
1 clove garlic, minced
1 8-ounce carton plain low-fat yogurt
2 tablespoons skim milk
1 teaspoon dried basil, crushed
½ teaspoon dried thyme, crushed
⅛ teaspoon dry mustard
⅛ teaspoon pepper

In a blender container or food processor bowl combine sunflower nuts and garlic. Cover and blend or process to a very fine powder (almost a paste). Add yogurt, milk, basil, thyme, dry mustard, and pepper. Cover and blend or process till smooth. Cover and chill. Makes 1 cup (8 servings).

DILLY SALAD DRESSING

This thick and creamy dressing also makes a great sauce for broiled fish or steamed vegetables.

¾ cup buttermilk
¼ cup reduced-calorie mayonnaise *or* salad dressing
1 tablespoon tarragon vinegar
1 teaspoon sugar
1½ teaspoons snipped fresh dill *or* ½ teaspoon dried dillweed
Dash pepper

In a bowl stir together buttermilk, mayonnaise or salad dressing, tarragon vinegar, sugar, dill or dillweed, and pepper. Cover and chill. Makes 1 cup (8 servings).

CUCUMBER-BLUE CHEESE DRESSING

1 8-ounce carton plain low-fat yogurt
½ cup crumbled blue cheese (2 ounces)
1 tablespoon sugar
1 tablespoon vinegar
Dash pepper
½ of a medium cucumber, shredded
Skim milk (optional)

In a bowl combine yogurt, blue cheese, sugar, vinegar, and pepper. Stir in cucumber. Cover and chill. Stir in 1 to 2 tablespoons milk to thin, if desired. Makes 1½ cups (12 servings).

CREAMY GARLIC DRESSING

½ cup plain low-fat yogurt
⅓ cup reduced-calorie Italian salad dressing
1 tablespoon grated Parmesan cheese
1 small clove garlic, minced

In a bowl stir together yogurt, salad dressing, Parmesan cheese, and garlic. Cover and chill. Makes 1 cup (8 servings).

Orange Sherbet Freeze and Pineapple Sherbet (see recipes, page 193) will satisfy your sweet tooth without adding extra pounds, as well as cool and refresh you.

DESSERTS

CHAPTER 5

Why did we include such things as cakes, pies, cookies, and parfaits in a cook book on healthy eating? Dessert-lovers, we did it for you! Rather than have you pay dearly for eating disastrous desserts, we've given you healthier alternatives that are just as tasty.

Perhaps your next question is "How did you do it?" Primarily, we limited sugar and fat, and consequently kept the calories to a minimum. You'll also find lots of recipes that use the natural sweetness of fruit to satisfy your cravings for dessert.

CONTENTS

	CALORIES	PROTEIN (g)	CARBOHYDRATES (g)	FAT (g)	CHOLESTEROL (mg)	SODIUM (mg)	POTASSIUM (mg)	PROTEIN	VITAMIN A	VITAMIN C	THIAMINE	RIBOFLAVIN	NIACIN	CALCIUM	IRON
	PER SERVING							PERCENT U.S. RDA PER SERVING							
Apricot-Sauced Baked Apples (p. 183)	179	1	46	1	0	5	474	2	37	15	2	3	4	3	8
Baked Papaya (p. 184)	52	1	13	0	0	5	346	1	46	120	2	3	3	3	3
Banana Pudding (p. 190)	167	3	33	3	1	69	242	5	5	6	4	8	2	8	2
Blueberry-Orange Sundaes (p. 193)	174	3	31	5	7	74	294	4	5	29	5	10	2	7	1
Cherry Cobbler (p. 182)	214	4	36	7	35	121	221	6	33	18	9	8	6	6	6
Chocolate Custards (p. 191)	112	7	17	2	6	116	198	11	3	1	2	15	1	10	1
Chocolate-Mint Pie (p. 179)	134	5	17	6	4	79	117	8	2	1	5	9	2	8	3
Chocolate-Orange Torte (p. 175)	152	3	24	6	0	107	81	4	4	13	6	5	3	4	4
Cocoa Macaroons (p. 187)	81	1	12	4	0	15	43	2	0	0	3	1	0	1	1
Crunchy Topper (p. 182)	35	0	4	2	0	12	18	1	1	0	1	0	0	0	1
Fruited Floating Islands (p. 181)	156	2	38	1	0	19	268	4	20	46	4	5	2	3	3
Honey-Pecan Cookies (p. 189)	181	3	15	13	0	90	106	4	6	0	11	2	3	1	4
Mango Ice (p. 191)	68	1	17	0	0	14	79	2	34	20	2	3	1	1	0
Marble Angel Cake (p. 176)	202	5	46	1	0	64	189	8	0	27	5	10	4	1	5
Mocha Meringues (p. 181)	149	3	35	0	1	56	112	5	2	1	1	6	0	7	1
Mocha Pudding (p. 190)	112	5	23	1	2	83	232	7	5	2	3	11	1	15	2
Oatmeal-Pear Cookies (p. 189)	126	2	17	6	0	76	54	3	2	1	5	3	2	1	4
Orange Sherbet (p. 193)	91	4	18	1	3	38	196	6	1	25	4	7	1	10	0
Orange-Yogurt Fruit (p. 183)	78	2	17	1	1	19	306	4	3	129	5	8	2	9	2
Peanut Butter-Oatmeal Cookies (p. 190)	114	3	13	6	17	89	81	4	3	0	4	2	5	2	4
Pineapple Sherbet (p. 193)	81	3	18	0	1	40	211	4	3	14	5	7	1	11	1
Pineapple-Wheat Cookies (p. 187)	116	1	15	6	15	65	42	2	2	1	5	3	2	1	3
Poached Pears (p. 183)	105	0	27	0	0	0	136	1	1	22	2	2	1	2	1
Raisin Squares (p. 186)	156	2	26	5	17	60	103	3	0	1	6	4	4	2	6
Raspberry Chiffon Pie (p. 178)	116	3	24	1	0	33	103	5	2	19	1	5	2	2	1
Spice Cupcakes (p. 176)	151	2	25	5	0	108	45	4	4	0	6	5	3	4	3
Spiced Rice Pudding (p. 191)	176	5	30	4	2	89	287	8	12	2	7	11	4	16	4
Summer Fruit Parfaits (p. 184)	175	4	28	7	22	120	317	6	13	19	6	8	4	5	2
Triticale-Oatmeal Cookies (p. 189)	174	3	22	9	23	145	86	4	7	1	7	4	3	2	6
White Mousse With Fresh Fruit (p. 184)	117	5	24	1	3	53	300	8	4	48	4	10	2	14	2
Yogurt Drop Cookies (p. 186)	117	2	15	6	16	69	29	2	2	0	4	3	2	2	3

CHOCOLATE-ORANGE TORTE

This torte—with almost no cholesterol and only 120 mg sodium per serving—calls for no salt or egg yolks, little baking powder, and cocoa instead of chocolate.

Nonstick spray coating
1 cup all-purpose flour
2 tablespoons unsweetened cocoa powder
1¼ teaspoons baking powder
¼ cup margarine
⅔ cup sugar
¾ teaspoon vanilla
½ cup ice-cold water
2 egg whites
1 1.4-ounce envelope whipped dessert topping mix
2 tablespoons unsweetened cocoa powder
½ cup skim milk
½ teaspoon vanilla
1 11-ounce can mandarin orange sections, drained

Spray a 9x1½-inch round baking pan with nonstick spray coating; set aside. In a small mixing bowl stir together flour, 2 tablespoons cocoa powder, and baking powder; set aside.

In a mixer bowl beat margarine with an electric mixer on medium speed for 30 seconds. Add sugar and ¾ teaspoon vanilla; beat on medium speed till well combined. Add dry ingredients and cold water alternately to beaten mixture, beating on low speed after each addition. Thoroughly wash beaters.

In a clean small mixer bowl beat egg whites on medium speed till stiff peaks form. Stir a small amount of beaten egg whites into flour mixture to lighten batter. Fold in remaining egg whites. Turn into the prepared pan. Bake in a 375° oven for 20 to 25 minutes or till cake springs back and leaves no imprint when lightly touched. Cool 10 minutes on a wire rack. Remove from the pan; cool completely.

Meanwhile, in the small mixer bowl combine dessert topping mix and 2 tablespoons cocoa powder. Add milk and the ½ teapoon vanilla. Beat on high speed till soft peaks form and mixture is light and fluffy.

Reserve 12 of the mandarin orange sections. Coarsely chop remaining orange sections. To assemble torte, use a sharp knife with a long blade to carefully cut the cake horizontally into 2 layers. Place the bottom half on a serving plate. Top with a layer of ⅓ of the dessert topping mixture, a layer of the chopped mandarin orange sections, and another layer of ⅓ of the topping mixture. Replace remaining cake layer, cut side down. Top with remaining dessert topping mixture. Garnish with reserved orange sections. Makes 12 servings.

Spread a thin layer of the dessert topping mixture atop the bottom layer of the cake. Place the chopped mandarin orange sections atop. Carefully spread another thin layer of dessert topping mixture over the orange sections. Then add the remaining cake layer. Decorate the top of the torte with the remaining dessert topping mixture, using the whole mandarin orange sections as a garnish.

MARBLE ANGEL CAKE

You'll notice that many of the cake batters in this chapter call for egg whites only. Although eggs have an important function in leavening and forming the structure of the cake, it's the egg whites that do most of the work. By eliminating the yolk, you also eliminate 253 mg cholesterol per egg.

For light-as-a-feather angel food cake, allow the egg whites to reach room temperature before beating them.

  1½ **cups sifted powdered sugar**
  1 **cup sifted cake flour** *or* **sifted all-purpose flour**
  ¼ **cup unsweetened cocoa powder**
  1½ **cups egg whites (11** *or* **12 large)**
  1½ **teaspoons cream of tartar**
  1 **teaspoon vanilla**
  1 **cup sugar**
     Strawberry-Banana Topper

Sift together powdered sugar and flour; repeat sifting twice. Sift together *half* of the flour mixture and cocoa powder.

In a large mixer bowl beat egg whites, cream of tartar, and vanilla with an electric mixer on medium speed till soft peaks form. Gradually add sugar, about 2 tablespoons at a time, beating till stiff peaks form. Transfer *half* of the beaten egg white mixture to a separate large mixing bowl.

Sift the plain flour mixture, about ⅓ *cup* at a time, over *half* of the egg white mixture, folding in lightly by hand after each addition. Set aside. Repeat with the cocoa-flour mixture and remaining egg white mixture.

Pour white batter into an *ungreased* 10-inch tube pan; spoon cocoa batter atop. With a knife or narrow metal spatula, swirl gently through batters to marble, leaving definite light and dark areas. Bake on the lowest rack in a 350° oven about 40 minutes or till cake springs back and leaves no imprint when lightly touched. Invert cake in the pan; cool completely. Loosen cake from the pan; remove from the pan. Serve with Strawberry-Banana Topper. Makes 12 servings.

STRAWBERRY-BANANA TOPPER: For topper, in a blender container or food processor bowl combine 2 cups frozen unsweetened *strawberries*, partially thawed; 1 tablespoon *honey;* and ½ teaspoon finely shredded *lemon peel.* Cover and blend or process till smooth. Slice 2 *bananas.* Arrange some of the banana slices atop each slice of cake. Spoon strawberry mixture atop the fruit and cake.

SPICE CUPCAKES

Remember to wash the beaters well before using them to beat the egg whites. Any fat left on them will prevent the whites from whipping properly.

  1 **cup all-purpose flour**
  1¼ **teaspoons baking powder**
  ½ **teaspoon ground nutmeg**
  ½ **teaspoon ground cinnamon**
  ¼ **cup margarine**
  ⅔ **cup sugar**
  1¼ **teaspoons vanilla**
  ½ **cup skim milk**
  2 **egg whites**
  2 **tablespoons sifted powdered sugar**

In a small mixing bowl stir together flour, baking powder, nutmeg, and cinnamon; set aside. In a large mixer bowl beat margarine with an electric mixer on medium speed for 30 seconds. Add sugar and vanilla; beat on medium speed till well combined. Add dry ingredients and milk alternately to beaten mixture, beating on low speed after each addition. Thoroughly wash beaters.

In a small mixer bowl beat egg whites on medium speed till stiff peaks form. Stir a small amount of egg whites into the flour mixture to lighten the batter. Fold remaining egg whites into flour mixture.

Line 10 muffin cups with paper bake cups; fill cups two-thirds full with batter. Bake in a 375° oven for 15 to 20 minutes or till a wooden toothpick inserted in center comes out clean. Cool on a wire rack. Sift powdered sugar atop cupcakes. Makes 10 cupcakes (10 servings).

RASPBERRY CHIFFON PIE

The name chiffon describes the light, delicate texture that develops from folding in beaten egg whites or whipped cream or dessert topping.

Meringue Crust
2½ **cups fresh *or* frozen red raspberries**
2 **tablespoons lemon juice**
¼ **cup sugar**
1 **envelope unflavored gelatin**
2 **egg whites**
2 **tablespoons sugar**
¼ **cup skim milk**
½ **of a 1.4-ounce envelope whipped dessert topping mix**

To shape the meringue crust, drop the beaten egg white mixture into the 9-inch pie plate by tablespoonfuls. Use the back of the spoon to spread the egg white mixture over the bottom and up the sides of the pie plate to form a shell.

Prepare Meringue Crust. Thaw berries, if frozen. Reserve a few berries for garnish; set aside. In a large mixing bowl crush enough of the remaining berries to measure 1¼ cups. Stir in lemon juice. Set aside.

In a small saucepan stir together the ¼ cup sugar and gelatin. Stir in ¾ cup *water*. Heat and stir till sugar and gelatin dissolve. Cool. Stir cooled gelatin mixture into berry mixture. Chill in the refrigerator till the consistency of corn syrup, stirring occasionally.

Remove from the refrigerator (gelatin mixture will continue to set). In a small mixer bowl immediately begin beating egg whites with an electric mixer on medium speed till soft peaks form. Gradually add the 2 tablespoons sugar, beating on high speed till stiff peaks form. When gelatin mixture is partially set (the consistency of unbeaten egg whites), fold in the stiff-beaten egg whites.

In the small mixer bowl beat milk and dessert topping mix on high speed till soft peaks form. Beat for 2 minutes more or till light and fluffy. Fold into gelatin mixture. Chill till mixture mounds when spooned. Pile mixture into Meringue Crust. Chill in the refrigerator for 3 to 4 hours or till set. Garnish with reserved berries. Makes 8 servings.

MERINGUE CRUST: In a small mixer bowl beat 2 *egg whites*, ½ teaspoon *vanilla*, and ¼ teaspoon *cream of tartar* with an electric mixer on medium speed till soft peaks form. Gradually add ⅓ cup *sugar*, beating with an electric mixer on high speed till stiff peaks form and sugar is almost dissolved.

Spray a 9-inch pie plate with *nonstick spray coating.* Spread egg white mixture over bottom and up sides of plate to form a shell. Bake in a 300° oven for 45 minutes. Turn off the heat and let dry in oven with door closed for 2 hours more. Cool thoroughly on a wire rack.

CHOCOLATE-MINT PIE

For a tasty, fat-reduced piecrust, try this version with cottage cheese.

> 2 **tablespoons shortening**
> ⅓ **cup all-purpose flour**
> ¼ **cup low-fat cream-style cottage cheese, drained**
> 1 **envelope unflavored gelatin**
> 2 **tablespoons sugar**
> ¼ **cup water**
> ¾ **cup skim milk**
> 1 **tablespoon unsweetened cocoa powder**
> 4 to 6 **drops mint extract**
> 1 **cup chocolate-flavored ice milk**

For crust, cut shortening into flour till pieces are the size of small peas. Add cottage cheese; toss till all is moistened. Form into a ball. On a floured surface flatten dough. Roll dough from center to edges, forming a circle about 10 inches in diameter. Fit into a 7-inch pie plate; turn under and flute edges. Prick bottom and sides with a fork. Bake in a 450° oven for 10 to 12 minutes or till golden. Cool.

Meanwhile, in a 1-cup measure stir together gelatin and sugar. Stir in water. Let stand for 5 minutes. Place the measure in a medium saucepan which contains 1 inch of *water.* Heat and stir till gelatin and sugar are dissolved.

In a blender container or food processor bowl combine gelatin mixture, milk, cocoa powder, and mint extract; cover and blend till combined. Gradually add ice milk, blending till smooth after each addition. If necessary, cover and chill in the refrigerator till mixture mounds slightly. Spoon into prepared crust. Cover and chill about 4 hours or till firm. Makes 6 servings.

To prevent your chocolate-mint mixture from seeping through the crust, make sure it's thick enough to mound when dropped from a spoon. If it isn't, chill the mixture in the refrigerator till it mounds, stirring frequently. Spoon into the cooled, baked crust.

MOCHA MERINGUES

Because Mocha Meringues are extra-special, our taste panelists gave them an outstanding rating.

- **2 egg whites**
- **½ teaspoon vanilla**
- **¼ teaspoon cream of tartar**
- **½ cup sugar**
- **¼ cup sugar**
- **2 tablespoons cornstarch**
- **2 tablespoons unsweetened cocoa powder**
- **1¼ cups skim milk**
- **½ cup water**
- **2 tablespoons coffee liqueur**
  Sliced fresh fruit (optional)

For meringue shells, cover a baking sheet with brown paper. Draw 6 circles, 3½ inches in diameter, on the paper. In a small mixer bowl beat egg whites, vanilla, and cream of tartar with an electric mixer on medium speed till soft peaks form. Gradually add the ½ cup sugar, beating on high speed till stiff peaks form and sugar is almost dissolved.

Immediately pipe or spoon beaten egg white mixture into a shell shape in each circle on the paper-lined baking sheet. Bake in a 300° oven for 30 minutes. Turn off the heat and let shells dry in the oven with the door closed at least 1 hour more. Peel off paper.

Meanwhile, for filling in a heavy medium saucepan combine the ¼ cup sugar, cornstarch, and cocoa powder. Stir in skim milk and water. Cook and stir over medium heat till thickened and bubbly; cook and stir for 2 minutes more. Remove from the heat. Stir in coffee liqueur. Pour filling into a bowl. Cover surface with clear plastic wrap. Chill in the refrigerator, without stirring, till serving time. To serve, spoon filling into individual meringue shells. Garnish with fresh fruit, if desired. Makes 6 servings.

FRUITED FLOATING ISLANDS

Surrounded by a sea of cherries, oranges, and apricot nectar, poached meringue puffs are the tasty islands.

- **2 egg whites**
- **3 tablespoons sugar**
- **3 cups water**
- **1½ cups fresh *or* frozen unsweetened pitted dark sweet cherries**
- **¼ cup sugar**
- **4 teaspoons cornstarch**
- **1½ cups apricot nectar**
- **1½ teaspoons finely shredded orange peel**
- **2 oranges, sectioned**

For meringue puffs, in a small mixer bowl beat egg whites with an electric mixer on medium speed till soft peaks form. Gradually add the 3 tablespoons sugar, beating on high speed till stiff peaks form. In a 10-inch skillet heat water to simmering. Drop egg mixture in 6 portions into water. Simmer, uncovered, about 5 minutes or till firm. Lift meringue puffs from water; drain on paper towels and place on waxed paper. Chill, uncovered, in the refrigerator till serving time.

Meanwhile, thaw cherries, if frozen. Cut cherries in half. In a medium saucepan stir together the ¼ cup sugar and cornstarch. Stir in apricot nectar. Cook and stir till thickened and bubbly; cook and stir for 2 minutes more. Gently stir in cherries, *1 teaspoon* of the orange peel, and orange sections. Cover and chill in the refrigerator till serving time. At serving time, spoon fruit mixture into 6 individual dessert dishes. Top each with a meringue puff. Sprinkle with remaining orange peel. Makes 6 servings.

For a meringue that fluffs rather than flops, follow these simple rules. Start with a clean bowl and beaters. Then beat the egg whites till soft peaks form (tips curl) before adding sugar. Beating the egg whites too much or too little before adding the sugar may give you less than the best possible volume.

After gradually adding the sugar, continue beating the egg whites just till glossy stiff peaks form (tips stand straight). Beat the whites too much at this stage and the baked meringue will be dull; beat the whites too little and the meringue will shrink excessively after baking.

·QUICK RECIPE·
CRUNCHY TOPPER

Serve this make-ahead topper on fresh or frozen fruit, ice milk, or sherbet.

2 **tablespoons all-purpose flour**
2 **tablespoons shredded coconut**
2 **tablespoons brown sugar**
2 **tablespoons chopped walnuts**
   Dash ground cinnamon
1 **tablespoon margarine**

In a small mixing bowl stir together flour, coconut, brown sugar, walnuts, and cinnamon. Cut in margarine till mixture resembles coarse crumbs. Spread evenly in the bottom of a foil-lined 9x5x3-inch loaf pan. Bake in a 350° oven for 8 to 10 minutes or till brown. Cool slightly at room temperature. Crumble mixture. Cover and store in the refrigerator for up to 2 weeks or in the freezer for up to 2 months. Makes ¾ cup (12 servings).

Healthy Fruit Options: When you crave your favorite fruit, the canned or frozen forms are tasty, year-round options. For low-calorie canned fruits, choose juice pack, water pack, or calorie-reduced pack (slightly sweetened). Or, drain regular syrup-pack fruits and rinse them with water before using. For low-calorie frozen fruits, look for the unsweetened loose-pack variety.

CHERRY COBBLER

Remember to spoon the batter onto a HOT cherry filling. That way, the biscuit topper cooks more quickly and evenly.

1 **cup all-purpose flour**
1 **tablespoon sugar**
1 **teaspoon baking powder**
¼ **cup margarine**
1 **slightly beaten egg**
¼ **cup skim milk**
4 **cups fresh *or* frozen unsweetened pitted tart red cherries**
⅓ **cup sugar**
⅓ **cup water**
1 **tablespoon quick-cooking tapioca**

For biscuit topper, stir together flour, the 1 tablespoon sugar, and baking powder. Cut in margarine till flour mixture resembles coarse crumbs. In a small mixing bowl stir together egg and skim milk. Add milk mixture all at once to the flour mixture, stirring just to moisten. Set aside.

For cherry filling, in a medium saucepan combine cherries, the ⅓ cup sugar, water, and tapioca. Let stand for 5 minutes, stirring occasionally. Cook and stir till bubbly.

Turn hot cherry filling into an 8x1½-inch round baking dish or a 1½-quart casserole. Immediately spoon biscuit topper atop the cherry filling to form 8 mounds. Bake in a 400° oven about 20 minutes or till a wooden toothpick inserted in center of topper comes out clean. Serve warm. Makes 8 servings.

·QUICK RECIPE·

ORANGE-YOGURT FRUIT

½ **of an 8-ounce carton (½ cup) vanilla low-fat yogurt**
¼ **teaspoon finely shredded orange peel**
2 **medium oranges, sectioned**
2 **cups sliced strawberries**

In a small mixing bowl stir together yogurt and orange peel. Arrange oranges and strawberries on 4 small plates. Spoon some of the yogurt mixture atop each. Makes 4 servings.

APRICOT-SAUCED BAKED APPLES

Apple varieties especially good for baking include Rhode Island Greening, Rome Beauty, Baldwin, Jonathan, McIntosh, Winesap, and Granny Smith.

4 **large baking apples**
½ **cup finely snipped dried apricots**
1 **5½-ounce can (¾ cup) apricot nectar**
2 **tablespoons brown sugar**
¼ **teaspoon ground allspice**

Core apples; peel off a strip around the top of each. Place apples in a 10x6x2-inch baking dish. Fill apples with apricots.

In a small saucepan stir together apricot nectar, brown sugar, and allspice. Bring to boiling. Pour nectar mixture over apples. Bake, covered, in a 350° oven 30 minutes. Uncover and bake about 30 minutes more or till apples are tender, basting occasionally with nectar mixture. Serve warm. Makes 4 servings.

·QUICK RECIPE·

POACHED PEARS

The pears you use should be ripe but still firm. Too-ripe pears won't stand up as well after they're cooked.

½ **of a medium lemon**
1 **cup water**
¼ **cup sugar**
2 **teaspoons lemon juice**
2 **large pears**

Use a citrus zester or vegetable peeler on lemon half to cut very fine julienne strips of peel. In a 10-inch skillet combine lemon peel, water, sugar, and lemon juice. Bring to boiling.

Meanwhile, halve pears lengthwise, leaving stem attached to one half. Carefully remove core, leaving stem attached. Use a sharp knife to cut pear into thin slices, cutting almost but not quite to stem. Place pear halves, skin side up, in sugar mixture in the skillet.

Bring to boiling; reduce the heat. Cover and simmer about 10 minutes or till pears are just tender. Use a slotted spoon to carefully remove pears from the skillet. Place pears on 4 dessert plates. Gently boil sugar mixture in the skillet for 4 to 5 minutes or till reduced to ¼ cup. Spoon sugar mixture over pears. Makes 4 servings.

SUMMER FRUIT PARFAITS

½ **of an 8-ounce package Neufchâtel cheese, softened**
2 **tablespoons skim milk**
1 **tablespoon honey**
½ **teaspoon finely shredded lemon peel**
2 **medium peaches, peeled, pitted, and cut into ½-inch chunks**
1 **tablespoon lemon juice**
2 **cups seedless grapes, halved**
½ **cup blueberries**

In a small mixer bowl beat Neufchâtel cheese, milk, honey, and lemon peel with an electric mixer on medium speed till smooth. Cover and chill in the refrigerator till serving time.

Toss peaches with lemon juice. In 4 wine-glasses layer grapes, peaches, and blueberries. Drizzle with chilled mixture. Serves 4.

BAKED PAPAYA

The papaya, a tropical fruit resembling a pear-shaped melon, has a delicate but rich flavor.

1 **large papaya (1¼ pounds)**
1 **tablespoon water**
1 **tablespoon lime juice**
1½ **teaspoons finely chopped crystallized ginger**

Cut papaya in half lengthwise. Peel and remove seeds. Cut into 1-inch pieces. Place papaya pieces in a 1-quart casserole. In a 1-cup measure stir together water, lime juice, and ginger. Pour over papaya; toss to coat well. Bake, covered, in a 375° oven for 15 to 20 minutes or till heated through, stirring twice. Makes 4 servings.

WHITE MOUSSE with FRESH FRUIT

Treat dinner guests to this citrus mousse topped with your choice of fruits—strawberries, orange sections, kiwi fruit, and/or seedless grapes.

1 **cup skim milk**
1 **envelope unflavored gelatin**
¼ **cup honey**
1 **teaspoon finely shredded orange *or* lemon peel**
1 **8-ounce carton plain low-fat yogurt**
2 **cups fresh fruit cut into ½-inch pieces**

In a medium saucepan stir milk into gelatin. Let stand for 5 minutes. Cook and stir over medium heat till gelatin is dissolved. Remove from the heat. Stir in honey and orange or lemon peel. Cool slightly; stir in yogurt till smooth. Pour into 6 individual molds. Cover and chill in the refrigerator about 3 hours or till set. To serve, unmold gelatin mixture onto 6 dessert plates. Spoon fresh fruit over each serving. Makes 6 servings.

Stock the cookie jar with Honey-Pecan Cookies, Triticale-Oatmeal Cookies, *and* Cocoa Macaroons *(see recipe, page 186).*

TRITICALE-OATMEAL COOKIES

Nonstick spray coating
¾ **cup quick-cooking rolled oats**
½ **cup all-purpose flour**
½ **cup triticale flour**
1 **teaspoon finely shredded orange peel**
½ **teaspoon baking soda**
½ **cup margarine**
½ **cup packed brown sugar**
1 **egg**
¼ **cup raisins**

Spray 2 cookie sheets with nonstick spray coating. Set aside. In a medium mixing bowl stir together rolled oats, all-purpose flour, triticale flour, orange peel, and baking soda. Set aside. In a large mixer bowl beat margarine with an electric mixer on medium speed for 30 seconds. Add brown sugar; beat till fluffy. Add egg; beat well. Stir in dry ingredients. Stir in raisins.

Drop from a teaspoon 2 inches apart onto the prepared cookie sheets. Bake in a 350° oven for 8 to 10 minutes or till done. Let cool on the cookie sheets for 1 minute. Remove from the cookie sheets; cool on wire racks. Makes 24 cookies (12 servings).

HONEY-PECAN COOKIES

½ **cup margarine**
¼ **cup honey**
1 **teaspoon vanilla**
1 **cup whole wheat flour**
¼ **cup toasted wheat germ**
¾ **cup finely chopped pecans**
Nonstick spray coating

In a large mixer bowl beat margarine with an electric mixer on medium speed 30 seconds. Add honey and vanilla; beat well. Add flour and wheat germ; beat well. Stir in pecans.

Divide dough in half; roll each half between 2 pieces of waxed paper to ⅜-inch thickness. Place dough flat in the freezer on a cookie sheet for 10 minutes. Spray 2 cookie sheets with nonstick spray coating. Working with half of the dough at a time, remove waxed paper. Use a 2-inch cookie cutter to cut dough into desired shapes. Reroll, freeze, and cut out dough scraps. Transfer to a prepared cookie sheet. Repeat with remaining dough. Bake in a 325° oven for 9 to 11 minutes or till done. Let cool on the cookie sheet for 1 minute. Remove from the cookie sheet; cool on a wire rack. Makes 24 cookies (12 servings).

OATMEAL-PEAR COOKIES

1 **large pear, peeled and cored**
1 **cup all-purpose flour**
½ **teaspoon baking powder**
½ **teaspoon baking soda**
¼ **cup shortening**
¼ **cup margarine**
⅓ **cup sugar**
⅓ **cup packed brown sugar**
2 **egg whites**
½ **teaspoon vanilla**
1 **cup quick-cooking rolled oats**

Chop pear to make ¾ cup. In a small bowl combine flour, baking powder, and baking soda. In a large mixer bowl beat shortening and margarine with an electric mixer on medium speed for 30 seconds. Add sugars; beat till fluffy. Add egg whites, vanilla, and 2 tablespoons *water;* beat well. Stir in flour mixture, oats, and pear. Drop from a teaspoon 2 inches apart onto an *ungreased* cookie sheet. Bake in a 375° oven for 9 to 10 minutes or till done. Remove from the cookie sheet; cool on a wire rack. Makes 36 cookies (18 servings).

You can freeze cookies "for a rainy day" either unbaked or baked. To freeze unbaked cookies, pack the dough in freezer containers or shape stiff dough into rolls and wrap securely in foil. Freeze for up to six months. To freeze baked cookies, place cookies in a single layer in the freezer about 1 hour or just till frozen. Transfer cookies to freezer containers, freezer bags, or foil. Return to the freezer for up to 12 months. (Pack fragile cookies in freezer containers.) Before serving, thaw cookies in freezer wrappings.

PEANUT BUTTER-OATMEAL COOKIES

To keep a "skin" from forming on top of the pudding as it cools, place a piece of clear plastic wrap or waxed paper directly on the surface of the hot pudding.

½ **cup all-purpose flour**
½ **cup quick-cooking rolled oats**
¼ **teaspoon baking soda**
¼ **cup margarine**
¼ **cup peanut butter**
½ **cup packed brown sugar**
1 **egg**
2 **tablespoons skim milk**
¼ **teaspoon vanilla**
2 **tablespoons chopped unsalted peanuts**
2 **tablespoons sifted powdered sugar**
1 **teaspoon unsweetened cocoa powder**
1 **to 2 teaspoons skim milk**

Combine flour, oats, and baking soda. Set aside. In a small mixer bowl beat margarine and peanut butter with an electric mixer on medium speed for 30 seconds. Add brown sugar; beat till fluffy. Add egg, the 2 tablespoons milk, and vanilla; beat well. Add dry ingredients, beating at low speed till combined. Spread in an 8x8x2-inch baking pan. Sprinkle with peanuts. Bake in a 350° oven for 20 to 25 minutes or till done. Cool.

In a small mixing bowl combine powdered sugar and cocoa powder. Add enough milk to make of drizzling consistency. Drizzle over cookies. Cut into bars. Makes 16 servings.

MOCHA PUDDING

¼ **cup sugar**
2 **tablespoons cornstarch**
2 **tablespoons unsweetened cocoa powder**
2 **teaspoons instant coffee crystals**
2 **cups skim milk**
1 **teaspoon vanilla**

In a heavy small saucepan combine sugar, cornstarch, cocoa powder, and coffee crystals. Stir in milk. Cook and stir over medium heat till bubbly. Cook and stir for 2 minutes more. Remove from the heat. Stir in vanilla.

Pour into a medium mixing bowl. Cover surface with clear plastic wrap. Chill in the refrigerator till serving time, without stirring. To serve, spoon into individual dessert dishes. Makes 4 servings.

BANANA PUDDING

For a lower cholesterol and sodium version of the classic recipe, we eliminated the egg and salt, and substituted skim milk for milk.

⅓ **cup sugar**
2 **tablespoons all-purpose flour**
1 **cup skim milk**
1 **tablespoon margarine**
½ **teaspoon vanilla**
1 **medium banana**
4 **teaspoons chocolate-flavored syrup**

For pudding, in a heavy small saucepan stir together sugar and flour. Stir in milk all at once. Cook and stir over medium heat till thickened and bubbly. Cook and stir for 1 minute more. Remove from the heat. Stir in margarine and vanilla.

Slice banana into 4 individual dessert dishes. Spoon pudding atop. Cover surface with clear plastic wrap. Chill in the refrigerator till serving time. Drizzle with chocolate-flavored syrup. Makes 4 servings.

SPICED RICE PUDDING

Whipped dessert topping gives extra-creamy texture to this rice pudding.

  2 **cups skim milk**
  2 **tablespoons sugar**
⅛ **teaspoon ground cinnamon**
⅛ **teaspoon ground nutmeg**
⅓ **cup long grain rice**
¼ **cup chopped mixed dried fruit**
  2 **teaspoons margarine**
¼ **cup frozen whipped dessert**
     topping, thawed

In a heavy medium saucepan bring milk, sugar, cinnamon, and nutmeg to boiling. Stir in rice and fruit. Cover; cook over low heat about 30 minutes or till most of the milk is absorbed, stirring occasionally. (Mixture may appear curdled.) Stir in margarine. Cool thoroughly. Fold in whipped dessert topping. Cover and chill in the refrigerator till serving time. Spoon into 4 individual dessert dishes. Makes 4 servings.

CHOCOLATE CUSTARDS

Instead of using four whole eggs, these cholesterol-curbed custards call for eight egg whites.

  8 **egg whites**
  2 **cups chocolate-flavored low-fat milk**
¼ **cup sugar**
  1 **teaspoon vanilla**
     Boiling water

In a large mixing bowl use a fork or wire whisk to lightly beat egg whites. Stir in milk, sugar, and vanilla. Place six 6-ounce custard cups in a 13x9x2-inch baking pan on an oven rack. Pour milk mixture into the custard cups.

Pour boiling water into the pan around the custard cups to a depth of 1 inch. Bake in a 325° oven for 25 to 35 minutes or till a knife inserted near the center comes out clean. Serve warm or chilled. To unmold chilled custards, loosen edges with a spatula or knife; slip point of spatula or knife down sides to let air in. Invert onto a serving plate. Serves 6.

MANGO ICE

Mangoes—one of the first fruits cultivated in India—have a distinctive, spicy flavor.

  1 **medium very ripe mango** *or*
     2 medium very ripe peaches
  2 **tablespoons sugar**
  1 **egg white**
  1 **tablespoon sugar**

Peel mango or peaches. If using mango, cut flesh from seed. If using peaches, remove seed. Cut mango or peaches into chunks. In a blender container or food processor bowl combine mango or peach pieces and the 2 tablespoons sugar; cover and blend till nearly smooth. Set aside.

In a small mixer bowl beat egg white and the 1 tablespoon sugar with an electric mixer on medium speed till stiff peaks form. Lighten mango or peach mixture by stirring in some of the egg white mixture. Fold mango or peach mixture into remaining egg white mixture. Pour into an 8x4x2-inch loaf pan. Cover surface with clear plastic wrap. Freeze about 3 hours or till firm. Scoop mixture with a small ice cream scoop or melon baller into dessert dishes. Makes 4 servings.

PINEAPPLE SHERBET

Because sherbet is made from milk, it's naturally lower in fat than ice cream. Make it with skim milk for an even bigger difference.

- 3 **cups skim milk**
- 1 **15¼-ounce can crushed pineapple (juice pack)**
- ¾ **cup evaporated skim milk**
- 1 **6-ounce can pineapple juice concentrate, thawed**
- ⅓ **cup sugar**
- ½ **teaspoon vanilla**
  Fresh mint (optional)

In a large mixing bowl stir together skim milk, *undrained* pineapple, evaporated milk, pineapple juice concentrate, sugar, and vanilla. Stir till sugar dissolves. Freeze in a 4- or 5-quart ice cream freezer according to manufacturer's directions. Serve scoops in dessert dishes. If desired, garnish with mint. Makes 7½ cups (15 servings).

ORANGE SHERBET

"Lots of zip" and "nice and spunky" were the comments from taste panelists when they sampled this orange-marmalade-sweetened sherbet.

- 1 **envelope unflavored gelatin**
- ¼ **cup cold water**
- ½ **of a 6-ounce can (⅓ cup) frozen orange juice concentrate, thawed**
- ½ **cup orange marmalade**
- 2 **8-ounce cartons vanilla low-fat yogurt**
  Orange slices, halved (optional)

In a small saucepan soften gelatin in cold water. Let stand for 5 minutes. Cook and stir till gelatin is dissolved. Stir in orange juice concentrate. Remove from the heat. Stir in marmalade. Stir in yogurt.

Turn yogurt mixture into a 9x9x2-inch baking pan; cover and freeze about 3 hours or till firm. With a fork break frozen mixture into chunks; place in a large chilled mixer bowl. Beat with an electric mixer on medium speed till fluffy. Return to pan. Cover and freeze at least 2 hours or till firm. Serve scoops in dessert dishes. If desired, garnish with orange slices. Makes 4 cups (8 servings).

·QUICK RECIPE·

BLUEBERRY-ORANGE SUNDAES

- 2 **tablespoons sugar**
- 1½ **teaspoons cornstarch**
- ½ **cup orange juice**
- 1 **tablespoon margarine**
- ½ **cup blueberries**
- 1⅓ **cups ice milk**
- 1 **medium banana**

In a small saucepan stir together sugar and cornstarch. Add orange juice. Cook and stir till thickened and bubbly. Cook and stir for 2 minutes more. Remove from the heat. Stir in margarine till melted. Stir in blueberries.

Place scoops of ice milk in 4 individual dessert dishes. Slice some of the banana over each serving. Spoon some blueberry-orange mixture over each. Makes 4 servings.

Which are you more concerned about—cutting calories or cutting fat? Here are some tips to help you make the best frozen dessert choice. To cut calories, choose ice milk. It has 199 calories per cup, compared with 257 calories in sherbet and 259 calories in ice cream. To cut fat, however, sherbet (with 2 grams fat per cup compared to 7 grams in ice milk and 14 grams in ice cream) is a better choice.

Got the urge for a snack? Try satisfying your snacking mood

with reduced-fat recipes, such as Thick Banana Milk Shakes

(see recipe, page 207) or Cranberry-Orange Dip with fruit

(see recipe, page 198).

SNACKS & BEVERAGES

CHAPTER 6

Snacks and thirst-quenchers can make or break your plans to eat wisely. The "makers" will boost your nutrient intake and tide you over until mealtime. The "breakers" will shoot your salt, fat, and sugar intake sky-high and ruin your appetite for a wholesome meal.

On the following pages you'll see scores of the good kind of snacks and beverages—homemade crackers and other munchables, spreads, dips, appetizer soups, frozen pops, fruit drinks, and milk shakes. Choose from elegant appetizers to informal grab-it snacks. Any will please hungry party guests, whether your guests are health-conscious or not.

CONTENTS

	PER SERVING							PERCENT U.S. RDA PER SERVING							
	CALORIES	PROTEIN (g)	CARBOHYDRATES (g)	FAT (g)	CHOLESTEROL (mg)	SODIUM (mg)	POTASSIUM (mg)	PROTEIN	VITAMIN A	VITAMIN C	THIAMINE	RIBOFLAVIN	NIACIN	CALCIUM	IRON
Banana-Melon Appetizer Soup (p. 197)	110	3	13	6	17	100	389	5	67	72	3	5	3	4	2
Carrot-Cheese Ball (p. 203)	58	2	2	5	15	100	61	4	22	6	1	3	0	4	1
Chicken-Curry Spread (p. 203)	46	4	1	2	15	78	64	7	2	1	1	3	7	3	1
Chili-Cheese Popcorn (p. 202)	114	3	10	7	2	133	56	5	10	1	3	2	2	5	2
Chocolate Pops (p. 203)	113	2	21	3	9	45	117	4	2	2	2	6	1	8	2
Chunky Radish Dip (p. 198)	35	2	1	3	9	52	62	2	3	4	0	2	0	2	1
Cranberry-Orange Dip (p. 198)	86	1	21	1	1	18	166	2	2	9	4	4	2	4	1
Dilly Dip (p. 200)	39	3	1	2	2	126	32	5	1	0	0	3	0	2	1
Fresh Tomato Juice Cocktail (p. 207)	32	2	7	0	0	69	320	2	19	48	5	3	4	3	6
Fruit-Cheese Dip (p. 200)	53	2	3	4	12	65	51	3	4	2	1	2	0	1	0
Fruit Cooler (p. 206)	65	3	13	0	1	48	102	5	2	34	2	7	1	5	1
Grapefruit Cooler (p. 205)	169	1	42	0	0	2	325	2	1	92	8	3	3	2	3
Gruyère-Apple Spread (p. 205)	66	4	2	5	14	82	38	6	4	1	1	3	0	8	0
Hot Chili-Cheese Dip (p. 198)	62	2	9	2	3	53	74	3	7	31	3	2	2	6	4
Hot Harvest Cider (p. 206)	116	1	29	0	0	11	258	1	1	24	3	2	1	3	5
Mexican Hot Chocolate (p. 207)	115	6	23	1	3	111	314	10	7	3	4	14	1	21	4
Nifty Nachos (p. 201)	95	5	12	3	8	77	72	8	9	51	3	4	3	15	5
Orange-Wheat Crackers (p. 201)	109	2	14	5	0	109	63	3	4	6	6	2	3	3	4
Oriental Fruit Soup (p. 197)	56	0	12	0	0	3	127	0	0	63	1	1	0	1	2
Rosy Berry Punch (p. 206)	97	0	25	0	0	1	64	1	1	20	1	1	1	1	2
Sage-Pork Pâté (p. 205)	35	4	2	1	22	21	68	6	21	4	4	10	5	1	3
Spicy Party Mix (p. 200)	133	4	13	8	2	156	78	6	3	9	10	2	14	3	8
Stuffed Mushrooms (p. 197)	47	2	7	2	0	53	285	3	19	6	7	19	15	1	4
Thick Banana Milk Shakes (p. 207)	141	7	28	1	4	155	476	11	9	15	4	14	4	12	2
Toasty Sesame Crackers (p. 201)	48	2	6	2	4	35	27	3	1	0	5	3	2	2	3
Tortilla Fruit Rolls (p. 202)	69	1	17	0	0	5	97	2	8	1	1	1	2	3	4

BANANA-MELON APPETIZER SOUP

This cold soup is a rich, fruity start to your meal.

> 3 cups cubed ripe cantaloupe
> 1 ripe small banana, sliced
> 1 tablespoon lemon juice
> ½ of an 8-ounce package Neufchâtel cheese, cut up
> 1 teaspoon poppy seed
>   Thin cantaloupe slices (optional)

In a blender container or food processor bowl place cubed cantaloupe, banana, and lemon juice. Cover and blend till smooth, scraping sides of container as necessary. Gradually add Neufchâtel cheese, blending after each addition till combined. Stir in poppy seed. Cover and chill in the refrigerator at least 1 hour. If desired, garnish with cantaloupe slices. Makes 2½ cups (5 servings).

·QUICK RECIPE·

ORIENTAL FRUIT SOUP

The skin of gingerroot wrinkles with age. So, look for a tuber with a smooth outer skin.

> ¾ cup apple juice
> 1 tablespoon dry sherry
> 2 thin slices gingerroot
> 2 thin apple slices (optional)
>   Fresh mint (optional)

In a medium saucepan stir together apple juice, sherry, gingerroot, and ¼ cup *water*. Bring to boiling. Reduce heat; cover and simmer for 1 minute. Remove the gingerroot and discard. Ladle soup into 2 small bowls. If desired, float an apple slice and fresh mint atop each serving. Makes 1 cup (2 servings).

STUFFED MUSHROOMS

Fines herbes (pronounced FENE zerb) is an herb blend. The combination of herbs varies but often includes parsley, tarragon, basil, thyme, and chives.

> 24 very large fresh mushrooms (2½ to 3 inches in diameter)
> ½ cup sliced green onion
> ½ cup finely shredded carrot
> ½ teaspoon fines herbes, crushed
> 1 tablespoon margarine
> ¼ cup Grape Nuts cereal
>   Nonstick spray coating
>   Paprika (optional)

Remove stems from mushrooms; reserve. Simmer mushroom caps in a small amount of boiling water for 2 minutes. Drain mushroom caps; invert caps onto paper towels. Cool. Finely chop stems to make about 1 cup. (Reserve remaining stems for another use.)

In a small saucepan cook and stir chopped mushroom stems, green onion, carrot, and fines herbes in margarine till onion is tender. Stir in cereal. Spray a shallow baking pan with nonstick spray coating. Spoon some of the mushroom mixture into each mushroom cap; place in the baking pan. Sprinkle with paprika, if desired. Bake, covered, in a 425° oven for 12 to 15 minutes or till heated through. Makes 24 (8 servings).

Keep Stuffed Mushrooms hot when serving them to a crowd by just heating one plateful at a time. Then, as the first round disappears, pull the next round piping hot from the oven. Or, you can use an electric skillet, hot tray, griddle, or bun warmer to keep them warm right at the serving table.

CRANBERRY-ORANGE DIP

Look for cranberry-orange relish in the freezer section of your supermarket.

  1 **8-ounce carton lemon** *or*
       orange low-fat yogurt
  ½ **cup cranberry-orange relish**
  ¼ **teaspoon ground nutmeg**
  ¼ **teaspoon ground ginger**
  1 **medium apple**
  1 **medium nectarine**
       Lemon juice
  2 **cups seedless grapes**
  1 **cup fresh pineapple cut into**
       chunks *or* **one 8¼-ounce can**
       pineapple chunks, drained

For dip, in a small mixing bowl stir together yogurt, cranberry-orange relish, nutmeg, and ginger. Cover and chill.

Just before serving, core apple and remove pit from nectarine. Slice apple and nectarine; brush with lemon juice. Serve dip with apple slices, nectarine slices, grapes, and pineapple chunks. Makes 1¼ cups (10 servings).

CHUNKY RADISH DIP

  ¾ **cup finely chopped red radishes**
  ½ **of an 8-ounce package Neufchâtel**
       cheese, softened
  ¼ **cup plain low-fat yogurt**
  1 **teaspoon prepared horseradish**
  ¼ **teaspoon dried dillweed**
       Dash garlic powder
       Assorted fresh vegetable dippers,
       low-sodium crackers, *or*
       breadsticks

For dip, in a small mixing bowl stir together radishes, cheese, yogurt, horseradish, dill-weed, and garlic powder. Cover and chill in the refrigerator at least 1 hour. Serve dip with fresh vegetable dippers, low-sodium crackers, or breadsticks. Makes 1¼ cups (10 servings).

HOT CHILI-CHEESE DIP

  8 **7-inch flour tortillas**
  1 **medium onion, chopped (½ cup)**
  2 **cloves garlic, minced**
  2 **teaspoons cooking oil**
  3 **large tomatoes, peeled, seeded,**
       and chopped
  1 **4-ounce can green chili peppers,**
       rinsed, seeded, and chopped
  ½ **teaspoon chili powder**
  ¼ **teaspoon bottled hot pepper sauce**
  1 **tablespoon cornstarch**
  1 **tablespoon cold water**
  ½ **cup shredded American cheese**
       (2 ounces)

For tortilla wedges, stack tortillas. Cut whole stack into 8 wedges to make 64 wedges total. Spread evenly in a single layer on 2 medium baking sheets. Bake in a 375° oven for 10 to 15 minutes or till wedges are dry and crisp. Transfer tortilla wedges to a rack to cool.

For dip, in a medium saucepan cook onion and garlic in hot oil till tender but not brown. Stir in tomatoes, chili peppers, chili powder, and hot pepper sauce. Boil gently, uncovered, over medium heat for 10 minutes, stirring occasionally. Stir together cornstarch and water; stir into tomato mixture. Cook and stir till thickened and bubbly. Cook and stir for 2 minutes more. Stir in cheese till melted. Serve dip warm with tortilla wedges. Makes 2 cups (16 servings).

The dipping mainstays— celery and carrot sticks—are conspicuously absent from our list of healthy vegetable dippers. Why? Because with 50 mg sodium per stalk of celery and 34 mg sodium per carrot, the two vegetables are higher in sodium than some other dippers.

Better choices are fresh mushrooms, cherry tomatoes, radishes, green pepper strips or rings, zucchini or cucumber spears, and green onions. Or, try crisp-cooked kohlrabi sticks, asparagus spears, or cauliflower or broccoli flowerets (you can serve them raw, too).

·QUICK RECIPE·
DILLY DIP

For an especially colorful trayful of dippers and dip, serve this creamy dip in a hollowed green pepper.

> 1 **cup low-fat cottage cheese**
> ¼ **cup reduced-calorie mayonnaise** *or* **salad dressing**
> 2 **teaspoons dried dillweed**
> 1 **tablespoon finely chopped green onion**
> 1 **to 2 teaspoons skim milk (optional) Assorted fresh vegetable dippers, low-sodium crackers,** *or* **breadsticks**

In a blender container or food processor bowl combine cottage cheese, mayonnaise or salad dressing, and dillweed. Cover and blend till smooth. Stir in green onion. If desired, stir in milk till of desired consistency. Serve with vegetable dippers, low-sodium crackers, or breadsticks. Makes 1⅓ cups (10 servings).

FRUIT-CHEESE DIP

This dip doubles as a delicious topper for fresh fruit.

> 1 **8-ounce package Neufchâtel cheese, softened**
> 1 **small banana, mashed**
> ¼ **teaspoon ground nutmeg**
> ½ **cup canned crushed pineapple** *or* **finely chopped fresh fruit, well drained Apple wedges, pear wedges, strawberries,** *or* **other fruit dippers**

In a small mixing bowl stir together Neufchâtel cheese, banana, and nutmeg till smooth. Stir in crushed pineapple or chopped fruit. Cover and chill in the refrigerator at least 1 hour. Serve with apple wedges, pear wedges, strawberries, or other fruit dippers as desired. Makes 1¾ cups (14 servings).

SPICY PARTY MIX

> 3 **cups bite-size shredded rice** *or* **corn squares cereal**
> 3 **cups bite-size shredded wheat squares cereal**
> ¾ **cup unsalted peanuts**
> ⅓ **cup cooking oil**
> ½ **teaspoon bottled hot pepper sauce**
> ⅓ **cup grated Parmesan cheese**
> 1 **teaspoon chili powder**
> ¼ **teaspoon garlic powder**
> 2 **cups chow mein noodles** *or* **unsalted pretzels**

In a large shallow baking pan combine shredded rice or corn squares cereal, shredded wheat squares cereal, and peanuts. In a 1-cup measure stir together cooking oil and hot pepper sauce. Drizzle oil mixture over cereal mixture, tossing to coat evenly.

In a small mixing bowl stir together Parmesan cheese, chili powder, and garlic powder. Stir into cereal mixture. Bake in a 300° oven for 20 minutes, stirring after 10 minutes. Stir in chow mein noodles or pretzels. Bake for 10 minutes more. Makes 7½ cups (20 servings).

NIFTY NACHOS

Each ounce of purchased tortilla chips contains 6.2 grams fat, compared to 1 gram fat in homemade tortilla wedges.

- **5 8-inch flour tortillas**
- **2 medium tomatoes, peeled, seeded, and chopped**
- **1 4-ounce can diced green chili peppers, drained**
- **½ teaspoon chili powder**
  Several dashes bottled hot pepper sauce
- **1 cup shredded mozzarella cheese (4 ounces)**

For tortilla wedges, stack tortillas. Cut whole stack into 8 wedges to make 40 wedges total. Spread evenly in a single layer on 2 medium baking sheets. Bake in a 375° oven for 10 to 15 minutes or till wedges are dry and crisp.

Meanwhile, combine tomatoes, chili peppers, chili powder, and hot pepper sauce. Spoon tomato mixture over wedges; top with cheese. Broil, 1 baking sheet at a time, 4 to 5 inches from heat about 1½ minutes or till cheese is melted. Slide onto a serving platter. Serve at once. Makes 40 nachos (8 to 10 servings).

TOASTY SESAME CRACKERS

To crisp crackers that have been around awhile, spread on a baking sheet; place in a 300° oven 5 to 10 minutes or just till warm. (Pictured on page 18.)

- **1 cup all-purpose flour**
- **3 tablespoons sesame seed, toasted**
- **2 tablespoons toasted wheat germ**
- **⅛ teaspoon salt**
- **3 ounces Neufchâtel cheese**
- **4 to 5 tablespoons water**

In a medium mixing bowl stir together flour, sesame seed, wheat germ, and salt. Using a pastry blender, cut in Neufchâtel cheese till mixture resembles coarse crumbs. Stir in water, 1 tablespoon at a time, till mixture is moistened. Form into a ball.

On a well-floured surface roll dough, half at a time, to a thickness of about 1/16 inch. Cut into 2-inch squares. Prick squares with a fork. Place on an ungreased baking sheet. Bake in a 350° oven for 12 to 15 minutes or till golden. Makes 72 crackers (18 servings).

ORANGE-WHEAT CRACKERS

These tasty wheat crackers have about half the calories and a third of the sodium of their off-the-shelf counterpart—graham crackers.

- **1 cup all-purpose flour**
- **1 cup whole wheat *or* rye flour**
- **¼ cup packed brown sugar**
- **2 teaspoons baking powder**
- **1 teaspoon finely shredded orange peel**
- **⅛ teaspoon salt**
- **½ cup margarine**
- **⅔ cup orange juice**

In a medium mixing bowl stir together all-purpose flour, whole wheat or rye flour, brown sugar, baking powder, orange peel, and salt. Using a pastry blender, cut in margarine till mixture resembles coarse crumbs. Stir in orange juice, 1 tablespoon at a time, till mixture is moistened. Form into a ball.

On a well-floured surface roll out dough, half at a time, to 1/16 inch. Use a floured 2½-inch round cookie cutter to cut crackers. Prick with a fork. Place on an ungreased baking sheet. Bake in a 350° oven for 12 to 15 minutes or till golden. Makes 72 crackers (18 servings).

After you cut out the crackers, use a fork to prick the dough three or four times to make about 16 small holes in each cracker. Without the holes, air and steam will build up during baking and cause the crackers to puff.

TORTILLA FRUIT ROLLS

**1 6-ounce package mixed dried fruit
    bits**
½ cup water
¼ cup sugar
**¼ teaspoon ground cinnamon
    Dash ground nutmeg**
**8 6-inch flour tortillas, cut in half
    Skim milk**

To fill Tortilla Fruit Rolls, *spoon a rounded tablespoon of the cooled fruit mixture along the cut edge of each tortilla half to within ½ inch of the ends. Starting from the cut edge, roll up each tortilla half.*

In a small saucepan combine fruit, water, sugar, cinnamon, and nutmeg. Bring to boiling. Remove from heat; cover and let stand about 15 minutes or till cool, stirring occasionally.

Meanwhile, wrap tortilla halves tightly in foil; heat in a 350° oven for 10 minutes. Remove *half* of the tortilla halves from foil; keep remaining tortilla halves wrapped till needed.

Spoon about 1 tablespoon of the fruit mixture along cut edge of each tortilla half; roll up. Brush curved edge with milk; press gently to seal. Place tortilla rolls, seam side down, about 1 inch apart in a 15x10x1-inch baking pan. Brush lightly with milk. Bake in a 350° oven about 15 minutes or till edges begin to brown. Makes 16 (16 servings).

·QUICK RECIPE·

CHILI-CHEESE POPCORN

Plain buttered popcorn seems ho-hum next to this zippy rendition.

2 tablespoons unpopped popcorn
1 tablespoon grated Parmesan cheese
½ teaspoon chili powder
**   Dash garlic powder**
1 tablespoon margarine, melted

In a heavy skillet pop popcorn, covered, over medium-high heat, using no oil and shaking constantly till all popcorn is popped. (This should make about 4 cups popped popcorn.)

Stir together Parmesan cheese, chili powder, and garlic powder. Stir in margarine. Pour over popcorn. Toss till well coated. Makes 4 cups (2 servings).

CHOCOLATE POPS

Use regular milk instead of skim milk. The added fat is necessary for a creamy, smooth frozen texture.

- ½ **cup sugar**
- 3 **tablespoons unsweetened cocoa powder**
- 2 **tablespoons cornstarch**
- 2 **tablespoons brown sugar**
- 2 **cups milk**
- 1 **teaspoon vanilla**
- 8 **3-ounce paper drinking cups**
- 8 **wooden sticks**

In a medium saucepan stir together sugar, cocoa powder, cornstarch, and brown sugar. Stir in milk. Cook and stir over medium heat till thickened and bubbly. Cook and stir 2 minutes more. Remove from heat; pour into a medium bowl. Stir in vanilla. Cover surface with clear plastic wrap; let cool at room temperature for 30 minutes without stirring.

Pour mixture into cups; insert sticks. Place in the freezer at least 2 hours or till firm. To serve, peel off cups. Makes 8 (8 servings).

CARROT-CHEESE BALL

- ½ **cup sliced carrot**
- 3 **tablespoons finely chopped green onion**
- 2 **tablespoons grated Parmesan cheese**
- ¼ **teaspoon dry mustard**
- ⅛ **teaspoon garlic powder**
- ⅛ **teaspoon ground red pepper**
- 1 **8-ounce package Neufchâtel cheese, softened**
- ⅓ **cup snipped parsley**
  Melba rounds, cucumber slices, *or* **zucchini slices**

In a small saucepan cook carrot, covered, in a small amount of boiling water for 15 to 20 minutes or till very tender. Drain. Mash carrot till nearly smooth. Stir in onion, Parmesan cheese, mustard, garlic powder, and red pepper. Stir in Neufchâtel cheese. Chill, covered, in the refrigerator for 2 hours.

Shape into a ball, then roll in parsley. Chill, covered, in the refrigerator at least 2 hours more or till firm. Serve with melba rounds, cucumber slices, or zucchini slices. Makes 1¼ cups (12 servings).

CHICKEN-CURRY SPREAD

Because not all yogurt is low-fat, you'll need to check the label carefully when looking for this product.

- 1 **cup finely chopped cooked chicken (5 ounces)**
- ½ **of an 8-ounce package Neufchâtel cheese, softened**
- 3 **tablespoons finely chopped green onion**
- 1 **tablespoon Dijon-style mustard**
- 1½ **teaspoons curry powder**
- ½ **cup plain low-fat yogurt**
  Melba rounds *or* **rye bread**

In a small mixing bowl stir together chicken, Neufchâtel cheese, onion, mustard, and curry powder. Stir in yogurt. Serve as a spread with melba rounds or rye bread. Makes 1¾ cups (14 servings).

Soften Neufchâtel cheese to make it easier to combine with other ingredients. Just let an 8-ounce package stand at room temperature for 30 minutes to 1 hour. When you're on a tighter schedule, soften the cheese quickly by stirring it vigorously. Or, if you own a microwave oven, unwrap the cheese and place it in a microwave-safe bowl. Micro-cook, uncovered, on 100% power (HIGH) for 15 to 20 seconds or till softened.

Gruyère-Apple Spread, Sage-Pork Pâté, *and* Hot Harvest Cider *(see recipe, page 206) make great autumn party go-togethers.*

GRUYÈRE-APPLE SPREAD

½ of an 8-ounce package Neufchâtel cheese
1 cup shredded Gruyère cheese (4 ounces)
½ cup low-fat cottage cheese
¼ teaspoon dry mustard
1 small apple, cored and shredded
2 tablespoons finely chopped pecans
1 to 2 tablespoons skim milk (optional)
2 teaspoons snipped chives
Low-sodium crackers

Bring Neufchâtel cheese and Gruyère cheese to room temperature. In a small mixer bowl combine the Neufchâtel cheese and Gruyère cheese; beat with an electric mixer on medium speed till nearly smooth.

Add cottage cheese and dry mustard; beat on medium speed till combined. Fold in apple and pecans. If necessary, stir in milk till of desired consistency. Transfer to a small serving bowl. Sprinkle chives atop. Cover and chill in the refrigerator at least 1 hour. Serve with crackers. Makes 2 cups (16 servings).

SAGE-PORK PÂTÉ

¾ pound lean ground pork
1 medium onion, chopped (½ cup)
2 cloves garlic, minced
¼ pound beef liver, cut up
¾ cup skim milk
2 egg whites
2 tablespoons fine dry bread crumbs
1 tablespoon cornstarch
1 teaspoon dried sage, crushed
Nonstick spray coating
1 radish, sliced (optional)
Chives (optional)
Low-sodium crackers

In a medium skillet cook pork, onion, and garlic till pork is browned. Add liver; cook and stir over high heat about 3 minutes or till liver is no longer pink. Drain well. Let cool for 10 minutes. In a blender container or food processor bowl combine pork mixture and milk. Cover and blend till smooth. Add egg whites, bread crumbs, cornstarch, sage, ¼ teaspoon *salt*, and ¼ teaspoon *pepper*. Cover and blend till smooth.

Spray a 7½x3½x2-inch loaf pan or a 3-cup ovenproof mold with nonstick spray coating. Transfer pork mixture to the pan or mold. Cover with foil. Place the loaf pan or mold in a shallow baking pan. Pour *hot water* around the pan to a depth of ½ inch. Bake in a 325° oven about 1 hour or till knife inserted near center comes out clean. Cool; cover and chill in the refrigerator several hours or overnight. Unmold. If desired, garnish with a sliced radish and chives. Serve with crackers. Makes 2½ cups (25 servings).

·QUICK RECIPE·

GRAPEFRUIT COOLER

1 6-ounce can frozen grapefruit juice concentrate, thawed
1 6-ounce can unsweetened pineapple juice
1 tablespoon sugar
1 28-ounce bottle ginger ale, chilled
Ice cubes
Fresh mint (optional)

In a large pitcher stir together thawed grapefruit juice concentrate, pineapple juice, and sugar. Slowly pour in ginger ale; stir gently to mix. Serve immediately over ice cubes. Garnish each serving with mint, if desired. Makes 5 cups (5 servings).

The nutrition analyses for dips and spreads (page 196) include the nutritional content of the dippers—either two low-sodium crackers per tablespoon of dip or spread, or ¼ cup vegetables or fruit per tablespoon of dip.

·QUICK RECIPE·
ROSY BERRY PUNCH

For a beverage that's hard to match, pour a glass of the original whistle wetter— water. And to make your glass of water even more refreshing, serve it over ice with a mint sprig or a lemon slice.

Pictured on the cover.

> 2 10-ounce packages frozen raspberries *or* strawberries, partially thawed
> 1 6-ounce can frozen pink lemonade concentrate, thawed
> 1 28-ounce bottle ginger ale, chilled
> Ice cubes *or* ice ring
> Lemon slices (optional)

In a punch bowl stir together *undrained* raspberries or strawberries and lemonade concentrate. Slowly pour in ginger ale; stir gently to mix. Add ice. Garnish with lemon slices, if desired. Makes 7 cups (12 to 14 servings).

·QUICK RECIPE·
FRUIT COOLER

Choose your favorite frozen fruit juice concentrate— grape, orange, apple, or pineapple—to make this slushy, hot weather drink.

> 1 cup skim milk
> 1 6-ounce can frozen grape, orange, apple, *or* pineapple juice concentrate
> 4 egg whites
> ¼ cup water
> 10 *or* 11 ice cubes (2½ cups)

In a blender container combine skim milk, frozen juice concentrate, egg whites, and water; cover and blend till well combined. Add ice cubes, one at a time through opening in the lid, blending till smooth. Makes 5½ cups (7 servings).

HOT HARVEST CIDER

To make this cider ahead, cover and refrigerate after straining. Later, just stir in remaining ingredients and heat. (Pictured on page 204.)

> 3 cups water
> ½ cup packed brown sugar
> 1 small orange, thinly sliced
> 6 inches stick cinnamon
> 1 teaspoon coriander seed
> 1 teaspoon whole allspice
> 1 teaspoon whole cloves
> 1 whole nutmeg
> 3½ cups water
> 1 12-ounce can frozen apple juice concentrate
> 1 6-ounce can frozen pineapple juice concentrate
> 2 tablespoons lemon juice
> Cinnamon sticks (optional)

In a large kettle or Dutch oven stir together the 3 cups water and brown sugar. Add orange slices, the 6 inches stick cinnamon, coriander seed, allspice, cloves, and nutmeg. Bring mixture to boiling. Cover; reduce heat and simmer for 20 minutes.

Strain; return liquid to the saucepan. Add the 3½ cups water, apple juice concentrate, pineapple juice concentrate, and lemon juice. Cook till heated through, stirring often. Serve with additional cinnamon sticks, if desired. Makes 9 cups (12 servings).

THICK BANANA MILK SHAKES

You'll find it's easier to peel and cut up bananas before you freeze them. (Pictured on the cover and on page 199.)

1¼ cups skim milk
2 medium bananas, peeled, cut up, and frozen
1 cup chopped fresh or frozen peaches *or* strawberries *or* 1 cup fresh or frozen blueberries
½ cup low-fat cream-style cottage cheese
1 tablespoon honey
5 large ice cubes

In a blender container or food processor bowl combine milk; bananas; peaches, strawberries, or blueberries; cottage cheese; and honey. Cover and blend till smooth, adding ice gradually. Makes 4 cups (4 servings).

MEXICAN HOT CHOCOLATE

¼ cup unsweetened cocoa powder
¼ cup water
3 tablespoons honey
2 tablespoons brown sugar
½ teaspoon finely shredded orange peel
¼ teaspoon ground cinnamon
1 quart skim milk
½ teaspoon vanilla
   Cinnamon sticks (optional)

In a medium saucepan combine cocoa powder, water, honey, brown sugar, orange peel, and ground cinnamon. Cook and stir over medium heat about 2 minutes or till smooth. Gradually stir in milk; heat just to simmering. *Do not boil.* Remove from heat. Stir in vanilla. Pour into 6 cups. If desired, serve with cinnamon-stick stirrers. Makes 4 cups (6 servings).

FRESH TOMATO JUICE COCKTAIL

Here's a vegetable drink that doubles as a zippy appetizer and as a nonalcoholic cocktail.

1 medium cucumber
3 large ripe tomatoes, cut up (1½ pounds total)
2 teaspoons lemon juice
½ teaspoon sugar
½ teaspoon Worcestershire sauce
⅛ teaspoon celery salt
   Few dashes bottled hot pepper sauce
   Dash onion powder
   Dash ground cloves
   Ice cubes (optional)

Halve cucumber lengthwise. Using half of the cucumber, cut it lengthwise into quarters. Cut 2 of the quarters into 1-inch pieces. Halve remaining 2 quarters crosswise to use as stirrers. (Reserve the remaining half of the cucumber for another use.)

In a blender container or food processor bowl place tomatoes; cover and blend till smooth. Add 1-inch cucumber pieces; cover and blend till smooth. Strain tomato mixture, pressing through a sieve to remove solids. Discard solids.

Stir lemon juice, sugar, Worcestershire sauce, celery salt, hot pepper sauce, onion powder, and cloves into tomato mixture. Cover and chill in the refrigerator or serve over ice cubes. Serve with cucumber-stick stirrers. Makes 2⅔ cups (4 servings).

THE GOOD AND BAD OF CAFFEINE AND ALCOHOL

Both caffeine and alcohol have been consumed in all kinds of societies in all parts of the world for centuries on end, yet people still debate about their value or harm. Scientifically, the two are in fact quite different. Caffeine mildly stimulates the central nervous system and alcohol depresses it.

No one needs to be told where caffeine appears in the daily diet. It is a key constituent in coffee, tea, and chocolate. Most recently, attention has been paid to its presence in soft drinks, especially colas, which are favored by children. Caffeine is the country's basic pick-me-up, and terms like "coffee break" and "kaffeeklatsch" have passed into the language—as has "teatime" in Britain.

Caffeine apparently does not work directly on the nervous system. Rather, it apparently blocks the action of a naturally occurring sedative compound called adenosine. By preventing the sedative action, it keeps us awake; it also is said to enhance mental performance. Although college students cramming for exams might agree, the claims do not stand up in controlled experiments.

Caffeine has been linked repeatedly to various forms of disease, but the findings have just as frequently been challenged. Moderate to heavy coffee drinkers were said to have more cancer of the pancreas, but later studies could not confirm the association. A pair of research papers presented at the same scientific meeting showed that caffeine consumption increased the chances of heart attack because it increased blood pressure and the heart's workload—while it also delayed the onset of chest pains in persons with heart disease. Another study has shown that depressed persons are more likely to be coffee drinkers—but it is said that drinking coffee may be the patients' way of coping with their illness, rather than a cause of it.

All of which has caused the U.S. Code of Federal Regulations to list caffeine as a multi-purpose GRAS substance—Generally Recognized As Safe. It appears in the U.S. National

Academy of Sciences/National Research Council reference text of substances as a flavoring agent and stimulant.

The evidence against alcohol is more compelling. Heavy users of beer, wine, and spirits have an increased risk of cancer, heart disease, brain damage, and liver damage. Alcohol is associated with half the motor-vehicle deaths in the U.S. and with a substantial proportion of violent acts, from homicide to arson. It even affects the unborn: A child born to an alcoholic mother has a characteristic dish-faced appearance and retarded mental and physical development. Even an expectant mother who drinks only moderately may have a low birth-weight child.

The Dietary Guidelines of the U.S. Department of Health and Human Services are emphatic on the subject: If you use alcohol, do so in moderation.

But as even the ancients knew, alcohol in small amounts—*in moderation*—can have a tonic effect on the heart and circulation, and research laboratories are now beginning to explain why. Alcohol apparently enhances the production of so-called "good cholesterol"—high-density lipoproteins, or HDL. Middle-aged men who drank one glass of wine a day have been shown to have higher HDL levels—and, presumably, greater protection against heart attack—than heavier drinkers or nondrinkers. With increased amounts, the benefits were offset by risk of other diseases.

Nutritionists point out that alcohol in all forms consists of "empty" calories—calories which put on weight but do not provide any essential nutrients. A single glass of wine for its health benefits is recommended by many health and fitness programs.

And a good way to enhance the flavor of foods is to use wine in cooking. The small amount of alcohol rapidly burns off, leaving behind the taste and bouquet. Several main-dish and dessert recipes in this book use wine as a flavoring and seasoning.

Couscous Seafood Salad is a good start toward a balanced

intake of all four food groups. (See recipe, page 62.)

EAT A VARIETY OF FOODS

CHAPTER 7

Variety in food is important to good nutrition, but it isn't that hard to achieve. Most of us eat a variety of foods every day, without thinking about it. If you pick different foods from within the four food groups, you'll get the nutrients you need. And over a period of days, you should achieve a balanced diet and come out right.

CONTENTS

ariety is not only the spice of life but the basis of a sound diet. The Recommended Dietary Allowances (RDAs) demonstrate that we need various nutrients in various amounts. But figures aren't always easy to translate into food on the plate. Hence nutritionists have devised food groups to help blend the right amounts of the right foods into a daily diet.

The best known of these food group plans is called the Basic Food Groups, and is illustrated in the photo *at right.* Food is classified into categories, with recommended daily servings of four groups.

Group 1 includes milk and milk products, including cheese, yogurt, cottage cheese, and ice cream. These foods provide calcium, protein, riboflavin, and thiamine. Adults need two cups or the equivalent a day; children, teenagers, and pregnant women, four cups; nursing mothers, six.

Group 2, meat and meat substitutes, includes beef, veal, pork, lamb, poultry, fish, eggs, and nuts and legumes. These furnish protein, iron, riboflavin, niacin, and thiamine. We need two or more servings a day.

Group 3, fruits and vegetables, gives us vitamin A, vitamin C, thiamine, iron, and riboflavin. We need four or more servings a day—a good source of vitamin C, such as citrus fruit, every day; a good source of vitamin A, such as carrots, broccoli, or cantaloupe, at least every other day.

Group 4, breads and cereals, includes rice, all baked goods, and pasta. They provide riboflavin, niacin, iron, and thiamine. We need four or more servings a day.

As nutritionists agree, these four groups have some flaws. For one thing, some popular foods aren't listed, even though they provide nutrients. Butter, margarine, salad dressing, and mayonnaise are dumped into a miscellaneous category that also includes soft drinks and alcohol (sometimes called a fifth food group). Another problem is that some dishes just don't fit neatly into any group—soup is an example. Finally, the Basic Food Groups stresses eating, rather than restricting intake. If you dutifully followed the program, you'd wind up consuming more than 2,300 calories a day, not exactly a weight-loss diet.

Another classification is called the Food Exchange Lists. It groups foods into six categories—milk, vegetable, fruit, bread, meat, and fats. Within each group, foods are grouped that have a similar nutrient content: A slice of bread or a small potato, for instance, has about the same amount of carbohydrate and protein, and each provides about 70 calories, so they can be exchanged for each other.

The exchange system also includes foods that needn't be counted, because they have negligible calories. They include diet drinks, coffee, tea, bouillon without fat, unsweetened pickles, garlic, lemon, lime, most condiments, and raw vegetables such as chicory, Chinese cabbage, endive, escarole, lettuce, parsley, and radishes. Some of these should be restricted for other reason, though. Pickles, for instance, are high in sodium.

This exchange system, worked out by the American Dietetic Association, American Diabetes Association, and several government agencies, doesn't prescribe daily servings but allows you and a diet counselor to tailor a meal plan according to your tastes and needs, and can be the basis for a weight-loss diet.

A modified Four Food Group Plan was suggested after new RDAs were listed for vitamins E and B_6, zinc, and magnesium. The new plan, proposed in the Journal of Nutrition Education but not yet widely adopted, suggests two daily servings of milk and milk products; two servings of meat, fish, or poultry; two servings of legumes; four servings of fruits and vegetables; four servings of whole-grain products; and one serving of fat or oil.

We hear and read so much about vitamins in pill form that we sometimes forget what vitamins really are: organic compounds found in food that help to facilitate key body processes and compounds that the body cannot make for itself. As the table at the right shows, there are 13 vitamins, each with its task to fulfill, each readily available in common foods. Vitamins come in two forms—water soluble and fat soluble. Vitamin C and all the B vitamins are water

	VITAMIN	FUNCTIONS
FAT SOLUBLE	A	Maintains mucous membranes and inner organs, helps build bones and teeth; promotes vision.
	D	Promotes absorption of calcium for strong bones and teeth.
	E	Prevents oxidation of essential vitamins, fatty acids. Needed for red blood cells, muscles, and tissues.
	K	Essential for blood clotting.
WATER SOLUBLE	Thiamine	Assists in release of energy from carbohydrates; helps synthesize nerve-regulating substances; promotes appetite.
	Riboflavin	Maintains skin and eye tissue; needed for energy release from macronutrients.
	Niacin	Works with thiamine and riboflavin to produce energy reactions in cells.
	Pyridoxine (B_6)	Participates in absorption and metabolism of fats and proteins; helps in formation of red blood cells.
	Cobalamin (B_{12})	Needed for building of genetic material and functioning of nervous system.
	Folic acid (Folacin)	Helps to form body proteins and genetic material; promotes growth; needed for formation of hemoglobin in blood.
	Pantothenic acid	Needed for metabolism of macronutrients, formation of hormones and nerve-regulating substances.
	Biotin	Needed for formation of fatty acids, release of energy from carbohydrates.
	C	Helps maintain bones, teeth, and blood vessels; helps form structural collagen.

DEFICIENCY SYMPTOMS	SOURCES
Night blindness, rough skin, poor bone growth, cracked and decayed teeth.	Carrots, broccoli, squash, spinach, liver, egg yolk, milk and dairy products.
Stunted growth, bowed legs, malformed teeth in children. Osteomalacia (bone loss) in older adults.	Fish, milk, eggs. Made in skin by direct exposure to sunlight.
Breakdown of red blood cells.	Green leafy vegetables, vegetable oil, whole-grain cereals and breads, liver.
Hemorrhage (especially in children).	Cabbage, brussels sprouts, kale; other green leafy vegetables; milk.
Mental confusion, muscular weakness, swelling of heart, leg cramps.	Pork, liver, oysters, cereals, nuts, legumes.
Skin disorders and cracking around lips; eye sensitivity to light.	Dark green vegetables, whole grains, pasta, mushrooms, milk, eggs, meat, fish.
Pellagra, diarrhea, mental confusion, irritability, skin disorders (especially in parts exposed to sun).	Poultry, meat, fish, tuna, peanut butter, dried beans and peas.
Skin disorders, smooth tongue, convulsions, dizziness, nausea, anemia.	Avocados, spinach, green beans, bananas, whole-grain cereals.
Pernicious anemia; degeneration of peripheral nervous system.	Kidneys, meat, fish, eggs, milk, oysters.
Anemia with large red blood cells, smooth tongue, diarrhea.	Dark green leafy vegetables, fruits, soybeans.
Not known in humans.	Nuts, eggs, liver, kidneys, whole-grain bread and cereal, dark green vegetables, yeast.
Not known in humans.	Egg yolk, liver, kidneys, green beans.
Scurvy: gums bleed, muscles degenerate, wounds don't heal, teeth loosen.	Citrus fruits, strawberries, tomatoes, melons, green pepper, potatoes.

soluble; they are readily absorbed by the body and just as readily excreted, which means they cannot be stored and (with the exception of B_{12}) must be replenished every day. The fat-soluble vitamins A, D, E, and K must be utilized in a much more complicated manner and, once in the cells, tend to become stored there. That means that they can accumulate in the body with life-threatening results, although few persons consume them in such large quantity.

Unlike vitamins, which are mere helpers in body processes, minerals become part of the human structure itself. They are not transformed as the body utilizes them and in many cases resemble the minerals taken from the ground. The table lists the minerals we need, where they are found in food, and the role they play in the body. We need seven of them in relatively large quantity, led by calcium and phosphorus for bones and teeth, and the electrolytes sodium, potassium, magnesium, and chlorine, which help to

	MINERAL	FUNCTIONS
MINERALS	**Calcium**	Needed for strong bones and teeth, muscle contraction, and normal heart rhythm, blood clotting, transmission of nerve impulses.
	Phosphorus	Works with calcium to promote strong bones and teeth; also needed for metabolism of fats and carbohydrates.
	Sulfur	Helps build proteins, especially hair, nails, cartilage.
	Chlorine	Part of fluid outside cells. Helps in formation of gastric juice and in digestive process.
	Magnesium	Helps regulate body temperature, nerve and muscle contractions, protein synthesis. Activates enzymes in carbohydrate metabolism.
	Sodium	Regulates water balance, muscle contraction, nerve irritability. Major component of fluid outside cells.
	Potassium	Works with sodium to promote fluid balance, regulate muscle contraction and heart rhythm. Major constituent of fluid within cells.
TRACE MINERALS	**Iron**	Part of hemoglobin in blood. Transports and transfers oxygen in blood and tissues.
	Iodine	Main constituent of thyroid hormones, which regulate basal metabolism and influence growth and development.
	Copper	Acts with iron to synthesize hemoglobin in red blood cells; helps form nerve walls and body's connective tissue.
	Zinc	Component of insulin and digestive enzymes; needed for protein metabolism.
	Fluorine	Component of strong teeth; prevents decay. May also be necessary for strong bones and to prevent bone loss in adults.
	Chromium	Metabolism of glucose and protein, synthesis of fatty acids and cholesterol, insulin metabolism.
	Selenium	Works with vitamin E to protect cells against oxidative damage.
	Molybdenum	Essential for function of certain enzymes, especially those needed in production of uric acid.

DEFICIENCY SYMPTOMS	SOURCES
In children, stunted growth and poor bone formation. In adults, bone loss and brittle bones.	Milk, cheese, small fish eaten with bones, dried beans and peas, dark green vegetables.
Rare in humans. Weakness, pain of bones.	Liver and kidneys, meats, fish, eggs, milk and dairy products, nuts and legumes.
Not known in humans.	Eggs, meat, milk and cheese, nuts, legumes.
Vomiting and diarrhea.	Table salt (sodium chloride).
Rare except in alcoholics or persons on limited diet. Weakness, tremors, dizziness, spasm.	Green leafy vegetables, whole grains, nuts, beans. (Magnesium may be lost in processing of packaged or canned foods.)
Deficiency is rare. Excess believed a factor in high blood pressure.	Salt, salted foods, soy sauce, monosodium glutamate, baking powder, cheese, fish, shellfish, poultry, eggs.
Muscle weakness, nausea, rapid heartbeat, possible eventual heart failure.	Fresh fruits (especially oranges, cantaloupe, bananas), dark green vegetables, liver, meat, fish, poultry, milk.
Faulty digestion, anemia, cell damage.	Liver, eggs, lean meat, legumes, whole grains, green leafy vegetables.
Goiter (enlarged thyroid). Birth defects in children if the mother is thyroid-deficient in early pregnancy.	Iodized salt, seafood, vegetables grown near the sea, butter, milk, cheese, eggs.
Unknown in adults. May cause anemia in infants. Excess: Wilson's disease, a metabolic defect.	Found in most foods *except* dairy products. Good sources: organ meats, shellfish, cocoa.
Rare in U.S. Can cause growth retardation, poor wound healing. Excess: nausea, vomiting, fever.	Wheat germ and bran, whole grains, legumes, nuts, lean meats, fish.
Tooth decay; possible bone loss in older persons. Excess: mottled teeth.	Water, either naturally or artificially added.
Poor use of glucose.	Corn oil, brewer's yeast, meats, whole grains.
Unknown in humans. Excess (shown in animals): nerve damage.	Seafoods, kidney, liver, some grains, depending on soil in which grown.
Not known in humans. Excess: loss of essential copper; gout-like syndrome with high uric acid.	Meat, grains and legumes.

maintain the body's fluid balance. Others are needed in far smaller amounts, but are no less vital. Minerals can accumulate in the body and some of them (including iron, copper, and selenium) can be dangerous if consumed in quantity.

Water is essential to our diets, and provides minerals necessary for good health.

Nearly two-thirds of the human composition is water; maintaining that proportion is even more important than eating the right foods. Water bathes the tissues, lubricates the joints, carries nutrients to the cells and takes the wastes away, and is built into the structures of many chemical compounds. But it is not just an inert lubricant or transport mechanism: Water makes possible the breakdown of disaccharides into two glucose molecules, for instance, by contributing hydrogen to each.

SOURCES OF WATER

We need two quarts of water daily. That seems like a prodigious amount of drinking, but in fact most of us don't take it all from the water cooler. Most comes from other liquids such as coffee, tea, soups, and soft drinks and from vegetables and fruits. Lettuce, for instance, is nearly 90 percent water. The supply is constantly being turned over as it passes out of the body via urine, feces, and perspiration. Keeping the body's fluids balanced is a delicate matter. That is why sodium, which regulates the transport of fluids into and out of the cell, is so important in the diet.

As every schoolchild learns, water consists of two parts of hydrogen to one part of oxygen. But the stuff we drink usually contains other substances as well. In some areas, a substantial percentage of the RDA for minerals may come in drinking water. To begin with, chlorine is added to most public water supplies for purification purposes, and fluoride to prevent tooth decay. Other minerals are found in greater or lesser amounts. Hard water, as every suds-seeking homemaker knows, is rich in calcium. Soft water is soft because it is laced with sodium. Recent studies have indicated that cardiovascular disease is more prevalent in soft-water areas, so the government now requires that public water supplies be tested for sodium content, for the protection of those with high blood pressure.

Concern over possible pollution of the water supply by chemical contaminants has caused many people to turn to bottled "spring" water. Whether this water is actually more healthful is unknown; some contains high sodium, so read labels carefully.

WHAT GOOD ARE VITAMIN PILLS?

Americans spend hundreds of millions of dollars annually to buy vitamin capsules, minerals, dietary supplements, and synthetic forms of various nutrients. Are they healthier as a result? The answer is a qualified but emphatic no.

Nutritional study after nutritional study has shown that eating a balanced diet provides all the vitamins and minerals we need; if anything, most Americans get more than enough. The complaint that foods are stripped of vitamins by modern processing doesn't hold up, either; canned and packaged foods provide their share of nutrients. And, as we have seen, most vitamins can't be stored in the body. Thus, most vitamin pills just pass innocuously, if expensively, through the body.

There are exceptions. A person on a very low-calorie, weight-loss diet may need vitamin supplementation because the quantities of food are so small that it is difficult to balance nutrients in proper amounts. But this is a matter for a diet specialist. Pregnant women usually need calcium, iron, and folic acid supplementation. Premenopausal women may be given calcium or vitamin D or both to combat osteoporosis, or bone shrinkage. Breast-feeding infants may need vitamin D.

Vitamin C has been touted by the Nobel laureate Linus Pauling for prevention and treatment for the common cold; other scientists dispute his conclusions. Vitamin E has been suggested for conditions ranging from aging to arthritis, but the claims have not received scientific support.

The term "protein" means "in first place," and there can be little doubt of protein's prominence in all biological life. Protein comprises our muscles, forms the framework of our bones, and is the primary component of our hair and fingernails and the lens of the eye. The disease-fighting antibodies are proteins; so are the enzymes. Protein helps the blood to clot and wounds to heal.

TORN APART, PUT TOGETHER

Before these miracles occur, however, some changes occur in most protein we eat. Protein in food consists of giant molecules made up of smaller molecules, called amino acids. Like other organic matter, the amino acids contain carbon, hydrogen, and oxygen, but they also include the element nitrogen. The body takes the protein in food, breaks it down into its constituent amino acids, then breaks it down further and uses the pieces to construct its own proteins. It is a bit like tearing down a colonial house and then reusing the lumber to build a contemporary dwelling on the same foundation and site.

Protein exists in all life, both animal and vegetable. Most of us can list the common sources of protein—beef, veal, lamb, pork, poultry, fish, eggs, milk, cheese, nuts, grains and cereals, beans and peas, and dark green vegetables. For centuries, humans obtained most of their supply from plants. With prosperity has come a shift in protein sources, which some nutritionists blame for the chronic-disease problems of the industrial world. Animal protein is thought to be tastier, and it certainly costs more and carries more prestige, so people who can afford it may turn their backs on beans and rice in favor of sirloin steak. In most cultures, protein accounts for about 10–13 percent of daily calories. Americans used to get half of that figure from plants and half from animals. Today's figures are 69 percent meat, 31 percent vegetables.

Not that animal protein itself is bad; in fact, it is the most concentrated form available. But protein is almost never found alone. It is almost always heavily larded with fat, and even if you trim the visible portions, fat still marbles the protein fibers. In fact it is fat that gives Brie cheese and beef their flavor and their moistness. Protein itself, if you could eat the stuff, is virtually tasteless and somewhat dry. But fat, particularly saturated animal fat, has been closely linked to cardiovascular diseases, so by eating more animal protein we may be increasing our risks of heart disease.

Moreover, the body has no way to store protein for use tomorrow. It must be replenished throughout the day. When the supply is greater than the body's needs, the nitrogen atoms are simply stripped away and flushed off in the urine. The remaining atoms are rearranged and placed in the body's future energy supply. Result: a further load of fat.

THE MYTH OF PROTEIN

Protein also is a substance surrounded by myth. Prizefight trainers and football coaches have traditionally stoked their tigers with red meat before sending them into the arena, in the mistaken belief that protein provides more energy and knockout power. In fact, protein is a poor source of energy. One gram of protein provides four calories, compared to nine calories per gram for fat. However, the body gives first priority to its energy needs, so a meal of protein must be complemented with carbohydrates and fats. Otherwise, the protein will be converted to use as energy, an inefficient process.

How much protein do we need per day? That depends on age, size, and body weight. Growing children need a higher proportion of their

Protein comes from many sources, including meats, cheese, fish, nuts, grains, legumes, and seeds.

calories in protein; persons over the age of 60 need less. The rule of thumb for adults established in the RDAs is 0.8 grams of high-quality protein for each kilogram (2.2 pounds) of ideal body weight. Thus, an adult woman whose ideal weight is 110 pounds requires 40 grams of protein a day. (The RDAs use ideal body weight because weight above that usually is fat, which requires no protein for maintenance.) Most Americans meet their daily protein needs, and then some. In fact, they may meet the requirement in a single meal featuring roast beef.

Is too much protein harmful? It certainly is wasteful: Nitrogen, the unique feature of protein, cannot be used by the body and is simply an expensive residue. Otherwise, an overload of protein does no harm to a healthy person, except possibly pile up fat. In persons with impaired kidneys (often unsuspected), the increased strain of excreting the excess nitrogen can be hazardous. Among the elderly, in whom kidney function declines, a low-protein diet may be recommended.

THE BUILDING BLOCKS OF LIFE

By count, there are 22 amino acids, known as the "building blocks of life." All of them are important for human existence and function. Some can be manufactured within the body itself, using the chemicals available. But others must be obtained from the food we eat, because the body cannot make them. Eight amino acids fall into this category; they are termed the essential amino acids. Their names are isoleucine, phenylalanine and tyrosine, valine, leucine, threonine, tryptophan, lysine and methionine, and cystine.

"Essential" doesn't mean that the other amino acids are less necessary. It does mean that these eight (plus histidine, for growing children) must be present in an adult diet if the body is to have the materials needed to build its own proteins. It is not enough that amino acids be present: they must be in excess of the minimum amount specific for each of the eight and all on hand simultaneously. Since the body can't store amino acids, the essential acids must be part of the same meal.

Three of the amino acids—tryptophan, lysine, and methionine and cystine—are labeled limiting amino acids. Unless these are available in the correct amounts, the value of the others is limited. If a meal contains 100 percent of the requirement for lysine, but only 70 percent of the tryptophan requirement, protein manufacture is limited to 70 percent of need.

A protein that contains all essential amino acids is called a complete protein. A high-quality protein not only is complete, but contains the eight essential amino acids in the optimum proportions for the body's use. And a true high-quality protein is one that also is easily digestible, so that all of it can be broken down into small fragments that can pass through the intestinal wall into the blood.

Egg white protein meets all these standards so successfully that the World Health Organization labels it a reference protein, against which all other protein values are measured. Egg white protein is assigned an arbitrary value of 100. An acceptable protein is one that scores 70 or higher. Fish has a rating of 75 to 90, rice a rating of 86.

Since the body does not utilize protein easily, it is better to eat small amounts at intervals through the day, rather than in one large serving. And one other item about protein on the dinner plate. It should always be eaten with enough calories from fats and carbohydrates so that it will not be used for energy.

PUTTING PROTEINS TOGETHER

Most animal proteins are complete, but most vegetable proteins are not. That doesn't mean vegetable proteins are any less valuable. Indeed, nutrition studies have shown that children grow equally well on meat or vegetable protein diets; however, if you stick to vegetables, you must be more selective in which vegetables you eat.

Fortunately, this idea of complementary proteins, or mutual supplementation, is easier to put in practice than it sounds. People have been doing it for centuries, without thinking about it. The Mexican staple dish of beans with corn tortilla is a classic example. Corn is low in lysine and tryptophan; beans have plenty of both but a scant amount of methionine. Put them together and the protein is as complete as if you were eating steak.

Similarly, the Japanese diet combines rice with tofu and the Chinese diet combines rice with leafy green vegetables. You probably practice mutual supplementation yourself: a peanut butter sandwich on wheat bread is an example of a complete protein. So is the old Southern staple of rice and black-eyed peas.

Virtually all plant products contain some protein, but often in such scant quantities that nutritionists disregard them. (It has been estimated that if you ate nothing but fruit, you would have to consume six pounds at a meal to obtain enough of the right protein.) But some plants are rich protein sources. At the top of the list are plant seeds, especially nuts. Legumes—dried peas, dried beans, lentils, kidney beans (but not fresh peas and beans)—rank next. Soybeans and products made from them, such as soy milk or bean curd, are the closest to an animal protein. Leafy vegetables such as broccoli and cabbage also contain usable protein.

Here are possible combinations to make up complete proteins:

• Leafy vegetables with grains and cereals.

• Legumes with corn, rice, wheat, or sesame.

• Soy with grains, sesame seeds, or peanuts.

Another way to obtain complete protein is to combine vegetable sources with eggs or milk. Many persons who avoid meat, poultry, and fish do this. Again, you may practice this form of mutual supplementation yourself: A complete protein at breakfast is cornflakes and milk. Finally, a time-honored way to obtain complete protein is to combine vegetables with a very small amount of meat—using the meat as a condiment, as Thomas Jefferson once wrote. That's the principle of much Oriental cooking, and you'll find many such recipes in this book.

COMPLEMENTARY PROTEINS

Combine with one or more in same meal

Legumes
Corn
Rice
Wheat
Sesame seeds
Barley
Oats

Rice
Wheat
Legumes
Sesame seeds
Peanuts

Wheat
Legumes
Soybeans and peanuts
Soybeans and sesame seeds
Rice and soybeans

For most of history, people all over the world have followed a vegetarian or near-vegetarian diet—not necessarily by choice. Plant food always has been more abundant than animal sources, and cheaper besides. After a swing toward meat and potatoes, many former beef-eaters are turning back to a simpler diet.

There are three basic forms of vegetarianism. Vegans strictly avoid all forms of animal food and eat only plants. Lactovegetarians allow themselves milk, cheese, and other dairy products. Ovolactovegetarians add eggs to the list. In practice, many other persons follow a vegetarian diet most of the time, while eating chicken or fish occasionally.

No one has ever proved beyond doubt that vegetarianism is healthier, but the evidence is compelling. For instance, Seventh Day Adventists, who follow an ovolactovegetarian regimen, have a far lower rate of heart disease and greater longevity than other Americans. Most countries where a plant diet predominates have lower death rates from heart diseases than meat-and-potatoes America.

Following a pure vegetarian diet isn't easy. Besides being sure to obtain complete protein, vegans must consume sufficient calories as fat and carbohydrate to prevent the protein from being utilized for energy. They also

must be careful about vitamins. B_{12} can be obtained only from fortified soybean milk or vitamin tablets. Without milk, calcium will have to come from dark green vegetables, soybeans, or dried fruits and nuts. Green vegetables also will provide riboflavin.

Here is a four-food-group plan to be recommended for vegetarians:

• Whole grains, breads, or cereals: four servings a day.

• Legumes, nuts, and seeds: two servings a day. (Four tablespoons of peanut butter counts as a serving.)

• Fruits and vegetables. Dark green or yellow vegetables: two servings a day. (Women should have one cup of dark green vegetables a day to meet needs for iron.) Citrus fruit, melon, or strawberries: one or two servings a day. Potato, tomato, cabbage, or spinach: one serving a day.

• Milk or milk products: two servings a day. (Soy milk fortified with B_{12} for vegans.)

You may also wish to add one to two tablespoons daily of vegetable oil or margarine.

Many of the dishes in this book meet vegetarian standards.

Everyone's dietary needs are different, but some are more different than others. At certain times of life, in certain jobs or occupations, because of certain illnesses or physical conditions, people require their own mix of nutrients or total intake of energy. The diet may be followed for only a short time, or for many years. On the next four pages are examples of these special needs.

PREGNANCY DIET

Because she's "eating for two," as the old saying goes, an expectant mother needs about 300 more calories a day than before she was pregnant. These usually come in the form of an additional quart of milk or equivalent dairy products, which also provide the added calcium needed for the developing fetus's bones and teeth. She also needs increased iron and folacin, which usually are given as supplements.

NURSING DIET

A new mother who's nursing a baby needs about 500 more calories than before she was pregnant, about 200 more than during pregnancy. She continues to need a daily quart of milk, but requires proportionately less protein and more vitamin-rich foods. Her diet resembles that of pregnancy—but with differences: Whereas the expectant mother needs about 30 grams a day more protein than before pregnancy, the nursing mother requires less—about 20 additional grams. She also needs less folic acid. However, she should eat more foods rich in vitamins A, E, and C and thiamine, riboflavin, and niacin. She also requires more zinc and iron than during pregnancy and marked amounts more than in her prepregnancy diet.

RUNNER'S DIET

Like many athletes, runners used to mistakenly rely on a high-protein, red-meat-and-milk diet for energy. Sports-medicine specialists now recommend a diet high in complex carbohydrates, because they are absorbed more slowly and provide a supply of glycogen throughout the exercise period. Chicken or fish, which is more easily digested, should substitute for red meat. Runners also are advised to shun the "quick fix" candy bar or soft drink as an energy source.

Long-distance runners usually carry only 4 to 8 percent body fat (contrasted with the average male's 12-26 percent). The runner's daily diet may break down to about 65-70 percent carbohydrates, 10 percent protein (mostly chicken and fish), and the balance in fat. The daily caloric intake of long-distance runners may approach a surprising 3,000 calories.

Although many athletes augment their diets with vitamins, minerals, and other supplements, they are not necessary for improved performance. The recommended way of replenishing vitamins or minerals is by adjusting the diet. Female runners often have amenorrhea—lack of menstrual periods. The condition usually corrects itself with the end of heavy training, or may be corrected by changes in diet.

ALLERGY DIET

Allergies to foods are far less common than people suppose, and when they occur, the allergy is usually to a single food or group of foods that may be readily avoided. (The technique of identifying the food is called an elimination diet, in which one food is removed from the diet at a time until the symptoms— usually digestive upset, occasionally skin soil and plenty of sun. Especially in cold climates, the greenhouse shelters the more delicate perennials, like rosemary, which can be damaged by winter winds.

The flavor in most herbs comes from oil glands in the leaves. Oil production reaches its peak when the plants blossom. Harvest them on a sunny morning, after the dew has dried off, then hang them in bunches or spread in an airy place to dry. When the leaves are crisp, strip them from the stems and store in airtight containers.

Herbs cultivated for their seed (like caraway) are harvested when the seeds begin to lose their green color. After harvesting, the seeds should be shielded from the sun and dried on a hot, low-humidity day. Afterward, they, too, should be stored in airtight containers.

You can harvest most herbs several times a year; pick mint almost continuously during the growing season. A clump of perennials like chives transplanted to a window pot will provide a supply all winter. Some gardener-cooks prefer fresh to dried herbs, which also allows for a constant supply.

Herbs add most zest to home-cooked vegetables but can be used as flavorings in all types of dishes. But remember that most herbs have a strong flavor, and a little goes a long way. Herbs should enhance the natural flavor of food, not overpower it. Season to taste, and remember: You can always add more, but you can't take it away!

	PER SERVING							PERCENT U.S. RDA PER SERVING							
	CALORIES	PROTEIN (g)	CARBOHYDRATES (g)	FAT (g)	CHOLESTEROL (mg)	SODIUM (mg)	POTASSIUM (mg)	PROTEIN	VITAMIN A	VITAMIN C	THIAMINE	RIBOFLAVIN	NIACIN	CALCIUM	IRON
Apple, 1 medium	89	0	23	1	0	0	173	0	2	14	2	1	1	1	2
Asparagus Spears, 1 cup fresh	29	3	5	0	0	1	265	5	26	63	15	15	10	3	5
Banana, 1 medium	109	1	28	1	0	1	471	2	2	18	4	7	3	1	2
Bean Sprouts, ½ cup fresh	18	2	3	0	0	3	117	3	0	17	5	4	2	1	4
Beef Flank Steak, 3 ounces broiled	167	26	0	6	80	45	207	40	0	0	3	12	20	1	18
Beef Sirloin Steak, 3 ounces broiled	176	27	0	7	77	67	307	42	0	0	5	13	27	1	18
Beer, 12 ounces	151	1	14	0	0	25	90	2	0	0	0	6	11	2	0
Beets, ½ cup cooked and diced	30	1	7	0	0	41	198	2	0	10	2	2	1	1	3
Bouillon Granules, 1 teaspoon	5	0	0	0	0	372	6	1	0	0	0	1	0	0	0
Bread, 1 slice white	73	2	14	1	1	137	28	4	0	0	7	4	4	2	4
Broccoli, ½ cup cooked	20	2	3	0	0	8	207	4	39	116	5	9	3	7	3
Bun, 1 hamburger	119	3	21	2	2	202	38	5	0	0	11	6	6	3	6
Butter, 1 tablespoon	102	0	0	12	31	117	4	0	9	0	0	0	0	0	0
Cabbage, 1 cup shredded raw	17	1	4	0	0	14	163	1	2	55	2	2	1	3	2
Cantaloupe, ¼ of a medium	47	1	11	0	0	12	414	2	86	94	3	2	4	1	2
Carrot, 1 medium raw	29	1	7	0	0	33	239	1	154	9	3	2	2	3	3
Cauliflower Flowerets, 1 cup raw	27	3	5	0	0	13	295	4	1	130	7	6	4	3	6
Celery, 1 large stalk	7	0	2	0	0	50	136	1	2	6	1	1	1	2	1
Cheese, 1 ounce American	106	6	0	9	27	406	46	10	7	0	1	6	0	17	1
Cheese, 1 ounce cheddar	114	7	0	9	30	176	28	11	6	0	1	6	0	20	1
Cheese from skim milk, 1 cup cottage	202	31	8	4	19	914	216	48	3	0	4	24	2	15	2
Cheese, 1 ounce Swiss	107	8	1	8	26	74	31	12	5	0	0	6	0	27	0
Chicken, ¼ pound roasted dark meat	234	31	0	11	106	106	274	48	2	0	6	15	37	2	8
Chicken, ¼ pound roasted white meat	188	35	0	4	97	84	292	54	0	0	5	8	78	2	7
Chicken Noodle Soup, 1 cup	74	4	9	2	7	1102	55	6	14	0	4	4	7	2	4
Cucumber, 1 cup sliced	16	1	4	0	0	6	168	1	5	19	2	2	1	3	6
Egg, 1 large poached	79	6	1	6	273	146	65	9	5	0	2	8	0	3	6
Grapefruit, ½ of a medium	38	1	10	0	0	0	167	1	3	69	3	1	2	1	1
Grapes, ½ cup fresh green	55	1	15	0	0	2	166	1	2	6	5	3	1	1	1
Green Beans, ½ cup cooked	16	1	3	0	0	3	95	2	7	13	3	3	2	3	2
Ground Beef, 4 ounces cooked, 10% fat	186	23	0	10	80	57	261	36	0	0	5	12	26	1	17
Halibut, 3 ounces baked	145	21	0	6	51	114	446	33	12	0	3	4	35	1	4
Ice Cream, 1 cup vanilla	271	5	32	14	60	117	259	7	11	0	4	20	1	18	1
Jelly, 1 tablespoon	49	0	13	0	0	3	14	0	0	1	0	0	0	0	2
Lemonade, 1 cup reconstituted frozen concentrate	109	0	28	0	0	0	40	0	0	29	1	1	1	0	0
Lettuce, ¼ of a medium head iceberg	8	1	2	0	0	6	112	1	4	6	3	2	1	1	2
Macaroni, ½ cup cooked	96	3	20	0	0	1	51	5	0	0	1	1	1	1	2
Maple Syrup, 1 tablespoon	69	0	18	0	0	3	48	0	0	0	0	0	0	3	2
Mayonnaise, 1 tablespoon	100	0	0	11	8	80	5	0	1	0	0	0	0	0	0
Milk, 1 cup skim	85	8	12	0	4	126	404	13	10	4	6	20	1	30	1
Milk, 1 cup whole	157	8	11	9	35	119	368	12	7	6	6	23	1	29	1
Mustard, 1 teaspoon prepared	4	0	0	0	0	63	7	0	0	0	0	0	0	0	1

	PER SERVING						PERCENT U.S. RDA PER SERVING							
	CALORIES	PROTEIN (g)	CARBOHYDRATES (g)	FAT (g)	CHOLESTEROL (mg)	SODIUM (mg)	POTASSIUM (mg)	PROTEIN	VITAMIN A	VITAMIN C	THIAMINE	RIBOFLAVIN	NIACIN	CALCIUM	IRON
Nectarine, 1 medium	66	1	16	1	0	0	286	2	20	12	2	3	7	1	1
Noodles, ½ cup cooked	100	3	19	1	25	2	35	5	1	0	7	4	5	1	4
Onions, 6 medium green	14	0	3	0	0	2	69	1	0	13	1	1	1	1	1
Orange, 1 medium	61	1	15	0	0	0	237	2	5	116	8	3	2	5	1
Peanut Butter, 1 tablespoon	93	4	3	8	0	97	104	6	0	0	1	1	12	1	2
Pickle, 1 medium dill	7	0	1	0	0	928	130	1	1	7	0	1	0	2	4
Pickle Relish, 1 tablespoon	21	0	5	0	0	109	31	0	0	2	0	0	0	0	1
Pineapple, 1 cup unsweetened canned	79	1	20	0	0	2	312	2	1	32	15	4	4	4	5
Potato, 1 medium baked	144	4	33	0	0	6	780	6	0	51	10	4	13	1	6
Raspberries, ½ cup red	30	1	7	0	0	0	93	1	2	26	1	3	3	1	2
Rice, ½ cup cooked white	112	2	25	0	0	0	29	3	0	0	8	1	5	1	5
Salad Dressing, 1 tablespoon Russian	60	0	4	5	0	125	9	0	2	0	0	0	0	0	0
Salad Dressing, 1 tablespoon Thousand Island	60	0	2	6	4	112	18	0	1	0	0	0	0	0	1
Shrimp, 3 ounces raw	80	18	0	1	106	107	173	27	1	16	1	2	14	7	8
Spinach, 1 cup chopped raw	14	2	2	0	0	39	259	3	89	47	4	6	2	5	9
Strawberries, 1 cup fresh whole	45	1	10	1	0	1	247	1	1	141	2	6	2	2	3
Tomato, 1 medium ripe	20	1	4	0	0	3	222	2	16	35	4	2	3	1	3
Tomato Soup with milk, 1 cup	163	6	23	6	18	940	453	10	17	114	9	14	8	16	10
Vegetable Soup, 1 cup	80	6	11	2	5	980	178	9	39	4	3	3	5	2	7
Wine, 4 ounces red	91	0	3	0	0	0	0	0	0	0	0	0	0	1	6
Wine, 4 ounces white	101	0	5	0	0	0	0	0	0	0	0	0	0	0	0
Yogurt, ½ cup plain low-fat	79	7	9	2	8	88	292	10	2	2	4	16	1	23	1

RECIPE INDEX

A-B

Tips:

NUTRITION INDEX

rash—subside.) The most frequent allergies are to nuts, eggs, and milk, followed by wheat flour, shellfish, and certain food dyes. (Certain fruits and vegetables, especially tomatoes, are said to cause skin reactions, but some allergists dispute this claim.) A few unfortunates are allergic to more than one food or food group.

THE ANTICANCER DIET

Despite numerous spurious claims, no one can prescribe a diet that will *cure* cancer—and it is dangerous to think so. But the American Cancer Society (ACS) has drawn up a set of nutritional guidelines that, it says, may help to reduce one's chances of getting the disease. The ACS said that some food constituents may cause or promote cancer, while others may protect against it.

Like other organizations, the ACS says that Americans should avoid obesity and eat less fat. The report also makes the following recommendations for the American diet:

• Eat more high-fiber foods.

• Include foods rich in vitamins A and C in the daily diet.

• Eat more cruciferous vegetables such as cabbage, broccoli, brussels sprouts, kohlrabi, and cauliflower.

• Be moderate in consumption of salt-cured, smoked, and nitrite-cured foods.

• Be moderate in consumption of alcohol.

Baked Parmesan Fish Fillets are lower in fat and calories than traditional fried versions. (See recipe, page 111.)

MAINTAIN AN IDEAL WEIGHT

CHAPTER 8

Losing weight is a goal for most of us, but maintaining the loss also is important. That can mean changes in your eating habits, but also in the amount of exercise you get. There's no quick way to get your weight down and keep it there. It should be a lifelong program to stay within sensible limits.

CONTENTS

The human body can be thought of as a machine, similar to the family car. You feed fuel into the mechanism and it performs work. In the case of the car, the fuel is gasoline and the work is a trip to the supermarket. In the case of the human body, the fuel is food and the work is all the activity of daily life—breathing and thinking and exercising.

We measure the fuel in food in terms of calories. Diet propaganda has made "calorie" a dirty word, associated with forbidden and fattening glop that causes clothes to fit too tight, but in fact it is a perfectly objective term of scientific measure. A "calorie" represents the amount of energy required to raise the temperature of one gram of water one degree Celsius. A kilocalorie represents the energy needed to raise a kilogram of water (1,000 grams) by the same temperature. The calories in food are actually kilocalories, often written kcalorie or Calorie, with a capital C, but the two terms continue to be confused. In any event, a calorie stands for the amount of work that can be performed on the basis of a given amount of food that has been eaten.

The amount of fuel the body needs varies at different stages of life. As parents know or their grocery bills soon tell them, teenage boys consume prodigious amounts of food in order to sustain growth and maintain their activities. Proportionately larger amounts of calories also are needed by infants, preadolescents, pregnant women, and nursing mothers. On the other hand, caloric needs gradually taper off with age. A man of 51 can get along on 90 percent of the number of calories he needed 25 years before.

Men, as a group, must consume more calories than women, because their frames usually are larger and contain a higher proportion of lean body mass to fat and water than do the bodies of women. Likewise, the number of calories necessary for an individual is influenced by body size and amount of physical activity. The more exercise you get, and the more weight you carry around, the more fuel you need to keep the machine humming.

As we shall see, we need fuel to power everything we do. Just lying in bed for eight hours, a man consumes 640 calories while his heart beats and blood pumps. On average, about two-thirds of the calories consumed are used up in basic body functions. The balance goes for more strenuous forms of activity, from walking to weight lifting.

How do you get a handle on how many calories you need each day? The Committee on Dietary Allowances of the Food and Nutrition Board, National Research Council, has drafted Recommended Dietary Allowances (RDAs) for daily energy consumption. These are shown on pages 16–17. The energy RDAs, however, are somewhat different from the RDAs for macro- and micronutrients. Like the other RDAs, they are calculated for infants, children, and six age categories of males and females above age 11. But energy RDAs are based on mean heights and weights for each sex at each age level. Whereas the other RDAs are set high enough to meet the needs of virtually all persons in each population group, the energy RDAs represent the *average* needs of people in each category.

Or, as the committee report states: "The energy allowance is established at a level thought to be consonant with good health of average persons in each age group and within a given activity category. A large number of individuals may require less energy than is recommended because they have sedentary work and leisure patterns. For individuals who are already obese, energy intake should be reduced below the suggested levels."

Ideally, the number of calories we consume should roughly match the number we need to keep the machine in proper operation. But for most men, women, and children in laid-back, twentieth-century America, establishing this equilibrium is easier said than done. Surrounded as we are by rich and tempting foods

Grabbing a meal at a fast-food restaurant is a quick way to pile on the calories. Here, according to 1983 figures from the American Council on Science and Health, is the calorie count on some of the popular selections:

Big Mac—563

Whopper w/cheese—740

Filet-o-Fish—432

Kentucky Fried Chicken,

2 pieces, regular—393

2 pieces, crispy—544

Taco Bell Burrito—466

French fries—220

Onion rings—270

Chocolate milk shake—383

Cola—145

Lowfat cottage cheese
63 calories per ½ cup

Peach lowfat yogurt
60 calories per ½ cup

Cheddar cheese
226 calories per 2 ounces

Strawberry ice milk
100 calories per ½ cup

Poached white fish
144 calories per 3 ounces

Roasted chicken
150 calories per 3 ounces

Boiled pinto beans
244 calories per 1 cup

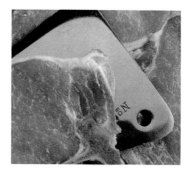

Broiled pork loin chop
251 calories per 3 ounces

Steamed asparagus
15 calories per ½ cup

Orange
64 calories per 1 orange

Banana
101 calories per 1 banana

Steamed corn
70 calories per 1 ear

Whole wheat bread
56 calories per 1 slice

Rye bread
61 calories per 1 slice

Corn bread
211 calories per 1 square

Buckwheat pancakes
292 calories per 2 pancakes

Where should the needle stop when you step on the scales? So-called "ideal" weights differ markedly, depending on how they were calculated. The table on this page was issued in 1983 by the Metropolitan Life Insurance Company, and is based on weights of policyholders with fewest illnesses and longest life. Figures are shown by small, medium, and large frames for both men and women. Height is measured with one-inch heels, and weight with five pounds of indoor clothing. Like other tables, they represent population averages; your ideal weight may differ.

	HEIGHT	SMALL FRAME	MEDIUM FRAME	LARGE FRAME
WOMEN	4'10"	102-111	109-121	118-131
	4'11"	103-113	111-123	120-134
	5'0"	104-115	113-126	122-137
	5'1"	106-118	115-129	125-140
	5'2"	108-121	118-132	128-143
	5'3"	111-124	121-135	131-147
	5'4"	114-127	124-138	134-151
	5'5"	117-130	127-141	137-155
	5'6"	120-133	130-144	140-159
	5'7"	123-136	133-147	143-163
	5'8"	126-139	136-150	146-167
	5'9"	129-142	139-153	149-170
	5'10"	132-145	142-156	152-173
	5'11"	135-148	145-159	155-176
	6'0"	138-151	148-162	158-179
MEN	5'2"	128-134	131-141	138-150
	5'3"	130-136	133-143	140-153
	5'4"	132-138	135-145	142-156
	5'5"	134-140	137-148	144-160
	5'6"	136-142	139-151	146-164
	5'7"	138-145	142-154	149-168
	5'8"	140-148	145-157	152-172
	5'9"	142-151	148-160	155-176
	5'10"	144-154	151-163	158-180
	5'11"	146-157	154-166	161-184
	6'0"	149-160	157-170	164-188
	6'1"	152-164	160-174	168-192
	6'2"	155-168	164-178	172-197
	6'3"	158-172	167-182	176-202
	6'4"	162-176	171-187	181-207

and lured by a life-style that minimizes physical effort, we consistently take in more energy than we are able to burn off.

When we eat, most of the food goes directly to meet the body's immediate needs. As we have seen, carbohydrate contains four calories per gram; being the nutrient most readily processed, it is utilized quickly to satisfy the cell's need for fuel. Protein similarly provides four calories per gram; most of it goes for body-building purposes, although in a pinch, it, too, can be used for energy. Fat contains nine calories per gram. It usually goes into storage for short- or long-term future demands. But all three macronutrients can be stored when not fully needed immediately, and that's where trouble starts.

STORING FUEL

Like any well-thought-out machine, the human body has a fuel storage area—a reserve tank. These are the fat, or adipose, cells. Dietary fat, as well as other nutrients that have been converted into a backstop energy supply, are stored there as a hedge against tomorrow. These cells seem able to expand almost limitlessly to tuck away fat; they apparently increase in numbers, too, as we send them more supplies.

To the despair of the appearance-conscious around the bathing-suit season, a dismaying number of these storage depots are concentrated in the most obvious and least flattering areas—around the waist, thighs, and hips, and in jowls and double chins. Most of us consider the cosmetic consequences of fat storage bad news enough. But as we shall see, there are medical troubles as well.

The ironic part of the unbalanced intake/outgo equation is that the average American consumes fewer calories than did the average American of yesterday. Statistically, caloric intake per capita is down about 10 percent from Grandpa's day—and that is an across-the-board figure, not simply among those who have become health- and weight-conscious. But the difference in physical activity between the generations is marked.

Instead of growing our own vegetables, bending and stooping and lifting to weed and seed, we take a package of frozen corn from the freezer. We don't walk to the neighborhood grocery, we drive (and try to park as near as possible to the entrance). Not many of us dig ditches or chop wood, either as a livelihood or a recreation; we are more likely to sit at a computer terminal. Even our pastimes are more likely to be passive rather than active—television instead of tennis.

With this kind of life-style, it doesn't take much to pile on the pounds. The myth that overweight people are voracious gluttons dies hard, but it is more often sloth, not stuffing yourself, that does you in. In fact, if you exceeded your recommended caloric intake by a mere 84 calories a day, without increasing your activity, you would gain ten pounds in a year. Eighty-four calories a day is about as much as half a banana or two-thirds of a can of cola—hardly an amount you would think about eliminating from your diet.

To lose a pound a week by diet only, you'd have to cut back 3,500 calories—500 calories a day. While not an impossible dream, this regimen would make many of us feel deprived, especially if continued long enough to achieve visible results. It's the reason people abandon diets quickly. Moreover, the fewer calories you consume, the more difficult to bring nutrients into balance.

Thus the most efficient way to reach ideal weight is to tackle both sides of the equation at once. Increase the work you do at the same time you reduce the amount of fuel. Actually, you probably would increase both exercise and intake, but not in equal measure; most serious runners, for instance, consume far more calories than their sedentary contemporaries, yet lose weight until they attain a stable optimum. A two-front attack will bring your weight into a healthy, life-sustaining balance.

How much energy you burn off in a day depends on how vigorously you exercise and on your body size. Here are caloric expenditures for typical activities for a 150-pound individual in an hour. The larger your frame, and the more zip you put into what you're doing, the more calories you'll use up.

ACTIVITY AND CALORIE EXPENDITURE

	Activity	Calories
LIGHT	Lying down or sleeping	**80**
	Sitting	**100**
	Driving an automobile	**120**
	Standing	**140**
	Domestic work	**180**
MODERATE	Walking, 2½ mph	**210**
	Bicycling, 5½ mph	**210**
	Gardening	**220**
	Golf	**250**
	Lawn mowing, power mower	**250**
	Bowling	**270**
	Rowing a boat	**300**
	Walking, 3¾ mph	**300**
	Swimming, ¼ mph	**300**
	Square dancing	**350**
	Volleyball	**350**
	Roller skating	**350**
	Badminton	**350**
VIGOROUS	Table tennis	**360**
	Wood chopping or sawing	**400**
	Ice skating (10 mph)	**400**
	Tennis	**420**
	Water skiing	**480**
	Cross-country skiing, 10 mph	**600**
	Squash and handball	**600**
	Bicycling, 13 mph	**660**
	Running, 10 mph	**900**

HOW MANY CALORIES DO YOU NEED?

Every person's need for calories is different because we all have individual appetites and activity patterns. Here's how the UCLA Center for Health, Enhancement, Education, and Research figures the number of calories you require each day to maintain proper weight:

First, compute your ideal body weight. For women, use the figure of 100 pounds as a base. Add five pounds for every inch of height above five feet. Thus, if you are 5 feet 5 inches tall, use the 100 base figure, add five times five pounds, for a total of 125 pounds. Depending on your frame, your weight should be within 10 percent of that figure—between 113 (slight frame) and 137 (large frame).

Men use the base figure of 106 pounds for five feet of height, then an additional six pounds per inch beyond that. The ideal body weight for a 5-foot-10-inch male would be 166 pounds—106 plus six times ten inches, or 60. Again, weight should be within 10 percent of that figure, depending on body build—150 to 182 pounds.

Now use the weight figure to determine how many calories you should consume.

Ten times your ideal body weight equals the rock-bottom amount necessary just to keep the body operating.

Thirteen times your ideal body weight gives you the number of calories needed to maintain a sedentary life-style, in which you work at a desk job and get very little exercise.

Fifteen times ideal body weight tells the number of calories needed to support a moderate program of exercise.

For example:

A 5-foot-5-inch woman would need 1,250 calories a day to support basic body function (125 pounds x 10 = 1,250); 1,625 calories for a sedentary life-style (125 pounds x 13 = 1,625); 1,875 for a moderate program of exercise (125 pounds x 15 = 1,875).

A 5-foot-10-inch male would need 1,660 calories a day for basic body function (166 pounds x 10 = 1,660); 2,158 for a sedentary regimen (13 x 166 = 2,158); or 2,490 for a moderately vigorous pattern of activity (15 x 166 = 2,490).

These numbers represent the amount of calories you'd have to consume each day to maintain your ideal weight. If you're currently consuming more, lowering your intake to these levels would help you to lose weight.

Remember, however, that weight loss optimally should be a gradual procedure. Cutting the number of calories you consume by 10–20 percent is more likely to be lasting and effective than trying to lose all weight beyond your "ideal" within a few weeks or months. As we shall see, most diets fail because people set unrealistic goals for themselves and quickly revert to their old eating or sedentary habits because they feel deprived or cheated.

Ideal weights usually are given for small, medium, and large frames, but it's sometimes difficult to know your category, especially if you've gained weight with age. One clue is in wrist-bones, where fat doesn't accumulate. Compare the size of your wristbones to others of your sex for a quick analysis of your frame.

Americans are fat and getting fatter. According to the latest national Health and Nutrition Examination Survey (HANES), the average American male weighs four pounds more than his counterpart ten years before, and the average woman, a pound more. The average man carries 20–30 more pounds than he should; the average woman 15–25. Even children are heavier these days. Depending on which standard is used, between one-fourth and one-third of Americans weigh too much.

Nobody in twentieth-century America likes to be fat, but that's not why an obese population should be a matter of concern; in other days and in other societies, weight was considered a mark of beauty. But much more critically, too much weight is a major American health problem—some physicians would say *the* American health problem. Obesity is closely linked to the most serious chronic diseases of contemporary society—heart disease, hypertension, diabetes, stroke, and perhaps some forms of cancer as well. Obese people have more osteoarthritis because of the overload of weight on their joints; they have more accidents and injuries because they are less agile about getting out of the way; they have more respiratory problems and more digestive difficulties. They have more trouble sleeping, and they snore more.

How do we define obesity? It's not simply a matter of being overweight as defined according to the height-weight charts. Anyone who has ever watched a professional football game (or a weight-lifting meet) knows that a human being can carry a prodigious number of pounds and scarcely be labeled obese. If you take the height-weight charts literally, a 6-foot-4-inch, 270-pound defensive tackle is 65 pounds overweight and therefore downright unhealthy. Try to give that kind of news to a sacked quarterback.

The terms overweight and obesity often are used interchangeably, but in fact the conditions are not the same. Obesity really means "overfat." The real standard of measure is the proportion of weight that is composed of fat, as compared to that representing lean muscle, bone, and water. Ideally, a man's body fat should be about 10–15 percent of his total weight, a woman's 15–20 percent (because women store fat around the hips, abdomen, and breasts in preparation for child-bearing). The average male, however, carries about 20 percent fat, the average female 30. Fully one-fourth of the population is higher than that.

OBESITY DEFINED

Generally, doctors define obesity this way: A man is obese if he carries 25 percent or more fat; a woman, if her proportion exceeds 30 percent. Anyone whose weight is 20 percent or more above the recommended amount for his or her height and build also is listed as obese. And anyone who is 50 percent above the recommended levels is morbidly obese.

Many obese people blame their glands or their genes for their pudgy midriffs, and to some degree they may be right. There appears to be no single explanation why some people are fat and some are not. Obesity definitely tends to run in families; members of these families seem to have larger and more numerous fat cells than members of other families. A Danish study of twins reared apart showed that children from obese families raised by thin parents tended to be obese, even though they followed their adopted parents' eating habits. Sex plays a part, too: More women are obese than men. So does age. The older we get up (to a point), the more likely we are to gain weight, as the basal metabolic rate slows down. Some races and nationalities have more obesity than others.

EATING MORE, EXERCISING LESS

Still, none of these fully explains the obesity epidemic. All matters of genes, sex, age, and race aside, obese people have been shown to eat more and exercise less than thinner people. Even the Danish twin studies showed that the heavier twins had bigger appetites and got less exercise than their siblings.

The way obesity produces health problems isn't fully established in all cases, but the association is clear. Hypertension is twice as common among obese persons, diabetes four times as prevalent. The obese are three times as likely to have heart attacks. Various explanations have been offered for the link between weight and disease. In the case of hypertension and coronary disease, it is believed that the heart must work harder and pump blood at a higher velocity in order to provide an adequate supply to the greater number of cells.

As for diabetes, it seems that the additional fat cells place too great a demand on the limited amount of insulin, the hormone that regulates the body's glucose level; glucose thus accumulates dangerously in the blood.

Doctors have been unable to show beyond question that gaining weight automatically predisposes a person to develop hypertension or diabetes. There are skinny victims of both diseases. But evidence is very strong that blood pressure drops, or insulin levels are better controlled, when weight is brought down. However, the association doesn't seem to be a linear one. Blood pressure doesn't automatically rise a given number of points for each pound gained. Rather there seems to be a "threshold weight" above which the health problems dramatically escalate.

But can one be too thin? From the outpouring of diet books and calorie-counting manuals, you wouldn't think so. Yet as the ancient Greeks knew, health is a matter of balance, rather than extremes. Television and popular magazines have familiarized Americans with the compulsive dieter, the young woman who literally starves herself to death in her mania for thinness. (See page 243.)

THERE'S GOOD NEWS (MAYBE)

And now the good news. Residents of Framingham, Massachusetts, have been participating in a long-term, government-supported study of health, illness, and longevity in their community. Recently, officials with the Framingham project were surprised to find that those who lived longest and had the fewest illnesses were slightly overweight by the standard actuarial tables. Persons whose weight was 5 to 10 percent above the recommended figures had better health records than those who were markedly overweight or those who were 10-15 percent underweight.

The Framingham group was cautious in its conclusions. However, they said that it appeared that Americans who were slightly overweight had little to worry about in terms of health.

Instant slimness, like instant riches, is difficult to achieve. America is overloaded with yo-yo fatties who have shrunk themselves to skinnies only to balloon back to their former weights when they return to their old eating and exercise habits. A suspicion is growing in medical circles that the yo-yo, gain-loss-gain cycle may be harmful, disrupting the body metabolism in damaging ways.

NO MIRACLE DIETS

Despite all the books and articles, there is no such thing as a miracle diet that will quickly melt away the pounds and keep them off. Achieving your optimum weight is a lifelong process; scaling down to it, a gradual one. Three elements must be changed: your dinner plate, your exercise pattern, and your way of thinking about food. It is a program that calls for patience, perseverance, and psychological support from family and friends.

There may be an additional reason why successful dieting is so elusive. Some doctors are beginning to suspect that the body has a weight set point, just as it has a temperature set point. By concerted effort you can bring your weight down below the set point, but as soon as you return to normal eating, you are likely to return to the same weight—just as a sauna elevates your body temperature, which then returns to normal when you step outside. Only a prolonged period of diet and exercise can lower the set point, in this view.

The arithmetic of weight gain or loss, as we have seen, is 3,500 calories per pound. To lose a pound you must make a shift of 3,500 calories, either by eating that much less, using up calories through exercise, or a combination of the two. That amounts to a shift of 500 calories a day for a week, not an insurmountable short-term goal as the food diary examples on pages 18–19 show. Many of us could cut out 500 calories daily, about 20 percent of our usual intake, by eliminating the afternoon soft drink, the drink before dinner, and the potato chips while watching television. The trick, of course, is to maintain this regimen day after day without feeling deprived.

The menus and diets throughout this book help to keep weight within desirable bounds. In general, they call for a caloric intake, based on frame and activity level, at about 2,000 calories a day for women and 2,500 a day for men. The guidelines call for larger amounts of carbohydrates to fill you up without mountains of calories, reduced intake of fats, and a sharp cutback in sugars and other sources of empty calories. And they call for greater emphasis on keeping yourself active.

EXERCISE VS. EXERCISING

Exercise is central to maintaining ideal weight, but there is a difference between exer*cise* and exer*cising*. A vigorous daily workout complete with calisthenics and a five-mile run certainly will swallow up the calories, but it also can make you feel martyred—and possibly bored, too. Ordinary activity that you enjoy, practiced on a regular schedule, can be equally helpful. The table on page 236 shows the number of calories burned off through some simple activities. A three-mile walk at a brisk pace can use up the calories you eat at a normal lunch. Duration and regularity of exercise are important. An occasional game of doubles tennis isn't enough. But yard work, weeding, and housework performed at regular intervals can consume calories at a healthy and weight-controlling rate.

TESTING YOURSELF FOR FATNESS

You can estimate the amount of fat your body carries in some rather complicated ways. The most objective method is to weigh the body while it is immersed in water. The amount of water displaced provides a measure of body density. Another technique uses calipers to gauge the thickness of a skinfold at the triceps, on the back of the upper arm. But both these methods are time-consuming, and expensive, and require interpretation by trained personnel. For most of us, they aren't necessary. There are some simple ways to know if you're too fat.

The pinch test is a simpler version of the caliper test, not requiring an instrument. Between your thumb and forefinger, grasp a fold of the triceps. If the pinch is more than an inch thick, you are probably too fat.

The ruler test requires that a man lie on his back and place a one-foot ruler lengthwise across the waistline. If the ends of the ruler don't touch the body, you can consider yourself too fat.

The girth test also is for men. Place a belt around your middle, and mark where it fastens. Then put it around your chest. If it takes more belt to encircle your waist than your chest, you are in the too-fat category.

The mirror test is the simplest—and most dismaying—of all. Take off your clothes and look critically at yourself in front of a full-length mirror. If you look fat— honestly too fat—you probably are too fat. Some persons, particularly teenage girls, may not appear too fat to others, yet regard themselves as overweight.

To protect your heart, lower your blood pressure, and improve your cholesterol levels, aerobic exercise is recommended. You can reach an accelerated heart rate by performing exercise at a steady, rhythmic, and prolonged pace. To bring energy consumption into line with food intake, however, an organized workout program may not be necessary. Dr. Peter Wood of the Stanford Heart Disease Prevention Program has said that healthy exercise should be "play." Bicycling, swimming, downhill skiing, and other recreational sports fit in here. If you don't enjoy your exercise program, Dr. Wood says, you won't continue with it.

And you can burn off calories in some simple, everyday ways. Here are a few tips:

• Walk up and down stairs whenever you can.

• Answer the farthest phone in the house; ask your friends to let it ring longer.

• Park in the area of the parking lot farthest from your destination, and walk.

• Walk instead of driving wherever you can.

• Get off the bus one stop early and walk the rest of the way.

• Get off the elevator one floor early and walk upstairs.

Losing weight is mental, too: You have to think thin in order to become thin. That means consciously changing some of your habits and attitudes about food.

For instance, in establishing your food diary, you recorded where you were and who your companions were while you were eating. Those entries help you to find unrecognized trouble spots in your eating habits and enable you to avoid them in the future or set up a substitute activity. The cocktail hour at the end of the day, with its companionship and conviviality, tempts many people off their diets. But a social substitute can be to run or to play racquetball with a friend just before dinner. When watching television or a tape on your videocassette player, you may find yourself unconsciously nibbling at snack foods simply to have something to do with your hands while your eyes and mind are occupied. Knitting or needlework can substitute for corn chips.

Here are additional tips to help you with your eating behavior and to aid you in sticking to a sensible diet:

• Eat only three meals a day, and at specified times and places. Sit down at a table, with a formal place setting complete with silverware, and don't dine in the den or library or at your desk.

• Use small plates and fill them up rather than large ones that can look half-filled and tempt you to pile on more food.

• Put specified servings on your plate and bring the plate to the table. Don't serve food family style, which can lead to large helpings—or seconds or thirds.

• Eat slowly, cutting your food deliberately, and set down the utensils after each bite. Chew slowly, and count the number of times you chew each bite.

• Never eat alone.

• Don't buy snacks to have "in case guests drop in"; keep food out of sight at home.

• Shop for groceries just after eating, to reduce impulse purchases. Prepare a shopping list in advance and stick to it.

• If you're the cook, don't sample the dishes you're cooking, and don't let yourself be tempted by the aroma!

HOW THIN IS TOO THIN?

To look at them, the last word you would use is "fat." Yet a small but growing number of Americans literally starve themselves trying to overcome an obesity that seems visible only to themselves.

Anorexia nervosa is largely confined to women, and mostly white, adolescent, middle-class and upper-middle-class girls with a perfectionist streak. (Only about 6 percent of the victims are boys, but a surprising number are women over 40.) The victims usually are described as quiet, obedient, and good students. They may begin to diet to lose only a few pounds, but soon become obsessed with dieting and thinness. Often they go without eating for days, claiming they are "not hungry" or that they "feel full" after only a few bites of food.

Many continue this compulsive fasting until they have lost as much as half their body weight. Often they become compulsive about exercise, too, engaging in hour after hour of running, jogging, or other strenuous solitary activity. Down to a mere 60 or 70 pounds, the emaciated girl may still contend that she is "too fat", or, at best, that she is "about right." About 10–15 percent of anorexics literally die of starvation.

Even when the consequences are not so dire, the girl may suffer physical harm. Her hair may drop out; she may have a low pulse rate, feel cold most of the time, and be constipated. Menstrual periods may stop completely, especially if she exercises a lot, and other functions of the endocrine system may be disrupted.

Although psychological, physiological, and emotional factors all interact, no full explanation for anorexia has ever been established. Some researchers believe that the early dieting either causes or accentuates a disturbance in the functions of the hypothalamus in the brain. The hypothalamus controls such important activities as maintenance of the body's water balance, regulation of body temperature, endocrine secretions, and sugar and fat metabolism.

Anorexics usually are treated with a combination of nutritional therapy, psychotherapy, and family counseling. In extreme cases, the girl may have to be hospitalized. If treatment is begun early enough, the outlook is good, but three to five years may pass before the girl is considered cured.

Another form of eating disorder is bulimia. Its victims usually are older. Unlike the shy, compliant anorexics, they are usually outgoing and overweight, and have huge appetites. Persons with bulimia go on huge food "binges," then force themselves to vomit immediately afterward, or purge themselves with laxatives. The binge-purge-binge cycle may go on for years, and is therefore difficult to treat by any known therapy.

Young athletes often want to gain weight, but go at it the wrong way. Instead of concentrating on "muscle-building" protein, they should increase carbohydrates and fats and add about 500 calories a day to their diet. Eat plenty of potatoes, rice, pasta, and bread; avoid foods such as cabbage that have lots of bulk but few calories. Add plenty of dressing to salads. Snack regularly, but two or three hours before meals so your appetite isn't spoiled. Continue to get exercise, so the extra pounds become muscle rather than fat.

The bulgur in Dill Vegetable Tabbouleh provides an abundance of fiber to this salad. (See recipe, page 162.)

EAT FOODS WITH STARCH AND FIBER

CHAPTER 9

The value of carbohydrates is being rediscovered, and for good reason. They provide bulk in the diet, and important nutrients as well. Eat carbohydrates and you automatically increase the volume of food, which crowds out appetite for less-nourishing dishes. There also is growing evidence that a high-carbohydrate diet may protect against some of the killer diseases.

CONTENTS

C arbohydrate, as the body's basic fuel supply, makes up the bulk of the American diet—even with today's changing tastes. Fifty years ago, 60 percent of Americans' calories came from carbohydrate. More recently, that proportion has dropped to about 50 percent. Still, a diet that is one-half carbohydrate adds up to a lot of pizza, Danish pastries, French fries, and cherry pie.

Although carbohydrate is a key ingredient in milk and is found in liver and a few other foods of animal origin, most of our supply comes from plants. Vegetables and fruits are primarily carbohydrate. But the richest source of carbohydrate is seeds, because they are packed with energy the new plant will need during germination. For this reason, the staple food in virtually every culture has been grain—wheat, rice, corn, millet, and others.

As we saw in Chapter 1, all carbohydrates are composed of sugars, arranged in various combinations. There are three single sugars or monosaccharides in the human diet. Glucose (also known as dextrose) is the "blood sugar" that powers most of the body's activities. Fructose is the fruit sugar you taste when you bite into a pear or peach; it is the sweetest of all sugars. It has the same chemical formula as glucose, although the molecular structure is different. The body rearranges the atoms to convert it to glucose. Galactose, the third simple sugar, is seldom found in its natural state, but is combined with glucose to form lactose (milk sugar).

Disaccharides, or double sugars, are pairs of single sugars linked together in specific ways. Sucrose is the one we know best. A combination of glucose and fructose, it is found in both beet and cane sugar in all the forms we use in cooking or at the table—white, brown, powdered, and granulated. Lactose is milk sugar, a combination of glucose and galactose, which the body breaks apart. Maltose, or malt sugar, consists of two glucoses. It occurs at only one stage in the plant's life. We find it in beer derived from malt, which is produced by germinating grains.

Both monosaccharides and disaccharides are thought of as simple carbohydrates. But the most significant form of carbohydrate in the diet is complex carbohydrate. The polysaccharides are combinations of simple sugars arranged in long and intricate chains. Some of them contain as many as 1,000 glucose units strung together as a single molecule.

The complex carbohydrates fall into three categories—starch, glycogen, and cellulose. Glycogen is not found in plants and actually represents a stage in the metabolism of carbohydrates, as we saw in Chapter 1. Cellulose is the woody, stringy part of plants known as fiber. Starch appears on most people's dinner plates every day. Broken down by the body into its glucose molecules, it is the body's chief source of energy.

To say that Americans today eat less carbohydrate than their grandparents did is not wholly accurate. Consumption of simple sugars has increased. But the sources have changed as Americans eat less fresh fruit and consume more candy bars, soft drinks, and the corn syrups and other sweeteners added to packaged foods. Meanwhile, there has been a marked decline in consumption of complex carbohydrates, especially whole grains and cereals that have been displaced by fat. That is the main reason the federal government's dietary guidelines call for more starch in the American diet for the 1980s.

Wheat is America's popular

grain, but grains popular in

other countries now are

appearing in our menus.

Bulgur is a Middle Eastern

staple. It is wheat that has

been parboiled, dried, and

cracked. It is usually sold

with the bran intact.

Couscous also is a Middle

Eastern form of cracked

wheat, usually more refined

than bulgur. Semolina is

made from durum wheat,

which doesn't rise, and is the

basic flour in pasta dishes.

Buckwheat, not technically

a grain, is eaten in

pancakes, as cereal, or even

as a vegetable side dish.

How can we put more complex carbohydrates into our diets? Let's begin by looking at the lowly potato. "Spuds" stoked the armies during World War I, but the brown-skinned tubers (except in the form of potato chips) fell into disrepute during recent decades. Figure-conscious women avoided them like the plague, under the misguided notion that potatoes are fattening.

Potatoes, of course, are *not* especially fattening, nor are other forms of starch. It's the butter and gravy and sour cream and other extras we pile on them that contribute the calories. The potato by itself is a primary source of starch, the ultimate complex carbohydrate. Indeed, potatoes are so loaded with starch that they provide the raw material for the stiffener that goes into shirt collars. Your basic medium-size baked potato weighs about 99 grams, of which 75 grams are water. Of the remaining 24 grams, 21 are pure carbohydrate, an amazing proportion.

And that's not all. Potatoes, including the skins, also contain three grams of high-quality protein, along with significant amounts of calcium, iron, vitamins A and C, and some of the B vitamins. In fact, an adult could live on an exclusive diet of potatoes, as Irish history proves. The Irish diet was so built upon potatoes that when a blight struck in 1846, one million Irish died and another million were forced to emigrate.

Sweet potatoes are another good source of complex carbohydrate, although they have slightly less starch, as well as less protein, than white potatoes. But they have more vitamin A and more calcium, iron, and other minerals than white potatoes. For all the baked sweet potato's nutritional value, it contains only 110 calories; a baked white potato only 90. All in all, potatoes in any form are among the most nutritious and least fattening vegetables around, especially when cooked with the skin intact, which preserves most of the nutrients.

Wheat flour is another neglected source of complex carbohydrate in the American diet, but for different reasons. That's because white flour, the kind most Americans prefer, has been stripped of most of its nutrients. Gone is the bran, the outer covering of the kernel, which primarily is cellulose fiber containing many vitamins and some protein. Gone also is the germ, the sprouting part of the kernel, which contains vitamin E, vegetable oil, protein, and some B vitamins. What remains is primarily starch, the food supply for the sprouting seed. It also contains protein and large amounts of the B vitamins.

WHAT THEY TAKE OUT OF BLEACHED WHITE FLOUR
True, most white flour has been enriched to restore many of the vitamins and minerals lost during processing. But none of the fiber is replaced. Bleached white flour loses even more of its nutrients. Not only are most American breads made from bleached white flour, but so are most pastries and cakes. And although some people sprinkle bran on foods in an effort to restore the loss, this does not replace other nutrients. Dr. Denis Burkitt, the British medical researcher who first focused attention on dietary fiber, has said that if he could make one change in the western diet, it would be to triple the amount of bread eaten—and that none of it would be white.

Stone-ground whole wheat flour preserves most of the kernel and therefore most of the nutrients and virtually all of the fiber. Other methods preserve slightly less of the nutrients and fiber. White flour (and white bread) is generally cheaper than whole-wheat products, but the latter are a better nutrition buy for the money. Many recipes in this book use whole wheat flour.

Cereals have been the food manufacturers' answer to suggestions that Americans should eat more complex carbohydrates. Every grocery shelf now groans with presumably nutritious products. Those that contain bran or whole grains are usually high in fiber, and some of them offer large amounts of protein as well. Others are fortified with vitamins, often in large amounts.

RETURN TO OLD FAVORITES

Actually, the best nutrition sources among cereals are some of the old standbys. Rolled oats contain more protein, ounce for ounce, than any other common cereal. The rolling process does the least damage to the nutrients. (But instant oatmeal does lack some of the basics.) Shredded wheat and dry cereals made from oats also are high in protein and fiber, and a good, if traditional, choice.

Granola often is touted as a health food. But it actually is high in sugar, from the honey and molasses, and high in fats, from the nuts, seeds, and oils. Granola bars are even higher in fats and sugars. According to one study, a honey and nut granola bar gets 35 percent of its calories from fat and 20 percent of calories from sugar.

Rice is the staple grain in much of the world, especially Asia, and is highly popular in the southern states. Brown rice is whole-grain rice that retains many of the natural nutrients, including the fibrous hulls. Most white rice is polished rice, which means that the original kernel has lost much of its protein and many other nutrients, especially B vitamins. As we have seen in Chapter 1, the dietary deficiency disease beriberi struck in epidemic form when polished rice supplanted the unpolished variety in the diets of many Asians. Instant and minute rice are the lowest in nutrient content. But any form of rice is a valuable source of complex carbohydrates.

Corn is another source of complex carbohydrate familiar to Americans. Most of what we eat is sweet corn, which has less starch and more simple sugars than field corn, the kind used in processed foods and in animal feed. In whatever variety, however, corn is rich in starch (cornstarch is a staple in cooking) and the kernels are a valuable source of fiber.

Fruits and vegetables also are primary sources of carbohydrates. They are high in fiber of various types, and although they do not provide the concentration of complex carbohydrates of grains and potatoes, they are rich in the simple sugars, too. Because they are high in water content (lettuce is 95 percent water), they are filling and help to prevent overeating. They are also good sources of bulk in the diet.

As a source of carbohydrate, vegetables and fruits are best eaten raw, because many of the nutrients and the caloric content are destroyed during cooking. Minimal cooking, such as steaming, is better than boiling, which destroys some of the food value. Stir-frying in a little oil also preserves the goodness and the nutrients. The crisper the vegetable, the more nutrients it is likely to retain.

Bugs Bunny was right.

Carrots are good for you.

Better, apparently, than

Bugs or our parents ever

realized. And so are some

other vegetables our folks

insisted that we eat—

spinach, broccoli, squash,

sweet potatoes, cabbage,

brussels sprouts, and

cauliflower. Bright orange

and dark green vegetables

are rich in vitamin A. But

these vegetables also contain

a substance called beta

carotene. Beta carotene gives

carrots, squash, and sweet

potatoes their bright orange-

yellow color. Beta carotene is

converted into vitamin A in

the body.

Dietary fiber has become a buzzword at American dinner tables and supermarket shelves. You find its healthful virtues trumpeted from bread wrappers and cereal boxes, often those with the highest price tags. Yet you will look for it in vain in any list of essential nutrients. So what is the stuff, really? And what good, if any, does it do in the body?

To begin with, the term fiber is itself a bit misleading. Most of what we call "fiber" doesn't look fibrous at all. True, the strings of celery or green beans come under the heading of fiber. (Celery actually contains less fiber than less stringy-looking parsnips or green peas.) But the definition also includes seeds, fruit skins, grains, nuts and kernels, and the hulls of beans and peas.

DIETARY FIBER DEFINED

The accepted definition of dietary fiber is those constituents of food that can't be broken down in the gastrointestinal tract. It is, in a way, the waste part of food, that for which we have no nutritional need. The human body lacks enzymes for this breakdown process. Some of the fiber is fermented by intestinal bacteria in the large intestine, but basically fiber passes through the body intact.

Most forms of fiber are complex carbohydrates. Cellulose, the woody parts of plant, is one form. Other forms include lignin, pectins, gums, mucilage, and hemicellulose. Most foods derived from plants contain some form of fiber, although the amount may vary from plant to plant and in fact may be changed by cooking. All share the property of absorbing water, and as a result they cause bulk in the stool.

The presumed value of fiber has a long history. Our grandparents made sure their families ate enough "roughage," another term for fiber, because they knew it had a laxative effect and promoted bowel regularity and therefore was considered essential to good health. "An apple a day keeps the doctor away" was another way of saying that pectin (fiber) prevented constipation. However, along with other changes in the American diet, the amount of roughage and fresh fruit eaten declined dramatically after World War II, as whole grain breads gave way to processed varieties and fresh fruits and vegetables were replaced by fats and sweets.

The current interest in fiber dates from the 1970s and the observations of Dr. Denis Burkitt, a renowned British physician. Burkitt was best known for his research on Burkitt's lymphoma, a form of childhood cancer common in Africa. While investigating the disease, Burkitt observed that intestinal and rectal cancers and certain other digestive ailments common in western countries were rare among tribal people who ate a high-fiber diet. Burkitt attributed these low rates to the fact that the Africans had frequent large bowel movements, induced by the amount of fiber they consumed. He said the movements removed cancer-causing and other harmful substances from the intestinal tract before they could cause damage.

Other doctors quickly disputed Burkitt's report. They pointed out that there were many differences between Africans and persons in the industrialized nations besides the amount of fiber in their diet, any of which might account for the difference in the figures. Not the least of these was that many of the tribal peoples did not live to the age at which such diseases normally develop. And the true cause of the diseases might lie in the foods that replaced fiber in the diet, not the lack of fiber itself.

However, the controversy generated interest in a nutrition topic that had laid dormant for years. And it led to a conclusion among doctors and nutritionists that, while Burkitt's claims had by no means been proven, increasing the amount of fiber to the level their grandparents ate would certainly do Americans no harm.

CAN DIETARY FIBER IMPROVE HEALTH?

Among the diseases that dietary fiber was said to offset were diverticulosis, an outpouching of the intestinal walls; diverticulitis, inflammation of the resulting pouches; stomach ulcers; appendicitis; hemorrhoids, gallstones, varicose veins, and heart disease. Most of these may have increased in incidence since Americans and others in the industrialized countries consumed less fiber, but no cause and effect had ever been shown. Ironically, an association between fiber and diverticulosis had already been suspected—but in reverse. Persons with diverticula had been placed on a low-fiber diet, to prevent the fibrous materials from irritating the intestinal walls. After Burkitt's studies became known, they were changed to a high-fiber diet.

Some of the mechanisms attributed to fiber by Burkitt have been largely agreed upon. A high amount of fiber does speed "transit time"—the time elapsed between the time food enters the mouth and the waste products are excreted at the rectum. Burkitt reported that African natives on a high-fiber diet had a transit time of 36 hours, whereas British men on a low-fiber diet recorded 77 hours. In addition, African bowel movements were four times as bulky as the British.

Why bowel regularity might promote good health is still argued. Burkitt said that slower transit times keep cancer-causing and harmful substances in contact with the intestinal walls for longer periods of time. Moreover, he said, there was more rapid passage of bile salts, associated with faster transit time, which was one means of clearing excess cholesterol from the system, and thus guarded against heart disease. Both of these conclusions are still controversial among physicians, although doctors agree that fiber can reduce constipation, and that, at least fiber-promoted bowel regularity is likely to make you feel more comfortable, whether or not it prevents disease.

SOURCES OF FIBER

If fiber is a good guy in the battle against many of the chronic diseases, how then should one get more fiber? Despite what you may have heard in the health-food stores, adding bran to other foods is not the answer. Indeed, one U.S.-sponsored study specifically stated that bran, which is mostly cellulose, did nothing to lower cholesterol levels. On the other hand, pectin, which occurs in fruits, and guar gum, found primarily in beans and other legumes, significantly reduced the amount of cholesterol in the blood. Reports on guar gum, in fact, were so promising that a nationwide study has been established to check its benefits.

For most of us, adding fiber to the diet doesn't call for any herculean measures or abrupt changes in what we eat. Eating a balanced diet, according to the Basic Four Food Groups or the food-exchange plans, will give us an adequate amount of fiber. Fresh fruits provide pectin, and vegetables are high in cellulose. Grains are still the leading source of fiber and other complex carbohydrates in the American diet.

Naturally low-fat, readily available ingredients team up in

Chicken and Fruit Salad. (See recipe, page 106.)

AVOID TOO MUCH FAT AND CHOLESTEROL

CHAPTER 10

Cardiovascular disease costs the country 550,000 lives and $72 billion in health care and lost output each year. Reducing those human and economic losses is a major reason why Americans are told to eat less fat. The high-fat American diet coincided with the rise in heart disease. Cause and effect hasn't been definitely established, but a low-fat diet is the best way to stay on the safe side.

CONTENTS

Fat is literally at the heart of America's concern about health. Over the past five decades, evidence has been steadily building that fats in the bloodstream are a major reason 550,000 Americans die of heart disease each year. More recently, suspicion has been raised that our high-fat diet also contributes to cancer, diabetes, and hypertension. Although the evidence is less compelling, the American Cancer Society, among others, has suggested that Americans reduce fat consumption as a potential protection against cancer.

The concern about fiber also reflects concern about fat. One reason for eating fiber is its bulk, which cuts down the appetite for fat. As for obesity, the very word means fat. The indigestible parts of plants presumably sweep harmful fat from the body. Although you needn't eat fat to be fat, fat remains the most concentrated form of energy in the diet, containing more than twice as many calories per gram as protein or carbohydrate.

Anyone who has ever smelled bacon frying on a cold winter morning knows, however, that fat has its good side, too. Fat flavors food and improves food's consistency; it is a major reason why we enjoy eating. Body fat serves as our storage depot for energy. Fat provides power for the muscles, including the vital heart muscle, when other supplies have been used up. Fat insulates against heat and cold, pads and protects the organs against shock and injury, lubricates the skin, and tones the hair. The fat we eat is the vehicle that transports the important fat-soluble vitamins.

Still, we don't need much fat. We can manage quite nicely on only about one or two tablespoonfuls of vegetable oil a day. (We can do without animal fat completely, as vegetarian societies prove.) Like other basic nutrients, fat is an organic compound of carbon, hydrogen, and oxygen, and the body can draw on other sources to manufacture the substances normally supplied by fat. Even the simple sugar glucose will serve as raw material in a pinch. Only one fatty acid, linoleic acid, has been deemed an essential fatty acid, one that must be obtained from the diet. The body lacks an enzyme to produce its own linoleic acid.

American consumption of fat, however, is the same old story of excess. If the fat in our food could be separated and measured in tablespoons, it would come to about eight times our daily need. About 42 percent of calories in the American diet came from fat at the time of the 1977 report of the Senate Select Committee on Nutrition and Human Needs. Although that proportion appears to be dropping, it is still believed to average above 40 percent. The committee recommended that the percentage of fat be reduced to 30, and the recommendation has since been endorsed by health agencies, led by the American Heart Association. Some believe that even 30 percent is too high, and have suggested that the percentage be lowered to 25, 20, or even 10. The recommendations also suggested that Americans reduce total fat (to combat obesity) and cholesterol, which has been implicated in heart disease.

To understand how fat helps us and sometimes harms us, we need to know a little about how it is utilized in the body. Fat metabolism differs significantly from that of other nutrients. The explanation is as near as the kitchen sink. Fats do not dissolve readily in water, as a greasy pan placed under the faucet clearly shows. The body is composed primarily of water. If the energy in fat is to be usable, it must be rendered soluble in water.

About 95 percent of fats are triglycerides, meaning that they consist of a backbone of glycerol with three fatty acids attached. Enzymes in the upper portion of the gastrointestinal tract break off two fatty acids. Bile, produced in the liver and stored in the gallbladder, surrounds the free fatty acids and the remaining monoglyceride exactly the same way that detergent coats the grease molecules in the frying pan. The now water-soluble substances are transported across the wall of the small intestine. There they are rebuilt into new triglyceride molecules, given a protein coat, and carried via the lymphatic system and the bloodstream to all parts of the body. Some are used for immediate needs by the cells; others are tucked away in the body's special storage areas—fat deposits—for future needs.

Coffee and cream go together, but Americans now use an artificial substitute to whiten the morning beverage. However, artificial creamers actually are a hidden source of fats. Many substitutes are based on coconut or palm oil, both of which are saturated fats. Before stirring, read the label carefully.

Broiled beef sirloin steak
7g fat and 77mg cholesterol per 3 ounces

Poached trout
8g fat and 47mg cholesterol per 1 fish

Shelled English walnuts
19g fat and 0mg cholesterol per ¼ cup

Cooked lima beans
0g fat and 0mg cholesterol per ½ cup

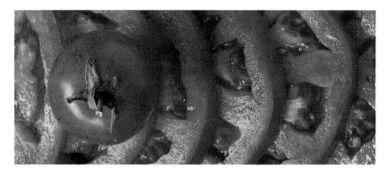

Sliced tomato
0g fat and 0mg cholesterol per 1 medium

Sliced avocado
35g fat and 0mg cholesterol per 1 medium

Cooked egg noodles
1g fat and 25mg cholesterol per ½ cup

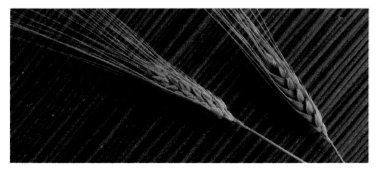

Cooked whole wheat spaghetti
0g fat and 0mg cholesterol per ½ cup

Most of us like the taste of fat, so cutting back on it can be less painful if done gradually. Here's a three-step method recommended by the American Heart Association:

• First, serve red meat only four to five times a week instead of daily. Substitute fish, chicken, or vegetable dishes. Choose lean meats rather than fat-streaked cuts when you do eat meat.

• After a month, cut back to three servings a week. At the same time, decrease the size of your meat portions.

(Continued opposite page)

To most of us, fat is fat. But nutritionally, there are important distinctions to be made among types of fat. Although triglycerides make up the overwhelming majority of total fats, the remaining 5 percent have an important role to play, too. Phospholipids are a combination of fats with phosphorus, which enables fats to travel through the blood. Sterols include cholesterol, a term just about all of us are familiar with. As with other foods, one cannot separate the three types. Triglycerides, cholesterol, and phospholipids often appear together in fatty dishes—an important bit of information for diet-watchers.

Triglycerides themselves are found in three different types. The distinction between them is a matter of organic chemistry, based on the number of openings in the fatty-acid molecule available for hydrogen atoms to attach to carbon atoms. The carbon atoms in fatty acids are arranged in chains of varying length; eight to ten is common, and the fatty acids in meat and fish contain 14.

One of the rules of nature is that a carbon atom has four bonding sites to other atoms. Commonly, each carbon atom in a chain is bound to two other carbon atoms and to two hydrogen atoms. However, this is not always the case in fatty acids. Sometimes a carbon may be joined by two bonds—double-bonded—to another carbon atom, leaving an opening where a hydrogen atom might otherwise be located.

HOW FATS DIFFER

Saturated fats have hydrogen atoms in all available positions. They are therefore said to be "saturated" with all the hydrogen atoms they could carry.

Monounsaturated fats have one pair of double-bonded carbon atoms in the chain, and thus one space remains open where a hydrogen atom could be attached.

Polyunsaturated fats have two or more—sometimes as many as five—openings without hydrogen atoms. ("Poly" means "many" or "multiple.")

Saturated fats, with some important exceptions, are primarily found in foods of animal origin and normally are firm or solid at room temperature—"hard fats." Monounsaturated fats usually come from vegetable sources, and are primarily liquid. Polyunsaturates are mostly vegetable, but also occur in fish. Most of them are oils, but they are sometimes "hydrogenated" or combined with saturated fat, to produce a fat that remains semisolid and keeps well without expensive refrigeration. Some brands of margarine are hydrogenated and usually are marked on the label.

Actually, many foods of various origin contain more than one type of fatty acid. They are classified by the predominant type, or by the P:S ratio, which shows the proportion of polyunsaturates to saturates.

Here are foods that are considered predominantly one type of fat. Some of the listings may surprise you:

Saturated: Butter, cheese, egg yolk, milk, lard, all types of meat, chocolate, and palm and coconut oil (widely used in food processing).

Monounsaturated: Avocados, cashews, olives and olive oil, peanuts and peanut oil, poultry, vegetable shortening.

Polyunsaturated: Almonds; corn, cottonseed, linseed, safflower, and sesame oil; soft margarine; mayonnaise made with vegetable oil; walnuts.

In terms of P:S ratio, freshwater fish, semisolid margarines, and chicken breast, skin, and thigh have about twice as much polyunsaturated as saturated fat. Beef liver, chicken heart, hydrogenated vegetable oils, peanut butter, and solid margarines are about equal in polyunsaturates and saturates. Chicken liver, lard, palm oil, and pork and veal have low P:S ratios; beef, lamb, egg yolk, and dairy products are very low in polyunsaturates compared to saturates.

But why should we nonchemists care whether fatty acids are saturated, monounsaturated, or polyunsaturated? What differences does it make whether the molecular arrangement of hydrogen atoms resembles an even row of shiny pearls, or a six-year-old's gap-toothed smile? One answer is fat's association with the presumed villain in heart disease, cholesterol.

Cholesterol keeps company with animal fat. It is found in comparatively large quantity in beef, lamb, veal, milk, and dairy products, and in eggs, shellfish, and liver. A serving of fatty meat like steak, indeed, is likely to raise blood cholesterol levels even more than foods lower in fat but higher in cholesterol, such as eggs. Polyunsaturated fats, on the other hand, tend to lower blood cholesterol. Monounsaturated fats appear to be neutral, with little or no influence on blood cholesterol.

FAT INTAKE ON THE RISE

Since the Department of Agriculture first began gathering statistics on the American diet in 1909, we have increased our intake of all three types of fat. Saturated fat, for instance, has risen from 45 grams a day to 55. Of the 42 percent of calories in the American diet that now come from fat, the Senate Select Committee on Nutrition and Human Needs reported in 1977 a breakdown like this:

Saturated fat.........................16 percent
Monounsaturated fat ....19 percent
Polyunsaturated fat.................7 percent

The Senate committee recommended that the three forms of fat be brought into balance. Of the proposed 30 percent of calories derived from fat, in other words, 10 percent should come from saturated fats, 10 percent from monounsaturated fats, and 10 percent from polyunsaturated fats. These standards have been adopted by several health agencies, including the American Heart Association and the American Cancer Society, and were incorporated in a statement by the National Institutes of Health Consensus Development Conference, which brought together some of the nation's most renowned researchers on the topic in 1984. (A few other agencies have suggested that *total* fat be reduced to 10 percent or less and that saturated fat be eliminated completely, but there is little evidence that most Americans would benefit from such a strict regimen.)

Gradually Americans seem to be trying to meet these standards. However, they have been more zealous in cutting saturated fat than total fat, which continues to be a worrisome problem in the view of many experts.

Although monounsaturates and polyunsaturates tend to keep blood cholesterol levels down, they can contain just as many calories as, or more than meat and dairy products. A handful of cashew nuts, the amount we might gobble unthinkingly while watching television, contain more than 75 percent monounsaturated fat but add up to 300 calories. A tablespoonful of safflower oil, a polyunsaturate used in cooking, contains 125 calories—or 25 more than an equivalent amount of butter. Thus, substituting polyunsaturated for saturated fats may aid the battle against heart disease, but loses ground against obesity, a health hazard in its own right.

Another aspect of polyunsaturates that causes concern is a possible link with cancer. This disturbing finding grows out of an experiment in which hospitalized veterans were put on a high-polyunsaturate diet in an effort to bring their blood-cholesterol levels down and reduce the risk of heart attacks. The veterans did have fewer heart attacks than a comparable group following a normal diet, but they also had more cancer. Later research indicated that polyunsaturates when heated to high temperatures may transform into fatty acids, which may produce cancer-causing substances. The results of the original study have been questioned, and meanwhile some doctors recommend that Americans not deep-fry with polyunsaturated oil.

• Ultimately, eat meat only in small amounts in combination with vegetables or starches, as in the stir-fried dishes in this book.

To change your taste from butter to margarine, prepare a half and half combination of the two, then gradually increase the margarine proportion.

Egg yolk is the most concentrated source of cholesterol in the biological realm. That's because a developing chick needs a bountiful supply to construct cell membranes and synthesize hormones for growth. Cholesterol is the building block for both. The demand can be traced clearly in the mother hen; lipoproteins, which transport cholesterol, increase markedly during ovulation, preparatory to storage in the egg. Something similar happens in pregnant mammals, including humans, but the process is more complex.

As with total fat, Americans consume more cholesterol than they need. This grayish-white substance is important to our bodies; it is an essential part of cell membranes, builds nerve sheaths, and is the raw material for hormones (including the sex hormones). The daily requirement is about 1,000 milligrams. The liver and other organs, however, can manufacture more than this amount from virtually any two-carbon molecule; certain cells of the body also can produce their own—all without drawing on the dietary supply. Most of the 450 or more milligrams of cholesterol that Americans consume daily is excreted.

The daily cholesterol requirements and the daily consumption are among the few facts about cholesterol that specialists agree upon. Another area of agreement is that cholesterol accumulating in the arteries, especially the coronary arteries, increases the risk of heart disease and stroke. In a process called atherosclerosis, the fat does its dirty work by building up plaques in the arterial walls and gradually narrowing the channel until the blood supply cannot squeeze by and is shut off to the heart. The result, which occurs 1,800 times a day in America, is a myocardial infarction—a heart attack.

DOES CHOLESTEROL CAUSE HEART DISEASE?

Does the fat we eat from the dinner plate translate into fat in the artery walls? On that point, doctors are still divided. Some point out that heart disease is caused by many factors, and that heredity, age, gender, obesity, high blood pressure, and smoking all contribute. Many people enjoy what doctors call the "Winston Churchill syndrome," referring to the former British leader who broke all the health and diet rules and lived to be 91. The case against dietary cholesterol has not been proven beyond question, it is said, and we are alleged to be victims of "cholesterolphobia," depriving ourselves of enjoying life for the sake of very dubious and distant gains.

A mammoth nationwide study completed in 1984 was to have settled once and for all the question of whether reducing cholesterol in the diet prevents heart disease. The Lipid Research Clinics Coronary Primary Prevention Trial enlisted 14 medical centers and 10,000 men aged 40-59, who had high blood-cholesterol levels. For ten years half were treated with cholestyramine, a drug known to reduce cholesterol levels in the blood. The other half received no cholestyramine. At the end of the experiment, the treated group had 19 percent fewer fatal and nonfatal heart attacks, and showed a 9 percent reduction in serum cholesterol, the levels in the blood.

X-ray angiography of participants' arteries in another clinical trial, completed shortly after the lipid trial, showed that progression of atherosclerotic buildup slowed down when blood cholesterol was reduced by drugs.

The leaders of this government-sponsored project declared emphatically that, for the first time, it had been shown beyond a reasonable doubt that reducing cholesterol in the blood lowered the risk of heart attack, at least in those at greatest risk. But the opponents remained unconvinced. They observed that cholesterol reduction had been achieved by drugs, not diet, and that it still had not been shown that a change in diet alone would achieve the same result.

The finding, however, was enough for an elite panel of cardiologists and preventive-health specialists assembled by the National Institutes of Health. The Consensus Development Conference on Lowering Blood Cholesterol stated flatly that cholesterol now had been shown to be a "major cause" of heart disease, and that every 1 percent reduction in blood cholesterol lowered risks by 2 percent. The committee acknowledged that drugs, not diet, had brought about the reduction. Since it was known, however, that reducing dietary cholesterol could lower blood cholesterol to some degree, the committee put its weight behind recommendations that Americans cut back on fat, saturated fat, and cholesterol.

Specifically, the committee endorsed the previous recommendations that fat intake be lowered to 30 percent of total calories, and that the 10-10-10 formula for saturated, monounsaturated, and polyunsaturated fats be followed. The committee also suggested that Americans reduce their daily cholesterol intake to 250 milligrams.

As a further recommendation, the committee said that all persons with a blood-cholesterol level higher than 260 milligrams per deciliter (mg/dl) of blood should be treated with drugs, and that those with moderately elevated cholesterol, defined as 220 mg/dl, be placed on a low-fat diet. Americans, the statement said, should reduce to their ideal body weight and exercise moderately.

The ink was hardly dry on the statement before a new controversy arose, this time from the opposite direction. Another faction of doctors suggested that the committee's recommended blood-cholesterol levels, as well as dietary-intake levels, were too high. Blood cholesterol should be brought down to 195 mg/dl, this group said, and Americans should keep their daily diet of cholesterol under 150 mg. Thus the quarrel rages on.

The concern over cholesterol, by whatever means it threatens life, is obvious because the stakes are so high. Heart disease in America began climbing steadily in the early 1900s and in the 1970s was claiming 750,000 victims, many in the prime of life. The rates began dropping in 1974 and within 10 years were nearly 25 percent lower, for reasons that are not clear. It is true, however, that the decline probably coincided with the emphasis on better diet, along with a reduction in cigarette smoking, more exercise programs, and better treatment and medication.

The focus on cholesterol as a possible culprit in heart disease began about the time of World War II. Quite accidentally, it was noticed that during the Nazi occupation of Europe, when meat, eggs, butter, and other fat-rich foods were unavailable, heart-disease rates and related deaths dropped remarkably. The famous seven-country study by Dr. Ancel Keys, a University of Minnesota epidemiologist, in which he compared heart-disease rates and fats in the diet across seven cultures, also had a major impact. He found that the Finns and the Americans, who ate the most meat and dairy products, had the most heart disease, and that the Japanese, who ate fish, rice, and vegetables, had the lowest. An in-depth study of one community, Framingham, Massachusetts, then showed that men under age 60 who had blood cholesterol higher than 260 mg/dl had triple the amount of heart disease of those at lower levels. The Framingham study, which is continuing, resulted in the definition of heart disease "risk factors," identified as blood cholesterol, cigarette smoking, heredity, gender, age, hypertension, obesity, and stress. The level of blood cholesterol was one of those considered a high-risk factor.

But not all cholesterol is alike, as scientists soon discovered. As a fat, cholesterol is not soluble in blood (see page 254), so it must be combined with a protein in order to be carried to the cells. Proteins that provide this transportation are lipoproteins—for lipids (blood fats) and protein.

Low-density lipoprotein (LDL) carries cholesterol to the cells, where it yields up its cargo via the cell gatekeepers, the receptor sites. These receptors admit molecules as needed, after which they effectively slam the door. High-density lipoproteins (HDL) collect the excess cholesterol from both the bloodstream and the artery walls and return it to the liver to be broken down and excreted.

HDL and LDL have been cast respectively as the good guys and the bad guys of heart disease. A high level of HDL appears to protect against heart disease, a high level of LDL appears to be harmful. More important than precise amounts, however, may be the balance between the two. Persons with high HDL and low LDL appear to be better off than those who have a higher HDL but a correspondingly high LDL.

The meat in your market isn't what it used to be. Under consumer pressure, ratings of meat have been changed to allow leaner cuts to receive top grades like prime or choice, once reserved for marbled (fat-streaked) cuts. Overall, the beef sold today contains 11.6 percent fat, compared to 15.4 percent 25 years ago. Pork contains less than half the fat of earlier years. Hogs are slaughtered at one-third the previous weight, instead of being fattened to higher figures.

The story doesn't end there, either. Scientists are discovering that several forms of both HDL and LDL may have greater or lesser protective effects; some forms have potentially damaging effects. Very-low-density lipoprotein (VLDL), for example, appears to be more harmful than LDL itself. Moreover, studies of families with genetically high cholesterol levels, a condition known as hypercholesterolemia, seem to show that the members of these families may inherit a defect at the cell receptor site, which could explain the high amounts of damaging LDL. Clearly, more is to be learned before the cholesterol controversy will end.

Ideally, of course, most of us would want an optimal HDL/LDL level to protect against heart disease. But how can we achieve it? To some extent, we may be endowed with it from birth. Dr. Nathan Glueck of the University of Cincinnati, for instance, has traced a number of families with markedly higher than normal HDL levels. They appear to live in good health until their 80s and 90s. Conversely, unfortunate families with genetically induced high cholesterol levels may die in their teens with cholesterol levels three times those of their contemporaries.

Women have high HDL levels, which may explain why they have less heart disease. Obese persons, diabetics, and heavy smokers have higher LDL and lower HDL levels. Persons who have heart disease or who have suffered heart attack have less HDL.

Running three or four times a week appears to raise HDL levels substantially. In one study of middle-aged men conducted at Stanford University, runners raised their HDL by 15 percent—"reaching women's HDL levels," Dr. Peter Wood said. Drinking a glass of wine a day also raises HDL (although drinking much more than that may have other harmful consequences).

Unfortunately, no diet has yet been devised that will keep HDL and LDL in a fine protective balance. Eating a lot of saturated fat raises HDL—but it raises LDL, too. Polyunsaturates lower LDL, but they also lower HDL. Fish oil may possibly help to lower LDLs while raising or not disturbing HDLs. This could explain why Eskimos, with their diet that is almost exclusively fat, have low rates of heart disease. Olive oil, a monounsaturate that is presumably neutral, is used for cooking in Mediterranean countries and could explain why Greeks and Italians have less heart disease than their neighbors in northern Europe.

If you can't zero in on the HDL/LDL equation, the next best step is to lower total cholesterol level, which is at the heart of all dietary recommendations of recent years. Despite the lack of incontrovertible scientific proof that cutting back on dietary fat reduces the heart-attack threat, most doctors believe that the circumstantial evidence is strong enough—the safety-in-numbers approach. They further point out that the 30-percent-of-calories limit actually is more fat than our forefathers ate before 1900 and considerably more than is eaten in most of the world today.

A 250-milligram-a-day consumption is by no means depriving yourself, and most of us could cut down to 200 mg a day with some simple measures.

The most concentrated form of cholesterol in the American diet is egg yolk. Each yolk contains about 250 milligrams, the entire recommendation for one day. Taking eggs off the breakfast table is one logical way to reduce cholesterol. (Americans have already cut down markedly on egg consumption—30 percent in ten years.) One way to cut back on eggs while still enjoying them is to use the egg whites, which are mostly protein. Scramble the whites and replace each yolk with a teaspoon of polyunsaturated oil, or combine a single yolk with two or three whites. You can provide yellow color with a pinch of saffron.

Cheese is another source of cholesterol and fat. Most cheese is about 28 percent fat; 3½ ounces of cream cheese has 120 mg of cholesterol. You can buy low-cholesterol and no-cholesterol cheese, but cheese sold as low fat still will contain about 21 percent fat. Here, in standard portions, are some other sources of cholesterol in the diet:
• Beef liver—300 mg
• Shrimp—125 mg
• Oysters—200 mg
• Lobster—300 mg
• Ice cream, rich—53 mg
• Whole milk—30 mg
Here are some foods low in cholesterol:
• Fish fillet—70 mg
• Skim milk—7 mg
• Chicken—60 mg
• Lean ground beef—63 mg
• Low-fat yogurt—14 mg

HOW ARTERIES BECOME CLOGGED

The buildup of plaque in the arteries, known as atherosclerosis, begins early in life. Autopsies of American soldiers killed in Korea and Vietnam disclosed diseased arteries even in 20-year-olds. About half of the American population have seriously damaged arteries by the time they reach their 55th birthday. Coronary bypass surgery is performed more than 150,000 times a year to detour the blockage.

How atherosclerosis begins isn't definitely known. One widely accepted explanation is the injury theory of Dr. Russell Ross of the University of Washington. Dr. Ross says the chain of events may be set in motion by injury to the delicate surface of the inner lining of the artery, the intima. In an attempt to repair the damage, platelets— blood cells that plug gaps in vessels to prevent blood loss—rush to the scene. They release a growth factor that causes cells in the area to proliferate and close the wound. Like debris collecting behind an obstacle in a brook, blood fats, fibrous material, and other substances pile up behind the "snag." The wall thickens, reducing the diameter of the channel further, increasing blood velocity, and causing more damage and more buildup. Eventually the entire channel may become blocked.

The culprit initiating the injury has not been identified. Among candidates are cigarette smoke, insulin, cholesterol or—possibly—a virus infection that sets up an immune reaction so that the body attacks and damages its own tissue.

Nature sweetens fruit so perfectly that only a kiss of honey is added to Summer Fruit Parfaits. (See recipe, page 184.)

AVOID TOO MUCH SUGAR

CHAPTER 11

We are a nation full of cookie monsters—not to mention soft-drink dragons and candy freaks. Even though we all like sugar, we consume too much of it for good health. Cutting back on sweeteners may be easier than you think. As a start, leave the sugar bowl off the breakfast table.

CONTENTS

WHAT'S WRONG WITH SUGAR?

Worried parents won't believe it, but candy contributes surprisingly little to children's sugar consumption. The biggest single source of kids' sugar is milk, which contains the natural sugar lactose. Next come soft drinks (14 percent) and cakes, cookies, and pastries (11 percent). Sweetened cereals account for 3.3 percent, and candy a mere 2.6 percent. Fresh fruit, an ideal source of natural sugar, makes up only 1.6 percent of the total.

The average American devours a sizable percentage of his body weight in sugar and sweeteners every year—125 pounds by one government estimate. That staggering total concerns many health experts, but the full consequences of our enormous sweet tooth aren't clear.

Sugar is *not* a poison, despite spurious claims in some health magazines, and it does *not* cause diabetes. (This myth may have grown up because many diabetics are obese, and they may be obese because they overdose on sweets.) Nor has sugar been linked to cardiovascular disease, research efforts to show a link between the two notwithstanding.

WHAT SUGAR OFFERS

But sugar may cause health problems. You may have heard that sugar provides "empty" calories. Refined sugar has no nutrients whatever to offer—no vitamins, no minerals, not even fiber. But it does have loads of calories. A teaspoon of sugar contains 16 calories; a cup of sugar, 770. Eating a lot of sugar can put on weight. Worse, though, it tends to replace more valuable foods in the diet. And because sweetstuffs seldom are filling compared with starch, one tends to gobble more sugar-loaded food and pack on more pounds.

The second problem is tooth decay, or what dentists call dental caries. Sugar, especially sticky forms of it, tends to cling to the surfaces and crevices of the teeth. Combined with poor dental hygiene, the sugar deposits establish a cozy environment where certain bacteria can flourish and attack the tooth's protective enamel and eventually destroy the tooth. Tooth decay is less a problem than in the past, thanks to the protective effects of fluoridated water and fluoridated dentifrices, but tooth decay in children, especially those who live in areas without fluoridation, still is a matter of concern.

Sugar, of course, is all around us, and just about everyone, including animals, loves it. One nutritionist has called sugar "America's favorite food additive." Not quite: As with salt, much of the sugar in the American diet comes prepackaged in foods bought off the supermarket shelf and not from table sugar added in cooking or stirred into coffee. Two-thirds of sugar consumption is in processed foods, including nearly one-fourth in soft drinks, and nearly another fourth in candy bars. Sometimes it appears as corn syrup or corn sugar added as a sweetener in baked goods.

Children get a lot of sugar from cereals—although less than parents think. Some cereals, by the manufacturers' own figures, contain as much as 60 percent sugar by weight. The American Dental Association (ADA) has recommended that cereals eaten by children contain less than 20 percent sugar. (A list of cereals with their sugar percentages is available from the ADA.

It's a common but mistaken belief that "raw" sugar, brown sugar, honey, and molasses are healthier sweeteners than refined sugar. All are sucrose, and, nutritionally, sucrose is sucrose. Each form of sugar contains the same number of calories per gram. Raw sugar has, in fact, been partially refined. Brown sugar is refined sugar that has been darkened with molasses. Honey, a concentrated form of sugar that helps bees survive through the winter, actually contains 18 more calories per tablespoon than table sugar. The nutrients in honey are negligible, and it can have serious side effects if given to infants. As forms of sucrose, both honey and refined sugar are composed of glucose and fructose molecules. The body breaks sucrose down into equal parts of fructose and glucose, and basically doesn't care where the glucose comes from.

Sugars occurring naturally in food are another matter. In concentrated form, fructose, the fruit sugar, also rots teeth, but the fructose you obtain in grapes or cherries is a dilute form. Fructose also is the sweeter form of sugar, although it contains the same number of calories per gram as glucose. You thus need less fructose and fewer calories to obtain a sweet taste. In addition, fresh fruit contains vitamins and other nutrients missing from table sugar.

Aristotle noticed it first. In the fourth century B.C., the Greek philosopher observed that people who ate a lot of ripe figs had more tooth decay than those who didn't. The great thinker didn't have all the answers, however. Sticky foods are only part of a complex process that culminates in tooth decay.

CUTTING BACK ON SWEETS

As we have seen, decay begins where food debris and bacteria accumulate and remain undisturbed. Prime targets are crevices between the teeth, pits, and fissures on the tooth surface under the gumline. The bacteria react with the carbohydrates of the foods to produce an acid that dissolves tooth enamel. The process usually starts with a single microscopic spot that gradually deepens and widens until it reaches the dentin within the tooth. At that point, pain strikes and we head for the dentist's office.

Sugar is a chief culprit because it coats the teeth and allows bacteria to flourish undisturbed. Many other factors contribute to tooth decay; tooth and mouth structure, inherited susceptibility, alignment of bite, and, of course, the presence or absence of tooth-strengthening fluoride in the drinking water all play a role. The strain of bacteria that causes decay never has been specifically identified. It may be that these bacteria proliferate in the mouths of certain persons and not in others. Variations in diet are critical. Aboriginal tribes in Africa and Australia who followed a grain diet had very few cavities—until the soft-drink sales force arrived with their cans and bottles.

Also important in cavity formation is *how* we eat. Americans may snack almost continuously from morning to bedtime. Each time we eat a food containing carbohydrates, the teeth are attacked by acid for 20 minutes or more. The more often we eat, the more frequently that exposure occurs.

The time needed to consume the food plays a part, too. Hard candy, cough drops, and mints remain in the mouth for a long time, coating the teeth and prolonging the siege.

What's on the rest of your dinner plate is important, too. Research has shown that carbohydrates eaten *with* a meal do less damage than those eaten alone, between meals. Apparently increased saliva in a full meal helps to neutralize the acid and clear the food from the mouth. Some foods may even have a protective effect. Cheese and peanuts, for instance, seem to act against the acid, especially if eaten after the carbohydrates. That may be one reason cheese and nuts have been a traditional dessert course.

Aristotle put his finger on another factor. Sticky foods—figs, dates, raisins, dried fruits, not to mention caramels, toffee, and other chewy candies—tend to cling to the teeth, especially in the crevices.

Even baby's formula has been shown to cause cavities. Dental researchers recently have identified a condition they call "nursing bottle mouth," caused when an infant is allowed to go to sleep with a bottle. The lactose, or milk sugar, bathes the teeth and remains in contact with them for hours, thus promoting cavity formation. If a baby is tucked in with a bottle, dentists say, the bottle should contain only water, or it should be removed after the baby has fallen asleep.

SUGAR AND OBESITY

Sugar itself doesn't make you fat. As we have seen, sugar contains less than half as many calories as fat, and the same amount as protein and other forms of carbohydrate. The problem is that sugar packs a lot of calories for its weight. Nutritionists use the term "caloric density."

In sweets, a large number of calories can be packed in a very small amount of food, with the result that you can consume a monstrous number of calories before you get that filled-up feeling. A handful of gumdrops, for instance, contains 400 calories; two handfuls of grapes, a mere 65. Yet you'd probably stop eating the grapes long before you finished them. You might chomp down all the gumdrops and go looking for more before you quelled your appetite.

Humans may not be born with a sweet tooth, but they develop it quickly. Studies have shown that not only human babies but infant animals will choose sugar water over other liquids once they have been introduced to it. Most of us prefer sweet tastes and associate sweetness with goodness—"How sweet it is!" "She's *such* a sweet person!" But we usually have a limit on how much sweet stuff we can consume. A few persons, however, go on periodic binges, eating a whole box of chocolates or a pound of cookies nonstop. Although a psychological explanation is suspected, there may be a neurological one as well.

SUGAR CONTROL

Cutting out sugar completely is not only unnecessary, but probably impossible. Just reading a food label will tell you that sweeteners are tucked away in some totally unexpected places, such as luncheon meats. Moreover, sugar often masquerades under other designations. You may find cookie labels that never mention sugar, but prominently list "corn syrup" or "corn sweeteners."

The best approach to sugar control might be called the snack attack. Most Americans get the bulk of their sugar between meals, in the form of soft drinks, candy bars, ice cream, cookies, and pastries. It is easy to consume virtually a third of the day's calories just during the coffee break.

Nutritious snacks include raw vegetables, unsalted nuts, unflavored yogurt, soda crackers, and toast. Cheese protects the teeth but contains both sodium and fat. Sugarless gum does not promote cavities and contains few calories. Coffee or tea without sugar substitutes for soft drinks.

Dental hygiene, of course, is the cornerstone of cavity control. Brush your teeth thoroughly at least once daily. If you can't brush after every meal or snack, rinse out your mouth with water to remove bits of food. Floss your teeth daily to remove plaque around the gumline and between teeth. And teach the lessons of proper toothbrushing to children.

ARTIFICIAL SWEETENERS

No-calorie and low-calorie sweeteners depend upon a whole galaxy of artificial compounds, some of them familiar, some not, many of them controversial.

Saccharin, which dates back to 1900, is about 300 times sweeter than refined sugar and is widely used in soft drinks and as a tabletop sweetener. It leaves a slightly bitter aftertaste. Large doses have been shown to cause cancer in laboratory animals, but sale is still permitted. Labels must carry the warning that saccharin "may be hazardous to your health."

Cyclamates are less sweet than saccharin, or about 30 times as sweet as sugar. They were widely used in the 1960s until laboratory tests implicated the cyclamates, too, in animal cancers. Cyclamates are now banned from sale in the U.S.

Aspartame was introduced in 1981 and given a renewed bill of health in 1985 by the national Center for Disease Control after a long investigation that found no evidence of a widespread health threat. The sweetener was first barred from soft drinks in fear that it might harm children but now is approved for both tabletop use and drinks. Aspartame contains the amino acid phenylalanine, and persons with phenylketonuria (PKU) are advised against its use.

Xylitol, sorbitol, and mannitol are sugar alcohols found in fruits. They are sometimes used in food for diabetics because insulin is not needed to metabolize them. They also are found in sugarless gum, because they appear to not cause tooth decay.

Diabetes affects 5 percent of the population; diabetes and its complications is one of the leading causes of death among Americans. The origins of diabetes aren't known, but heredity apparently plays a part. In the most prevalent form of the disease, overeating also plays a role. Nine of 10 older diabetics are obese—half of them seriously obese.

The disease is an inability of the pancreas to produce any or enough of the hormone insulin, which helps the body to use glucose; or of the tissues to use the insulin production properly. With too little insulin, glucose builds up in the blood and spills over into the urine. If no insulin is being produced by the pancreas,

daily shots of insulin are needed to control glucose levels (insulin-dependent diabetes). In non-insulin-dependent diabetes, some insulin may be produced—even in normal amounts—but other metabolic defects may prevent proper use. In many of these cases, exercise, the proper diet—and especially losing weight—may control the disease.

The proper diet for diabetics resembles that for all healthy persons. The American Diabetes Association has recommended that 50–60 percent of the diet come from complex carbohydrates, such as rice and grains; 12–20 percent from protein; and less than 10 percent from saturated fat, and more than 10 percent from vegetable fat. Depending on age and activity level, daily calories should number from 1,500 to 2,000.

Restricting fat is particularly important for diabetics, who have a higher rate of cardiovascular complications than the general population. The recommendation that diabetics eat plenty of starch represents a change from past thinking, but is based on the fact that complex carbohydrates both speed digestion and are filling, therefore cutting back on the desire for other foods.

Is eating simple carbohydrates—sugars—a no-no for diabetics? In one widely quoted study of Yemenite Jews who migrated to Israel, it was found that a higher rate of diabetes occurred among those who adopted Israeli sugar-consuming habits than among those who continued with the sugar abstinence of their homeland. Other scientists dispute the presumed link between sugar consumption and diabetes. Dr. Edgar L. Bierman of the University of Washington, after exhaustive research, has stated flatly that there is "no evidence" that excessive consumption of sugar causes diabetes.

For most diabetics, it is not necessary to resort to artificial sweeteners or dietetic foods. The system of food-exchange lists, cosponsored by the American Diabetes Association and the American Dietetic Association, enables diabetics to follow a normal diet.

Seventy percent of the salt has been slashed from this flavorful Swiss Rye Bread. (See recipe, page 135.)

AVOID TOO MUCH SODIUM AND SALT

CHAPTER 12

Salt is on every table, and in a lot more dishes than you might suspect. It plays an important role in diet—but can play a harmful one as well. One sure way to cut back on the amount you eat begins at the shopping cart. Instead of processed foods, with their high salt content, choose fresh fruits and vegetables and omit the salt when you cook.

CONTENTS

Animals, including humans, need salt. Sodium, which makes up 40 percent of the salt (sodium chloride) molecule by weight, plays a vital role in the biological process. Its positively charged ion sets off the electrical impulses in the nervous system that contract the muscles. Sodium touches off the heartbeat and controls its rhythm. Sodium also regulates the body's fluids outside the cells. Without sodium, we would literally drown internally.

The value and importance of sodium is not something the world learned only yesterday. Cattle instinctively seek salt sources in hot weather, so ranchers provide them with salt licks. The role of salt is embedded in human folklore. We sometimes call people "the salt of the earth," seat important guests "above the salt," or say someone "is not worth his salt." Even the word "salary" derives from the Latin word for salt. Caesar's legions were partly paid in salt because it was such a valuable commodity.

Sodium salt is intricately intertwined with two other elements, potassium and calcium. Together, they are known as the electrolytes and they perform an intricate little ballet around each cell. Sodium controls the fluids outside the cell, potassium controls fluid intracellularly, and calcium preserves the cell membrane that separates the two. The excitability of a nerve impulse or a muscle movement involves a temporary exchange of ions across the membrane. When the balance is out of synchronization, we feel a cramp or twitch.

Sodium has a delicate role in maintaining the fluid balance. Sodium ingested in food is easily absorbed in the intestinal tract and passes through the bloodstream to the kidneys, which extract precisely the amount needed to control fluids and excrete the unused sodium. Maintaining the balance is a continuous process. When we eat salted peanuts or potato chips, we feel thirsty and gulp a soft drink or a beer. The refreshment restores the balance between sodium and the extracellular fluid.

Sodium also is an important regulator of the blood volume and therefore the blood pressure. Blood is two-thirds water, and most of the fluid outside the cells is blood. When the body gets an increase of sodium, or maintains too much of the element, the blood volume increases to restore the proper proportion. The increased amount of blood must fit through the same blood vessels; pressure therefore increases until the volume drops. Likewise, a loss of sodium or salt can reduce the blood volume and pressure, which is why some people faint after losing salt during a siege of perspiration.

As important as sodium is, however, we need surprisingly little of it. The "safe and adequate" level proposed in the Recommended Dietary Allowance is only 1,100 to 3,300 milligrams (1.1 to 3.3 grams) a day. Since sodium is two-fifths of the salt molecule, that translates to about 2.75 to 8.25 grams daily, an amount the National Research Council says would more than amply supply the needs of virtually everyone in the U.S. population. Only those persons who did heavy physical work in hot weather would need more.

The 1977 U.S. Senate select committee report on Americans' nutrition status (see page 12) report and health agencies such as the American Heart Association have said that five grams a day would be a generous supply on which no one would feel deprived. Persons on a low-salt diet for medical reasons get along nicely on a gram a day. Yet the average American consumes 16 grams of salt daily.

There's no doubt that salt gives a flavor to food, and that most of us have learned to like that flavor. On a balanced diet, we would get an adequate supply of sodium from natural sources in food, such as kale and spinach, oysters and eggs. But two-thirds of the salt we consume comes from processed foods: from bacon and processed meats to canned soups and vegetables, where salt is used not only as a flavor enhancer but as a preservative. And the other third of the daily salt diet is added in cooking or at the table. Our liberal use of the saltcellar may be endangering our health.

Rosemary

Basil

Thyme

Oregano

Mint

Sodium and potassium are part of a duet, and some specialists believe America's high-sodium problem may actually be a low-potassium problem. As consumption of fresh fruit and vegetables has declined and processed food has increased, Americans get less potassium; one study shows we get one-sixth the potassium eaten by our ancestors. Good sources of potassium include potatoes, bananas, melons, skim milk, and citrus fruits. Citrus fruits should be in the diet every day.

Hypertension in America has been called an epidemic. Between 24 million and 60 million Americans are said to have blood-pressure readings high enough to endanger their health, the figure varying according to who's counting and how high is considered too high. The consequences of elevated blood pressure, as Americans have been reminded frequently, can be dire indeed. Hypertension is associated with the big killers of the 1980s, including heart disease, stroke, and kidney damage.

Blood pressure represents the amount of pressure against the artery walls as the blood is pumped through by the heart. It usually is expressed in two figures. The first, and larger number is systolic pressure, when the heart is pumping. Diastolic pressure is pressure when the heart is at rest. Blood pressure is considered normal when it ranges between 100/60 and 130/80. Blood pressure among Americans usually rises with age. Most doctors think a reading of 160/90 is too high.

Where does sodium fit in? The evidence against it is circumstantial but convincing. Sodium certainly plays a role in regulating blood pressure, although it may not be the only one. Public-health specialists say widespread hypertension in industrialized countries coincides with increased consumption of salt.

In parts of the world where people consume little salt, blood pressure readings are low, and they remain low throughout life. Alaskan Eskimos are practically free of hypertension. So are Congo pygmies, Kalahari bushmen, and numerous other tribal peoples who lead hard, simple lives and follow a low-sodium diet. But when these people adopt urban ways and take up an urban diet, their blood pressures come to resemble those of their city neighbors. When Kenyan herdsmen who had followed a low-sodium diet were drafted into their country's army, their blood pressure began to rise within two years.

On the other hand, some Japanese farmers consume almost twice the U.S. average of 16 grams of salt daily, and they have the world's highest rate of hypertension. Forty percent of these Japanese farmers over 40 have elevated blood pressure.

The explanation for the presumed link between high sodium intake and high blood pressure goes like this: Although the kidneys normally excrete any excess sodium not needed by the body, some people are not able to dump all the unneeded sodium. Genetic reasons or kidneys weakened by a lifetime of sodium overload may be the cause of kidney malfunction. The body responds by increasing the fluid volume to dilute the sodium. Like water pounding against the banks of a flood-swollen stream, the increased volume pushes against the walls of the vessels. In an effort to conserve fluid, the vessels constrict, which increases the pressure. The heart rate rises and the heart enlarges because the heart has to pump more blood around the body. Constant high pressure damages the vessel walls; the heavy workload weakens the heart.

OBESITY AND HYPERTENSION

Obesity is another factor in hypertension. An adult who is carrying 20 percent too much weight is at increased risk for high blood pressure, and at markedly increased risk if 50 percent overweight. Some doctors think sodium is the villain here, too, maintaining that obese people eat more, which means they consume more salt. In fact, a double whammy may be at work: Some people may be genetically programmed to be *both* hypertensive and obese.

Not everyone who is hypertensive is fat, but blood pressure does drop when obese people shed weight. In the same way, when sodium intake goes down, blood pressure goes down with it. Still, no one has ever been able to prove absolutely that overconsumption of salt *causes* high blood pressure. The matter may be more complicated, a consequence of that ballet among the electrolytes. Some doctors theorize that the real problem isn't high sodium, but low potassium. Some recent research implicates calcium, showing that blood pressure appears to rise when calcium intake begins to drop.

Blood pressure can be lowered with the use of drugs, and this is the usual treatment for serious hypertension. Doctors differ about whether to treat mild hypertension, since drug therapy is for a lifetime, and the drugs may cause side effects. The person who previously felt well without drugs may feel sick with them. Thus many doctors prefer to treat mild hypertension with diet. They recommend losing weight and restricting salt.

Can a restricted-salt diet prevent hypertension in a person whose blood pressure is in the normal range? Like many other dietary recommendations for the 1980s, no one knows for sure. However, the tendency is to play safe. Reducing your consumption of salt certainly won't threaten your health, and the chances are good that it may help.

The best advice for cutting down on sodium is simply to throw away the salt shaker. If you do not add salt to food while cooking, or at the table, you can easily drop below five grams a day. If you feel that food is simply too bland without the taste of salt, try a salt substitute. Usually based on potassium, these are available in most supermarkets. Lemon juice also is an excellent replacement. (Sea salt, sometimes sold as a substitute, is chemically identical to table salt, and actually may lack some nutrients destroyed in processing.)

Unless a doctor prescribes otherwise, it's seldom necessary to buy low-salt or salt-free foods. Just follow a few commonsense rules. Avoid foods that are cured in salt, such as pickles, olives, bacon, and sausage. Be cautious about packaged foods, many of which contain large amounts of salt. Canned soups, for instance, have as much as 1,000 milligrams of salt, virtually a day's whole ration. Canned vegetables contain far more salt than fresh or frozen varieties. Salt also turns up in quantity in cereals and baked goods, where it is used as a preservative as well as a flavor enhancer. You now won't find as much salt in canned baby food as there was in the past; manufacturers have recently reduced it or eliminated it altogether, under pressure from parents and from child nutritionists.

Don't be deceived into thinking that salty food necessarily *tastes* salty. You'll want to watch your consumption of thirst-provoking chips, pretzels, and salted nuts, yet some cereals contain more salt, gram for gram, than snack foods. Over-the-counter medicines like aspirin can be a hidden source of sodium. And fast-food restaurants can be a real trap for the unwary. A typical fast-food cheeseburger contains 1,400 milligrams of sodium, enough to destroy a low-sodium regimen.

SOURCES OF SODIUM IN FOOD

Consult package labels for other sources of sodium. Some nutritionists say that when salt is listed among the first three ingredients, you should choose another product. Sodium may be listed in many other ways: monosodium glutamate, sodium benzoate, sodium nitrate or nitrite. Remember that soy sauce is a concentrated form of salt. Worcestershire sauce, ketchup, and mustard also contain salt.

A surprising source of sodium is drinking water. Although the amounts are seldom a problem for healthy people, they can be sufficiently high in some localities to affect those on a low-sodium diet. Water suppliers are now required to notify customers if the sodium content exceeds 20 milligrams per liter. Another way in which sodium may creep into drinking water is in passing through a water softener. Some softeners substitute two sodium ions for a calcium ion to increase softness. Persons under treatment for hypertension should have a system in which the drinking water bypasses the softener.

Bottled waters may be high in sodium, especially club soda, and so are soft drinks. According to the National Soft Drink Association, some 12-ounce cans contain as much as 83 milligrams of sodium.

A tasty way to compensate for reduced salt or sugar in your diet is to flavor with herbs and spices—and to raise your own supply. Most herbs are surprisingly easy to grow and produce a bountiful harvest.

The most popular herbs for cooking are chives, mint, rosemary, sage, and thyme—all perennials—and dill, marjoram, parsley, and basil—annuals. All love sun and will thrive in almost any well-drained soil. In fact, experienced herb gardeners say that a highly fertile soil is counterproductive: Plants grow tall and leafy, but they have less bouquet and flavor.

Start the plants from seed indoors, in a sunny place, and transplant outdoors as soon as the soil is warm. A sheltered spot near the kitchen is best for an herb garden, because plants are within easy reach of the cook. Leave plenty of growing room, because some plants, particularly mint, spread rapidly. Many gardeners transplant annuals into small clay pots in the fall and place them indoors on a sunny windowsill to extend the growing season.

Some gardeners like to try an indoor herb garden, locating it in a kitchen greenhouse window. That makes the herbs even handier for cooking, although indoor cultivation is more difficult and the yield not so great. The most successful indoor efforts approximate the "ideal" outdoor conditions—well-drained